MW01519294

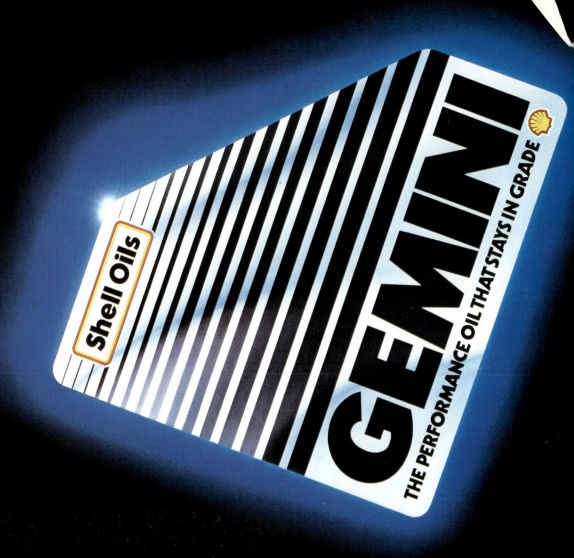

Protection above all.

No conventional oil can meet the demands of hard driving quite like Gemini. Above all, Gemini, the latest and most advanced formula from Shell, sets new standards in protection. Through high revs and fierce temperatures Gemini stays in grade. Mile after mile, day after day, protection beyond the capabilities of conventional oils.

Technology you can trust

In the three years it's been rallying, the Audi Quattro has, in fact, come in first an amazing 80 times in national and international events.

Which is something no car has ever done before.

In 1982, it won the World Rally Championship.

In 1983, Quattro driver Hannu Mikkola won the World Driver's Championship.

Drivers of competitive cars still don't know what's hit them. Or, should we say, overtaken them.

To be fair, the Audi Quattro does have something of an unfair advantage.

And that's its unique permanent 4-wheel-drive system.

In rallying, as in any driving, having an engine capable of producing phenomenal power isn't enough.

Somehow, that power has to be transmitted to the road.

Now you don't have to belong to Mensa to work out that a car transmitting power through four wheels rather than two is going to transport you from A to B more effectively.

The Audi Quattro also enjoys all the better known characteristics of 4-wheel-drive.

Like twice the ability to stick to the road, even when the road is awash with rain, gravel, ice or snow.

*SOURCE: WHAT CAR?   URBAN 18.3MPG (15.4L/100KM), 56MPH 34.9MPG (8.1L/100KM), 75MPH 27.4MPG (10.3L/100KM).   PRICE £20,402. NUMBER PLATES AND DELIVERY EXTRA. BROCHURE

It also comes in black,

And a talent for scaling minor mountains, should the occasion arise.

Ah ha, you may say, but how alike are Hannu Mikkola's Quattro and the Quattro we mere mortals can buy?

In its unique difference, the permanent 4-wheel-drive system, the rally and the road cars are identical.

It's true that whereas the rally Quattro develops 350bhp, the road Quattro has to be content with 200bhp.

But that's quite enough to get you from 0 to 60 in 6.7* seconds and on up to 137mph anywhere speed limits don't clip your wings.

Naturally, we're as keen to save your skin as we are Hannu's.

Hence the 1984 road Audi Quattro is fitted with a virtually skid-proof second-generation Anti-locking Braking System.

Fortunately, there's no comparison between the two cars as far as petrol consumption goes.

The government figures for the road model are 18.3mpg urban cycle, 34.9mpg at 56mph and 27.4mpg at 75mph.

Hannu? He averages 5mpg. But then, rally drivers will be rally drivers ■

FROM AUDI MARKETING, YEOMANS DRIVE, BLAKELANDS, MILTON KEYNES MK14 5AN. TEL: (0908) 679121. EXPORT AND FLEET SALES, 95 BAKER STREET, LONDON W1M 1FB. TEL: 01-486 8411.

blue, white, silver and first.

A picture of the Toyota Corolla winning the Rothmans RAC Open Rally Championship Manufacturers Award for the second successive year.

With maximum points and outright victories in 5 of 6 events, near standard 1600GT Corollas, won the Group A title in the 1984 Rothmans RAC Open Rally Championship.

A performance that not only won Toyota this year's Manufacturers Award by an incredible 9 point margin, but also won (as you can see from the picture) a lot of admiring glances from our competitors. **TOYOTA**

FINAL SCORES: TOYOTA 75 PTS. OPEL 66 PTS. AUDI 60 PTS. TALBOT 52 PTS. FORD 37 PTS. TOYOTA (GB) LTD., THE QUADRANGLE, REDHILL, SURREY RH1 1PX.

Add a Touch of Style with Accessories from Hella

HELLA®

Ideas today for
the cars of tomorrow

Hella SPORT

With a Hella Auxiliary Lamp Grille Set your car will look better and you'll see better.

Add good looks and safety to your car with a Hella auxiliary lamp grille set. Give it that individual, dynamic look. Hella are Europe's leading quality lighting manufacturer, so you can be sure you are buying the best. Grille sets are available with driving or fog lamp patterns for more than 25 popular car models.

Hella Front and Rear Spoilers – more style, less drag.

Extensive windtunnel and rigorous road tests ensure that Hella spoilers are well-designed and aerodynamically efficient. The advantages are: reduction in drag (Cd) leading to better road-holding and fuel economy. Hella spoilers are easy-to-fit and can be painted to match your car colour. A front spoiler complete with halogen fog lamps will give you extra safety as well as good looks.

Hella Car Stripes – the finishing touch.

Give your car a sporty, distinctive look to set it apart from run-of-the-mill models. Hella stripes come in custom or universal kits to suit all vehicles.

Fit Hella Wheel Trims – for that individual look.

Hella wheel trims are superbly styled with very smooth surfaces for aerodynamic efficiency. Finished in silver metallic colour, these sporty trims, in three distinctive designs, are available in 13 and 14 inch sizes for all vehicles with steel wheels.

Ask your local dealer for details of the Hella Accessory Range or write to:

Hella Ltd., Daventry Road Industrial Estate, Banbury, Oxon OX16 7JU Phone: (0295) 5 63 81, Telex 8 37 418

Hella Ireland Ltd., Newtown Industrial Estate, Coolock, Dublin 5, Ireland. Phone 47 33 11

BF GOODRICH UPDATE:

FOR THE FIRST TIME EVER, AN AMERICAN DRIVER AND STREET RADIALS WIN A MAJOR EUROPEAN RALLY.

Motorsports are the largest spectator events in Europe, and rallying is the largest motorsport in Europe. It is not uncommon to find a million or more spectators lining the courses of some European rallies.

It is extremely uncommon, however, to find an American driver winning a European Championship Rally. Likewise it is extremely uncommon to find a street radial winning such an event. In fact, neither had ever happened before the ECR Rally on the isle of Cyprus in the

RUNNING AT A DISADVANTAGE.

Few expected Buffum and BFGoodrich to win at Cyprus. Buffum's car was a turbo-charged 4WD long-wheelbased Audi Quattro. Yet the Cyprus Rally course is not congenial to such a car. (Indeed, it was the first time a Quattro had ever run the Cyprus Rally). A competitor described the course as "one continuous hairpin." To make matters worse, the mountain

On the other hand, the competition was in smaller cars and quite intense. It included the Lancia Rally driver who was then merely one point away from ECR leadership points, and it included the 1984 British Rally Champion (who was also last year's winner of the Cyprus Rally).

Likewise the competition for BFGoodrich was intense, since the Buffum car was the

John Buffum at the wheel of his Audi Quattro on BFGoodrich T/A Radials at the Rothman's Cyprus Rally.

eastern Mediterranean on September 30, 1984.

The driver was John Buffum, winner of seven U.S. Pro Rally Championships. The tyres were BFGoodrich T/A® Radials.

roads were extremely narrow, with some scarcely wider than the cars. The Quattro was thought too big for such roads. Buffum found that much of his driving was in 1st and 2nd gears, with turbo boost barely coming on before he would have to brake for the next corner.

only major competitor not running on special-purpose rally tyres.

PUNISHING CONDITIONS.

Conditions were intense too. The course, in fact, was so punishing that out of 76 cars

BF GOODRICH T/A® RADIALS

starting the rally, only 30 finished.

Yet John Buffum with Navigator Fred Gallagher of

of the road. So in the mountains we used the Radial Mud-Terrain T/A.® It has a really aggressive tread pattern that

there are times when this puts T/A Radials at a disadvantage to pure rally tyres. But not always. Because in developing the entire line of T/A Radials, many combinations of designs and materials were explored to develop the optimum combinations for a variety of high-performance needs and driving styles.

A case in point is the fact that T/A Radials were on every winning car in every U.S. Pro Rally this year. Equally impressive was the first American victory in European rallying, and John Buffum's highly respected finishes of fifth overall at the Acropolis Rally and fourth overall at West Germany's Hunsruck Rally – on BFGoodrich T/A Radials.

John Buffum (right), winner of the Cyprus European Championship Rally with Navigator Fred Gallagher (left).

Scotland managed to lead the entire distance of the rally. In the end, their Audi Quattro on BFGoodrich T/A® Radial tyres finished 7.88 minutes ahead of the second-place car.

"I've never rallied on tougher roads," Buffum said. "They were covered with a layer of dust a half-inch to an inch thick. Beneath that was a lot of loose stuff, and then about three inches beneath that was hard igneous rock, which was not at all forgiving to tyres."

In a previous interview with BFGoodrich, Buffum had explained how a controlled slide was the safest way through most corners in rally special (racing) stages. When asked if that was the case in Cyprus, Buffum replied: "Only on the plains. We used the BFGoodrich Radial All-Terrain T/A™ there, where you had room to slide through and where its bigger footprint was to our advantage. But the mountain roads were just too narrow. You can't do much sliding when the length of your wheelbase exceeds the width

cuts down into the road and pulls you along. Those BFGoodrich tyres really came through for us. Some of our competitors had awful problems with tyres. In Cyprus, with all its jagged rocks, you've got to expect punctures unless you're running on tank treads. But we only had two, due to encounters with roadside boulders. With one, we were able to drive the car about three miles to the end of the stage. With the other, we were far enough ahead so we could afford to spend a couple of minutes changing tyres. Others weren't so lucky."

TECHNOLOGY PUT TO THE TEST.

BFGoodrich has never built a special rally tyre. No doubt

But more important to you is knowing that a street radial can offer the traction and durability to perform well against highly specialized non-street tyres. And even more important yet is knowing that the BFGoodrich rally and racing efforts are in fact testing grounds for our continuing research and development of high-performance tyres for your car or truck.

At BFGoodrich, we believe in putting our technology to hard use so you can put it to good use.

Winning examples of BFGoodrich T/A® Radial technology.

WE MAKE CARS PERFORM™

Southam Tyres Ltd., Sparkbrook St., Hillfields, Coventry, West Midlands, CV1 5LA. Tel: 0203-555541. Telex: 851-31669.

Isaac Agnew (Distribution) Ltd., 45 Mallusk Rd., Newtonabbey, Co. Antrim, BT36 8SP, Northern Ireland. Tel: 02313-7111. Telex: 74-7330.

Watling Tyre Service Ltd., West Street, Gravesend, Kent DA11 0BN. Tel: (0474) 534692. Telex: 965672 CRAWLY G.

Audi Sport
World of Rallying
7

Martin Holmes

Published in Great Britain by
David Sutton Publications Limited
Colville Road,
Acton, London. W3 8BN.

Distributed by
Blandford Press Limited,
Link House,
West Street,
Poole,
Dorset,
BH15 1LL. England.

ISBN 0 9509286 0 8

Written and compiled by Martin Holmes

Designed by Ron Jones
Design and production in association with
Book Production Consultants, Cambridge

Typeset by Goodfellow & Egan, Cambridge
Printed in Italy
by Tipolitografia G. Canale & C. S.p.A. - Turin
in association with Keats European Limited

Acknowledgements

It has only been possible to compile this issue of Audi
Sport World of Rallying 7 through the help of friends in
many countries.

Special assistance has been given by Colin Taylor
Productions for pictures and Colin Wilson for information
from rallies in the Open British championship and
Graham Cooke for preparing the diagrams of four-wheel
drive transmission systems. Once again we have also
received considerable help from members of the RALLY
PRESS ASSOCIATION and many photographic
contributors as well as colleagues in other countries,
including:

Argentina (RA)	Eduardo Neira
Australia (AUS)	Stewart Wilson
Austria (A)	Axel Hofer
Belgium (B)	Willy Weyens
Brasil (BR)	Joaquim Cunha
Cyprus (CY)	Tony Christodoulou
Czechoslovakia (CS)	Jiri Prikryl
Finland (SF)	Esa Illoinen
Greece (GR)	Stergios Manolis
Hong Kong (HK)	Phil Taylor
Hungary (H)	Andreas Fekete
Iceland (IS)	Gunnlaugur Rognvaldsson
Ireland (IRL)	Brian Patterson
Ivory Coast (CI)	Gerard Lallemant
Japan (J)	Toshiyuki Iijima
Jordan (HKJ)	Derek Ledger
Kenya (EAK)	Mike Doughty
Malaysia (MAL)	Chips Yap
Mexico (MEX)	Guy Lassauzet
Netherlands (NL)	Vincent Van Danzig
New Zealand (NZ)	David McKinney
Norway (N)	Bjorn Lie
Oman (OM)	Stuart Gray
Paraguay (PY)	Gabriel Gonzalez
Poland (PL)	Stanislav Szelichowski
Portugal (P)	Fernando Petronilho
South Africa (ZA)	Jannie Herbst
Soviet Union (SU)	Margus Kuuse
Spain (E)	Maria-Angeles Pujol
Sweden (S)	Per Lidstrom
Switzerland (CH)	Peter Wyss
Turkey (TR)	Berkan Kilic
United States of America (USA)	Cam Warren
Uruguay (U)	Mario Uberti
West Germany (D)	Jurgen Schwarz
Yugoslavia (YU)	Branko Bozic
Zimbabwe (ZW)	Peter Mayes

Contents

Foreword

by Stig Blomqvist
1984 World Champion Driver

It was a long road but finally we reached the end! I am not just talking about the Ivory Coast Rally where my co-driver "Captain" Cederberg and I won the world championship, but our whole career beforehand. 1984 was a year with its ups and downs. After the Swedish I never thought I would ever get another good result; then the Acropolis put us back on the winning road again. But of all these events nothing ever seemed so long, so never-ending, as the Ivory Coast. All I had to do was finish in the top three places, everyone especially Hannu Mikkola was helping us along, but it was the loneliest few days of my life.

Rallying has changed so much since the old days back in Sweden with the Saabs. It seems only yesterday that my father and I entered our first few events together; little did we think I would never grow out of this senseless, expensive sport! But rallying has been my life. It is the best way I know to travel, meet people all over the world, know and work with people from different backgrounds. Nowadays we have a chance to think about the next generation, and even though the cars are completely different, you need the same enthusiasm and determination to succeed as we did all those years ago.

I am happy to be given these two pages in Audi Sport World of Rallying 7. David Sutton has always been an expert in building rally cars and I hope he will continue to command respect with his second venture into the publication world. I am reputed not to say too much in public, so my message must be short. Thank you everyone for the help and encouragement in my career, whatever your involvement and interest in rallying. I hope rallying gives you as much pleasure in the future as it has given me in the past.

Stig Blomqvist

Did you know . . .

Geography

. . . the longest rally in the world was the 1977 London-Sydney marathon, at 19,329 miles won by Andrew Cowan, Colin Malkin and Mike Broad in a Mercedes 280E.

. . . rallying is held in the six inhabited continents of the world. The most northerly event each year is the Arctic Rally in Finland, starting at Rovaniemi and held mostly north of the Arctic Circle, and the most southerly is the rally in Tierra del Fuego, running from San Pablo in Argentina across to Porvenir in Chile, and back.

. . . the highest rallies in the world take place over the Passo di Ticlio in Peru, the best known nowadays being the Marginal de la Selva. This goes up to 4843 metres above sealevel. The Himalayan Rally in India goes to about 3955 metres – weather permitting. The lowest rally in the world was the 1979 Jordan Rally, which went down to minus 750 feet at South Shuna 10km north of the Dead Sea.

People

. . . who is the most successful driver? Walter Rohrl is so far the only driver to be world champion twice (1980 and 1982), although when the European series used to be the premier series, the Pole Sobieslav Zasada won or shared the title three times. Up till the 1984 Swedish Rally Hannu Mikkola had 16 world championship wins and his regular codriver Arne Hertz 15. Mikkola had by then entered more world rallies than anyone else – 85 – but has had more than his fair share of retirements. Bjorn Waldegard had actually finished 47 times, more than anyone else. Hertz finished 44 times, more than any other codriver.

. . . the oldest man to win a world event is codriver Bjorn Cederberg. When he won in Ivory Coast 1984 he

was 47y.03m.12d. Oldest first-time winner is Ulster co-driver Terry Harryman (Safari 1983; 44y.07m.08d). Drivers come younger: oldest winning driver was Joginder Singh (1976 Safari; 44y.03m.15d) and the youngest winner was another driver, Henri Toivonen (RAC 1980; 24y.02m.06d) compared with the French girl codriver 'Biche' who won the 1973 Monte Carlo Rally when 24y.03m.29d.

. . . the most successful rally driver ever is probably Belgium's Gilbert Staepelaere, who claims 89 rally wins – all but one in Ford cars and mostly in his home country. France's Bernard Darniche can claim over 50 international wins, including four European championship wins, in four weeks, in four different countries – and two different Lancia Stratos cars, during 1977. That season he won ten ECR events, the Tour de Corse world event and also the French championship.

HOLMES

... some drivers keep on going. Celebrated veterans include the Greek Johnny Pesmazoglou who won the Acropolis Rally in 1953 in a Chevrolet and started the 1984 event one month after his seventieth birthday. The Swedish codriver Fergus Sager has competed in the Monte Carlo Rally 25 times and the Kenyan driver Prem Choda has entered 23 Safaris to date.

... lady drivers have been popular since the start of the sport. Michele Mouton has scooped most of the records; she first won a world event at Sanremo in 1981 though 'Biche' was the first lady to win a world event – the 1973 Monte Carlo as codriver to Andruet. Pat Moss gained her great successes before the world series started, but probably her best result was winning the Spa-Sofia-Liege in 1960. Mouton's codriver Fabrizia Pons is one of only two people who had scored world points both as driver and codriver, the other being Jean-Claude Lefebvre.

... Shekhar Mehta won the Safari four times in succession (1979–82) whilst event hattricks have been won by Makinen (RAC 1973–75), Munari (Monte Carlo 1975–77), Alen (1000 Lakes 1978–80), Darniche (Corsica 1979–81) and Rohrl (Monte Carlo 1982–84). Blomqvist became the first driver to win three consecutive world events in Acropolis, New Zealand and Argentina 1984, as well as the first to win 5 world events in one season (1984).

... the unluckiest driver in the world series must be Jean-Luc Therier, who failed to reach the end of 19 consecutive events between 1975 and 1980 – but who has achieved a remarkable winning rate of one in three – of those events he has finished. The most accident-prone (till the end of 1983) are Ari Vatanen who has crashed 14 times out of 29 retirements in the world series and Adartico Vudafieri (nine out of fourteen).

BELOW
World's winning-most rallyman? Gilbert Staepelaere gained most of his wins in Belgium, but here he is winning in Hungary in 1976.

ABOVE
Fiat at their most expansive. Just a small proportion of the Fiat Abarth 124s in the workshop in Turin in 1975.

Cars

... the Fiat/Lancia group have been the most successful in world rallies, between them winning almost 30% of the events. The Fiat Abarth 131 alone won 20, but the Audi Quattro's twenty-first win in Argentina 1984 put them equal, with the record held by Ford Escorts.

... four-wheel drive was first allowed in world events in 1979 when two Range Rovers entered the Bandama Rally. First world success for a 4x4 car was Hirabayshi's group 1 win in a Subaru on the 1980 Safari and the first outright win was by Mikkola's Quattro on the 1981 Swedish.

... "grand slam" results were gained by various models of Datsun on the Safari in 1981 (1st, 2nd, 3rd, 4th; also wins in groups 4, 2 and 1 – no group 3 cars entered). Top four places have also been taken by Lancia Stratos in Sanremo 1976, Mercedes 450SLC 5.0 in Ivory Coast 1979, various types of Audis in Sweden 1983, Quattros in Argentina 1983 and Lancia Rallys in Corsica 1983.

... Talbot Sunbeam Lotus cars won group 2 six times in a row in 1981 (a total of nine times out of 12 in all) and Datsun 160J cars won group 2 five times in as many world events in 1979.

... the most powerful cars in world championship rallies are nowadays the Sport Quattros. Most powerful normally aspirated car has been the BMW M1 used in France by Bernard Darniche and Bernard Beguin (about 420bhp) and the Dodge Ramchargers brought from USA to Kenya for the Safari, about 440bhp.

... the Opel Ascona 400 is probably the most versatile car. It won its second world event Swedish (1980), Monte Carlo (1982) and on its final works appearance, the Safari (1983).

Events

... the oldest event is the Targa Florio in Sicily; in 1984 they ran their 68th edition but for most of this time it was held as a road race.

... the fastest stage in the world championship was the first stage in Argentina, 1983. This was won by Stig Blomqvist in an Audi Quattro – who had never seen the stage before and who used pacenotes prepared (in a different language) by Hannu Mikkola, at an average speed of 189.53kph.

. . . the slowest rally in a FISA championship is probably the Cyprus ECR event, on which the fastest times on several stages are gained at less than a 30mph average speed.

. . . the biggest scandal must have been the 1966 Monte Carlo Rally when the top four cars were excluded for using a revolutionary lighting system and then in 1973 when many privateers were excluded after the route had been blocked by snow. The 1981 Acropolis Rally saw the leading Quattro cars forbidden from continuing at mid-distance due to regulation infringements.

. . . the biggest entry for a world rally was the Monte Carlo in 1982, with 299 starters. The smallest was 39 at Quebec in 1979 which immediately disqualified the event from the series the following year. The smallest number of finishers was three in Poland in 1973.

. . . what was the first ever rally? The first major trial as opposed to open road races was the Herkomer Trophy in Germany in 1904. The oldest event in the world series is Monte Carlo, which was first held in 1911 and which celebrated its 52nd edition in 1984.

. . . some rallies proved rather too tough. No crews

ABOVE
The world's most wasted car? The Fiat X1/9 2-litre had all the attributes of the Lancia Stratos – and light weight as well, but after six prototypes were built the project was cancelled.

BELOW
Traditions die hard. Jean-Claude Andruet drives his Ferrari through Collesano on his way to winning the 1981 Targa Florio – a rally rather than a roadrace.

reached the end of the 1972 Bandama Rally The same happened in a club event in the Republic of Ireland in 1962.

. . . other events have regularly been won by visiting drivers. Australia's Southern Cross was six times won by Andrew Cowan, who travelled there each time from his native Scotland.

. . . the best seeding in a world championship rally: the first five cars which finished the South Pacific Rally in 1977 carrying the numbers 1, 2, 3, 5 and 6, car number 4 retiring at an early stage. The worst seeding must have been the 1974 Safari in which the winner (Joginder Singh) started number 46!

. . . the closest world championship rally was the 1973 Safari, in which cars were timed to the minute, both Mehta and Kallstrom finished equal on points, the former being given victory under tie deciding rules. The 1976 Sanremo Rally was won by Bjorn Waldegard by 4 seconds, in front of Sandro Munari and the 1979 Monte Carlo by Bernard Darniche 6 seconds in front of Waldegard.

National Scenes

. . . probably the most successful driver at his own event is Franz Wittmann, who has now won the Janner Rally in Austria nine times.

. . . though seldom competing outside his own country, Kyosti Hamalainen has been a Finnish rally champion ten times at the start of this season – though often this series is divided into different groups and top group cars are excluded from the series.

. . . Sarel van der Merwe has been overall South African rally champion eight times. He is just as talented on the racetracks as in the special stages. He won the IMSA 24 hours endurance race at Daytona in 1984 in a March Porsche.

. . . French drivers have always been as good on circuits as stages. Andruet, Nicolas, Therier and Ragnotti have all won world rallies in France as well as important categories at the Le Mans 24 hour race. Andruet has also won the 24 hour race at Spa. Walter Rohrl, Vic Elford and the ex Renault competition chief, Gerard Larrousse, have all won international championship rallies and races.

. . . many countries have such specialised rallies it is unknown for foreigners to win. The Swedish was held for 30 years before a non-Swede (Mikkola, a Finn) won; the highest place by a central European on that event was Mouton's second in 1984. The 1000 Lakes has always been won by a Finn or a Swede.

. . . although they have produced many fine drivers, the Italian Sanremo Rally has usually been won by a visitor. Since the start of the world series it has only twice been won by a "native" – Munari and 'Tony' Fassina, and the RAC Rally has only been won by ONE home driver, Roger Clark, since Peter Harper in 1958.

Teams

. . . few private teams have ever won world events. David Sutton provided the winning Escort for Hannu Mikkola on the RAC in 1979 (the year the factory went on strike), all four wins (including two consecutive Acropolis rallies) for Ari Vatanen in the Rothmans Escort and Blomqvist's RAC winning Quattro in 1983. Almeras Porsche cars have won the Monte Carlo (Nicolas) and the Tour de Corse (Therier), Stratos cars from Jolly Club ('Tony') the Sanremo and from Chardonnet (Darniche) the Monte Carlo and Tour de Corse. Walter Boyce's POR win in 1973 and Singh's first Safari win, in 1974, were also private efforts.

BELOW
Franz Wittmann on his way to winning the 1977 Janner Rally with Helmut Neverla in a group 4 Opel Kadett GT/E.

ABOVE   ARCHIVES
The world's craziest jump? Jussi Kynsilehto with the author on the 1975 1000 Lakes Rally . . .

BELOW
Underground rallying. The finish of this special stage on the Swedish Rally was at ground level!

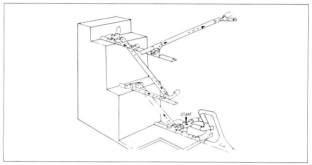

. . . which was the biggest team of all? Fiat admitted running over 30 Abarth 124s during 1975, as competition or training cars. For some time the honour of being the biggest private team was shared between unlikely places; Dr Pappalardo's Tape Ruvicha team of Escorts in Asuncion, Paraguay and Dr Miguel Oliveira's Diabolique team in Porto, Portugal.

. . . one of the most unusual sponsors for a private team comes from Czechoslovakia. Agroteam, for whom Vaclav Blahna won the national series in 1983, is run from the agricultural cooperative at Slusovice, near Gottwaldov.

. . . here today, gone tomorrow. One of the strangest "one-rally stands" was the Dodge Ramcharger team from Detroit. Originally to be sponsored by Chrysler, the team led by David Ash continued their 1981 Safari attempt even when the factory pulled out. Of four cars, two finished in the top ten – gaining the only world championship points for an American manufacturer.

. . . teams thrown out before they ever began. The two Vauxhall Chevette 2300HS cars were rejected by the organisers of the 1978 Portugal Rally for using the wrong kind of engine, the night before the start.

. . . thrown out after they won. The works Sunbeam Tiger of Peter Harper was excluded from the 1966 Alpine Rally, because it used inlet valves smaller than homologated. The Ford Lotus Cortina of Vic Elford which was excluded from the Sanremo Flowers Rally in 1966 when it was discovered that the wrong number of gear teeth were written on the homologation papers.

Favourite Photos of . . .

There are so many top-class photographers in rallying these days that we do not pretend that the people invited to contribute in Audi Sport World of Rallying 7 are alone in their work, or even in the quality. The selection has been based on many factors, their geographical spread – we have worked with them all before and can vouch for their professional attitude.

For TONY NORTH, rallying provides a working holiday! Being chief photographer for the Visitor newspaper at Morecambe, Lancashire, he began taking pictures of rallies in the mid-sixties as a way of becoming involved in the sport. These days he is responsible to Autosport for their national championship pictures but also works in his holidays for Colin Taylor Productions. Taylor has often sent him to far-flung areas of the world including the Middle East. A Nikon user, Tony normally uses Tri-X black/white and Fuji 100 colour film though his picture in this feature was taken on Kodachrome.

Thirty-seven year old MICHEL MORELLI, lives with his wife Michele Bertier at Monteux, near Carpentras in the south of France. For fifteen years they have together concentrated on motor sport photography. Working entirely freelance, they now command a wide respect among their clients enjoying the challenge of the production and supply of pictures, night and day. The "two Michels" have created standards through their reliability and quality of work which many younger French photographers seek to emulate.

With so much interest from the oriental car manufacturers in rallying, it was not surprising we soon met some photographer friends from Japan. The first to emerge was TAMOTSU FUTAMURA who had first ventured outside Japan to see the Mexico Grand Prix, which Surtees' Honda won. He came into rallying as mid-season break from covering Grands Prix. For years he was quite the most widely travelled of rallying's photographers though for the past four years he has lived in Vienna.

He spends half his time as photographer and half working with cine for television. He is freelance and uses Nikon F2 and F3 cameras with Kodak Professional Ektachrome film. His love of long lenses (600 and 800mm in particular) created a special style in his work which many have tried to copy but seldom equalled.

ROMANO POLI is based at Bologna, the centre of Italy's automobile journalism industry and concentrates solely on photography. He has an agency called Photo Quattro (Photo 4) which offers a wide range of motor sporting coverage. 27 years old, Romano employs three photographers as well as freelancers from event to event, but he is never happier than operating the shutters himself. Nowadays half his work is in the industry and half in journalism, and his eternal aim is to present a sense of fun and interest in the shots he takes.

FRANCISCO ROMEIRAS operates in Lisbon, Portugal under the name of "Photo Slick". A photographer by profession he started work eight years ago and concentrates on motor sport, mainly in Portugal. He uses Nikon cameras, Ilford black/white and Fuji colour film; his ambition is to expand and form an international agency. For the present he has an enviable knowledge of the roads of Portugal!

WILLY WEYENS has been working as a photographer, journalist and promoter in rallying for ten years, starting in national events in Belgium, working upwards through European championship rallies (which in the mid seventies enjoyed much greater interest) and on to world events. He is the leading rally correspondent in the Flemish language and his primary responsibility, as journalist, is to Nieuwsblad newspaper. Born in 1951 and single, Willy lives at Heusden-Zolder, the twin town which hosts Belgium's grand prix circuit.

GERHARD DIETER WAGNER left his work as an Opel mechanic and took up professional rally photography in 1977, after his father died. Based at Bad Soden between Wiesbaden and Frankfurt, 27 year old Gerhard is ideally placed to travel round his native West Germany and to go abroad. The energetic German motor sport journalism business offers an important basis for his work, though his first loyalties are to the monthly magazine Rallye Racing for whom he provides most of their world championship pictures.

TONY NORTH

One of the after effects of the South Atlantic dispute was that British journalists have found it very hard to get authority to go back to Argentina, indeed the author was the only British rally reporter at either of the last two world championship rallies in South America. One person who has been disappointed not to return is Tony North and this picture shows the reason why.

Argentina is a large country where distances and heights have a different dimension. This shot was taken back in 1981 when the rally was run in the Tucuman region, some way up in the Andes foothills. It is splendid territory, with long testing special stages where the fainthearted do not venture. This shot shows Timo Salonen's lonely Datsun Violet GT shortly before the car broke down with transmission failure. After that Argentina's expanse took on another aspect; it was very many hours before mechanics were able to rescue him!

Future Argentina rallies seem likely to be based at Cordoba, in less mountainous country and nearer civilisation, but for those who had seen the events at Tucuman nothing will ever be quite so impressive.

MICHEL MORELLI

A truck in a World Rallying annual? One of the reasons for this feature was to break away from the hard-news emphasis which our limits on pictures demands. Michel reckoned he searched through 25,000 transparencies before finding something DIFFERENT, a picture which portrayed movement and had a harmony of colour at the same time. The perfect picture is never taken, however hard a photographer tries. Maybe the solution to the quest for a photographer's fulfillment is not to expect a picture to be perfect. So long as it creates interest and has an element of good fun, what more is necessary?

This shot was taken on the 1982 Paris-Dakar Rally, but during a publicity stage in France rather than on the sandy pistes of Africa. Trucks are accepted as competition vehicles on this event for two reasons, firstly because the event offers them a unique competition opportunity, and for the professional crews to overcome the ban on independent service vehicles.

TAMOTSU FUTAMURA

The annual Safari Rally in Kenya offers the widest opportunities for rally photographers. It is full of action, people, places and above all nature. A lot of the pictures of animals with rally cars are specially staged, so when there is a chance of taking a genuine picture like this it is a dream for a photographer. Shekhar Mehta is seen passing some friends on the section halfway down towards Mombasa. Taken with 80/200mm zoom lens, Tamotsu has forsaken his usual long lens to good effect.

The Safari is however probably not Tamotsu's favourite event – that is the Monte Carlo Rally. In 1972 it was the first big rally he had covered, and he discovered the real challenge of rally photography. In rallying, you only get one chance to take each shot. It is so much more difficult than racing! But the chances of taking pictures like this make the whole world of rally photography rewarding.

13

ROMANO POLI

There is no shortage of good locations at the Monte Carlo Rally but it is always difficult to take a good selection of pictures. 1984 was the first time in many years there had been plenty of snow, and of course everyone wanted to get as many snow pictures as they could. At this rally this is never easy; because of the mountains and the closed roads it is an event where it is difficult to catch the cars up again. By the time you have the chance to overtake the cars the event will have moved away to a different area and the weather changed! Furthermore so much of the event is held in the dark and then denies you the chance to capture the character of the countryside in a photograph.

This shot shows Bruno Saby in the Philips Renault 5 Turbo heading into the light on stage 15. Run south of Gap, this was the sunniest and snowiest of them all and went over the Col des Garcinets. The camera was a Nikon F3 and the film was Fuji 50. The lens was standard focal length.

SLICK (FRANCISCO ROMEIRAS)

Although the Rally of Portugal produces some of the nicest pictures of the season, sometimes a picture taken elsewhere is of more interest to the photographer, especially if there is some unusual interest attached to it. One of rallying's great characters is Adartico Vudafieri who has an extraordinary propensity for accidents. On this occasion he left his braking a fraction later than other drivers had done, with the result you can see. Happily the incident damaged pride more than bodies, though the camera tripod owned by British television filmman Barrie Hinchliffe was never the same again.

The picture was taken in Italy where the competition is always exciting and in Tuscany the scenery especially attractive. The old Roman system of building roads on the top of hills rather than hidden in valleys, is one reason why few pictures at Sanremo are boring, because so many views show behind the cars.

Francisco, who operates under the name "Photo Slick" has an unrivalled knowledge of the roads in his native Portugal, and hopefully next time we can enjoy the benefits of this experience – if Mr Vudafieri does not do anything too exciting in the meantime!

WILLY WEYENS

This picture was not taken on a rally at all! It was taken near Touggourt in Algeria in December 1983 when Guy Colsoul was testing his tyres before the Paris-Dakar Rally-Raid. This is an area famous for its dunes and the very special character of the sand. At dawn the sand is hard and firm, by 11 in the morning the heat has made it very soft.

Colsoul was taking the event very seriously and eventually finished fourth, the best two-wheel drive entry – despite an accident on the first day in Africa when he hit another competitor who had stopped because of dust. The testing itself was a success even though the experiment of using twin-tyres on each rear rim did not work. The best solution for driving on sand was the oldest – simply by letting air out of the tyres.

African photography is so difficult by comparison with working in Europe. Everything takes ten times longer, things go wrong through no fault of your own. Traditional events like the Safari and Ivory Coast are difficult enough to cover, rallies like Paris-Dakar are a hundred times worse. Unusual pictures help to make it all worthwhile.

GERHARD DIETER WAGNER

Normally Gerhard's greatest ambition is to take a picture which tells you what a country is like. For him the job of a photographer is to say in a picture what a journalist cannot say in words. Having already had one Argentina picture in this collection he selected this shot – which shows more about the excitement of rallying than its location. It was taken in South America in 1984 and shows Jorge Recalde going flat-out through a water splash. For Gerhard the challenge was to use back lighting to best effect, bearing in mind that this is seldom very helpful when publishers often prefer front-lighting, to illuminate the car better.

For Gerhard the move to Cordoba took away many of Argentina's former photographic possibilities; he had enjoyed Bariloche's mountains and clean air. In his work he often uses a longer lens. This shot was taken with a 300mm f2.8 lens fitted to a Nikon F2 on Fuji 50 film, which like many rally photographers he has been using since early 1984.

The Total Traction Revolution

Four-wheel drive is rallying's most important revolution in memory. Nearly every world championship rally has now been won by a car with four-wheel drive and a growing number of production cars use this system. Its development is giving manufacturers a major justification for involvement in motor sport, and rallying will eventually take the credit for the development of total traction in road car design. However although rally and road cars are heading in the same direction, it does not mean they have to overcome the same problems. Some of the reasons rallying has turned to total traction have nothing to do with production car problems at all!

The most obvious reason for four-wheel drive is to improve traction and braking on slippery surfaces. The world championship for rallies is run with a huge percentage of competition on gravel rather than asphalt so, as Audi proved in 1982 and 1984, a world championship winning team has been able largely to ignore asphalt road inadequacies. Although factors such as improved tyre and suspension design have contributed, the most dramatic reason for the reduction of special stage times has been the improved traction which four-wheel drive offers. Stage times have come down despite increased limitations on engine modifications and without any apparent improvement in cornering power.

The second reason for four-wheel drive in rallying is that cars have recently broken through the three-hundred horsepower mark, for several years rallying's "sound barrier". Now four hundred horsepower is necessary to be competitive. Tyres have never really coped with more than two hundred going through the front axle or three hundred through the rear, so now tyres have become the limiting factor in rally car performance. Four-wheel drive eases the burden. Thirdly the doubling of tyre area used for traction gives a chance to build cars with narrow wheels and the cars can then be smaller and lighter than possible in two-wheel drive form.

BELOW
Too much to do? The front wheels on Mouton's Audi Quattro on the Swedish Rally show that it is difficult to put a lot of power through the front axle – and steer at the same time.

HOLMES

The Challenge of Four-Wheel Drive Systems

The problem with creating a design revolution is that drivers cannot readily adjust their skills, and fresh drivers are not available at short notice. One happy coincidence for the Audi Quattro was that a driver experienced in front-wheel drive rallying could adapt with relative ease. One inevitable consequence with original four-wheel drive designs was that better traction compromised cornering capability and driver control. When wheels were being asked to do more than before something had to be sacrificed. With two-wheel drive a rally driver could use the facilities at his command for more than their originally intended purpose, for example the brakes and the accelerator pedal were used to steer the car. With four-wheel drive there are changes in the traditional concept of dynamic balance. Furthermore the problems of setting-up a car have become increasingly more complicated, particularly because now there are three, not one, differentials which have functions to be adjusted.

Another disadvantage, which Audi did not originally appreciate, is that four-wheel drive requires more mechanical parts, each carrying additional weight and these cannot be under-engineered just because torque is put through more wheels. Because of Appendix J's engine size/minimum weight formula the projected weight of the final car is fundamental to the choice of engine capacity to be used. Four-wheel drive is nevertheless worth the effort because traction on world championship events is so important.

Designs for Success

When Audi entered the scene in late 1980 with a competition version of the Quattro road car, they were so far ahead of the opposition in taking advantage of the newly-permitted four-wheel drive facility that guidelines were hard to find. There was also great confusion because they were also the first team to break through the 300bhp barrier. It was difficult to know whether their excellent stage times were due to greater traction or to superior power or a combination of both. Furthermore they came on the rally scene at a period of design stagnation due to impending changes in Appendix J so some success had been due to natural advancement.

It has taken the Peugeot 205 Turbo 16 to make us realise how primitive was the Quattro! As can be seen from its rear wheel lifting tendencies the Quattro is essentially a front-wheel drive car with an added facility for driving the rear wheels. It uses a simple system of design by placing the engine outside the lines of the axles, but suffers the consequent high polar moment of inertia, an anathema to good handling in competition cars. If it was ever in doubt, this deadly effect was shown during the 1984 Sanremo Rally when water shot

ABOVE
Another advantage of total traction: the car still has traction through three wheels when there is a problem with the fourth! Martin Schanche surprised the locals at Pikes Peak.

Rohrl's Sport Quattro off the road at a tangent and Vatanen's Peugeot simply spun, and when patches of ice put Mouton's Quattro into a house on the 1982 Monte Carlo Rally. Having the engine outside the axles however means that the torque does not have to turn so many corners between the engine and the driven wheels and in theory not so much power should be lost in the transmission.

The Porsche 911s which entered rallycross in 1984 are other cars that have the engine outside the axles, virtually being Quattros in reverse. In rallycross power is even more important than in rallying and traction consequently vital. But when Martin Schanche's 4x4 Escort started winning with up to two hundred horse-power less than some rivals, it was obvious that cleverness could still beat force. The Peugeot by beating the Sport Quattro in rallying with a hundred horse-power less has developed this theme. The most pressing question when design work began in the early 'eighties was what layout would be the best.

These days there are two main questions to face – whether or not to place the engine within the axle lines and how to reduce the problems of putting too much power through the front wheels. To achieve better handling most designers have opted for an engine between the axles and this begs a supplementary decision, whether to use front or mid engine locations. Originally it was assumed that a front engine would under acceleration give all four wheels an equal chance of gripping to best effect; it also avoided the heat build-up from a mid engine. There seemed to be no inherent weight advantage with either layout. Many companies have traditionally preferred front-engined cars for marketing reasons or because drivers, feeling safer with an engine in front, would go faster if psychologically happier. Furthermore there was less wasted space with a front engine as the gearbox casing could encroach into the passenger area more easily.

With the advent of 400bhp plus cars, conventional four-wheel drive was getting out of hand. The front axle could not cope and the cars would not steer under acceleration. Therefore more power had to be directed to the rear axle and the rearward weight bias from a mid engine helped. Mid engines were also preferred for reasons of improved handling.

Handling was a high priority in the design of Schanche's 500bhp car, because rallycross demands a special ability to corner effectively when off-line. The Peugeot is the first car in rallies to split the torque unequally between the axles and immediately this pleased the drivers. Ari Vatanen was asked in Sanremo to explain how he could drive the Peugeot so easily when he had found the Manta 400 difficult. He said the Peugeot handled like the old Escort RS; the Opels had been too stable for his liking. When the torque should be split – and how this happens – are where things get complicated.

Enter the Scientists

What happens in a four-wheel drive transmission system is complex. From the earliest times the problems of making one axle speed up when going round sharp corners had indicated that a central differential was important. In situations where wheels are spinning

ABOVE
Ford constructed four-wheel drive Capri rallycross cars in 1971. Roger Clark is seen leading a group at Cadwell Park. Thirteen years later Ford are again involved in total traction for sport – and production cars as well.

BELOW
The man who started things off. Gene Henderson seen winning the 1972 Press-on-Regardless Rally in Michigan, USA (a qualifying round on the International Championship for Makes) – beating the works Lancias! The vehicle is a Jeep Wagoneer.

KEMPER

ABOVE
Some little explored four-wheel drive alternatives. In the early sixties BMC produced some twin-engined Mini prototypes, to obtain better power-to-weight ratios. In 1984 Lancia's engineer Giorgio Pianta made (in his spare time) a twin-engined Trevi, one object of which was to provide Pirelli with some experience of four-wheel drive tyre testing for the Delta Rally 4x4.

much of the time, as now happens with a high-powered rally car on gravel, it is important to be able to lock up this differential, but even so each axle must be strong enough to withstand all the shocks and snatches, or perhaps a breakage in part of the transmission. Wheel snatch when landing one-axle first or driving from a slippery track on to a more abrasive surface is doubly severe when using a freely running central differential. For these reasons the tricky problem was to combine the functions of an epicyclic coupling with the central differential. The object is to decide when to speed up the slower axle, to slow down the faster axle, to lock up

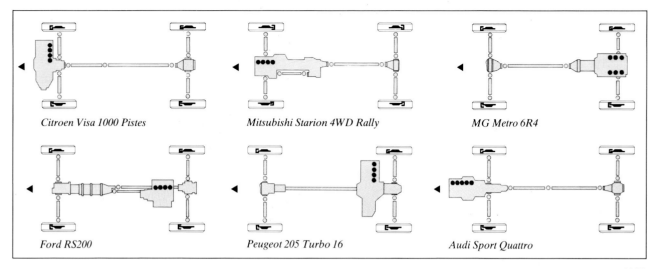

Citroen Visa 1000 Pistes   *Mitsubishi Starion 4WD Rally*   *MG Metro 6R4*

Ford RS200   *Peugeot 205 Turbo 16*   *Audi Sport Quattro*

COOK

the axles or ask the central differential to allow them to run free. The most promising solution to this challenge is clearly to be found in Schanche's European Rallycross car, but the way it is achieved is highly secret!

Virtually all four-wheel drive systems use a viscous coupling adjacent to the central differential. Developed by the British Ferguson company this mechanism uses a series of clutch-type plates which spin freely close to each other. When the spinning becomes excessive the fluid in which they spin changes viscosity and restricts the spinning, which progressively locks up the plates. This can be used in a variety of ways. Opel for example have used it so that only the rear wheels take up the drive from a standing start and the front axle only engages once the car is under way.

Having decided when the central differential should be locked comes the choice of how it should work when it is still operating freely. The degree by which the torque should be split between the front and rear axles can be pre-set, ranging in the case of Peugeot from 25/75 front/rear for asphalt, through 33/67 for gravel to 50/50 for sheet ice. Ford however are entering the scene with a disconnectable front axle – a 0/100 torque split system while the rallycross Porsches have a primitive automatic front wheel engagement system – a freewheel placed in the front axle transmission line. This may have certain attractions but leads to questions as to whether optional four-wheel drive is worthwhile in a competition car. If a car has to offer both four-wheel and rear-wheel drive, it must surely be unnecessarily heavy.

The Future

Coping with power outputs of over 500bhp and torque figures of over 55mkg yet still getting the car round corners like a two-wheel drive model is the next challenge for group B rallycar engineers. Differentials are under constant development and electronics provide new opportunities – like speed sensors. These have not yet been used in rallying but would permit a far more efficient system of differential. As the need increases for splitting the torque to give a rear-axle bias, so comes the need to discover if it is possible – or desirable – to lock the axles with a torque bias. Still very few rally cars have been designed from scratch to use four-wheel drive to full advantage. The Mitsubishi Starion 4WD, not yet homologated, is a rear-drive car adapted to take a normal Pajero utility transmission system; the forth-coming Lancia 038 could be said to be a mid-engined car adapted so the front wheels are also driven. Still the Peugeot 205 Turbo 16 is the only homologated purpose-built rally 4x4, and even so it has the constraint of having to LOOK like the mass production version.

The question of what the car must look like created difficulties for Austin-Rover's MG Metro 6R4. This demanded a very short wheelbase and therefore insufficient space to put its special V6 engine fully inside the axles. AR also chose not to use a turbocharger and this meant a larger and heavier engine and a less easily balanced car. Ford finally decided to have a mid engine and to use a transaxle system to create an equivalent mass centre at the opposite end of the car. Gradually engineers are emerging from the dark ages when four-wheel drive cars had hopeless control and could never steer under acceleration. Improvements are becoming visible all the time. Four-wheel drive enables cars to run softer compound tyres, and equivalent tyres can last more than twice the distance on four-wheel drive cars. The Peugeot has shown that 4x4 cars can handle in an acceptable way and not demand violent action by drivers to change their attitude. One day we will sit in production road cars and never notice the difference. Then we shall know that rallying's biggest revolution has been for everyone.

A Week at the Peak

Pikes Peak Auto Hillclimb went international in 1984 when Michele Mouton was sent by Audi to try to break the outright hill record with a Sport Quattro rally car. This unique event is held on gravel roads, the competition divided into three classes for Open wheelers, stock cars and rally cars and competitors have just one shot at the hillclimb each year. In fine American style, the competition is turned into a week-long show with

BELOW
In the midday haze, Rod Millen slides his Mazda RX7 4x4 into a sharp corner with nothing but the view behind.

early morning practice and qualifying, a rest day and then, on the Saturday, the race itself. For enthusiasts it is hard going. Every morning it is necessary to rise before four o'clock in order to arrive at the hill before the road closes, but only by staying the whole week is it possible to enjoy watching from a variety of locations.

The thinness of the air at the summit takes your breath away and makes life hard-work for competition cars, but for viewing, particularly in the early morning, it is without compare. If the weather is clear you can see the whole range of Colorado's Rocky Mountains, or on a cloudy day you will watch the cars climb through the clouds and beyond. At midday when the

official races are held the freshness of the morning breaks to haziness and in late afternoon, when the hill is crowded in a very long traffic jam as spectators head homewards, the weather turns and most bizarre rain-cloud patterns can be seen.

Michele was not the only intruder. Norwegian rally-cross champion Martin Schanche, hopeful of impressing sponsors, brought along his four-wheel drive special. Whereas Audi took the whole exercise so seriously the locals began to wonder if this was some form of invasion, Schanche was relaxed and hopeful, even driving his 500bhp Escort on the interstate highway the sixty miles from Denver when he had no trailer waiting for his car at the airport. And Mouton and Schanche were not the only visitors, for the event has in recent years attracted the American rally fraternity which includes various New Zealanders.

At first sight there seemed little reason for hope among the rallymen. Their cars were considerably less powerful than the locally run open-wheelers and stock cars, but rallymen had weapons denied to the others, four-wheel drive and turbocharging. In theory the changing altitude (from 9402 feet at the startline to 14110 at the summit) should prove ideal turbocharger territory, of which competitors in the Colorado mountain hill climb championship had little experience. For them the solution was to prepare their carburation for the average altitude and hope for the best. For Audi the operation was something far more than a one-shot record attempt, it was a chance to engage in a week of testing in unique conditions. Interestingly the event was sponsored by Predator Carburettors whose involvement in the event was a pay-off for being allowed to test on site themselves. Audi fitted a 100kg computer in the car, which noted out endless data and even led engineers at one point to ask Michele why she kept on lifting off the throttle . . .

Michele looked and acted a sensation. Lady drivers are seldom seen on the hill and her declaration of intent to take Fabrizia Pons on her record attempt sent Pikes Peak officials rushing to their rule books – to find they had never covered that eventuality! Michele said she would feel happier with Fabrizia but would not necessarily go faster. The weather never failed in raceweek so there was no chance of bad visibility, but there were one or two critical fast, blind bends further up the hill where pacenotes, in the absence of landmarks, would help greatly. Michele was battling against tradition as much as her opposition. This was the 62nd Race to the Clouds, folk heroes like Andretti and Unser are written large in the Colorado archives. After two attempts at

RIGHT

Point-and-Squirt. This Sprint car driver finds corners MOST inconvenient.

ABOVE   HOLMES

Michele Mouton attacks a hairpin at the "W's". Despite the view, this is only halfway up the hill!

the hill, John Buffum had sewn the seeds of curiosity back in Germany, however. He had proved that an Audi Quattro was not far off the pace, that specially designed Goodyears were not the only tyre for the course, that a V8 was not the only power unit capable for staying the course at racing speeds.

ABOVE
Gary Eaton's Peugeot's turbo kept over-spinning and failing.

BELOW
Bill Brister, overall winner, with his 600bhp Wells Coyote Special, failed to beat the outright record held by Al Unser Jnr in a similar car.

ABOVE
American motorsport is colourful. Fabrizia Pons finds local buffalo farmer, Jeep competitor Don Adams full of charm and stories.

Every day the stubby Audi, still an unfamiliar sight even on Europe's special stages, went up and down the hill. Michele Mouton spent spare moments driving her roadcar alone, committing every curve and brow to memory. Come raceday the one-shot was all that counted. "I felt confident in myself but not in the car. I actually sat on the starting line wondering if it would last the 12.4 miles. Normally you never think like that. If something happens on a stage on a rally there are so many more stages where you can catch up again". On the test days drivers practised different sections of the hill, hoping that mechanical problems would not upset their plans. For many it did, none more so than Gary Eaton in a Peugeot 505 Turbo which had a turbo failure on almost every outing. It was strange to watch the driving styles. The open-wheelers were potentially the best but only a handful were well driven. Many were old-fashioned sit-up-and-beg front-engined Sprint cars, and these were some of the worst offenders for point-and-squirt. They accelerated like mad, but only in between losing control and regaining it on the corners. The stockers burbled upwards, handling better by virtue of their ballasted chassis, but as with all the rear-wheelers, it was traction which let them down.

25

Amidst the spectacle the four-wheel drive rally cars looked tame, perhaps the tamest being Schanche's rallycross car. Built to the new "silhouette" formula, the car was designed as a derivation of a group A Escort XR3 and looked it. No wings, no wheel arch extensions, no air dams, many of the modifications being fitted to save damage when racing in close company with other cars. Just an ordinary Escort, fitted with four-wheel drive – and an engine from a C100 endurance car. It was only when practice times were published that Schanche's performance became notable. If anything went wrong with Michele's car (perish the thought) and Rod Millen's 4x4 Mazda RX7 was off-song, perhaps the Norwegian would save the honour for the special stage men? Maybe, wondered the real sliderule experts, the Escort might even challenge the Quattro if all went well.

Things were very worrying for Mouton as raceday grew near. The car never ran so well as it did the day it had arrived. Two days before the event Audi had brought journalists from Europe, the night before at a private dinner party a powerful "no-excuses" speech was delivered to the team by the American importers. The team slept uneasily in the few hours before the early start on raceday, knowing they would not be welcome again if things went wrong. What they had to achieve was never specifically defined. Of course to win

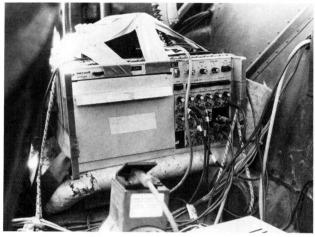

ABOVE
Audi's computer

the rally car category was number one ambition but little short of an outright hill record would please Michele.

It was an eerie experience racing that hill. High winds frightened all but the bravest helicopter pilots

BELOW
Organisers run competitors in order, depending on qualifying times but taking care to ensure the dust blows away before sending another car up the hill.

Larry Carnes's Pontiac, final car up the hill, receives the chequered flag as it made best stock car time.

from approaching the peak, drivers on the course reported an odd sense of isolation. "We drove up the hill wondering where all the spectators had gone. They had parked their cars so far off the track I never saw them, and maybe I was just concentrating too hard to notice them standing by the side of the track," said Michele. But record numbers were alright. The rally cars went first up the hill, finding that loose gravel had slowed their times. Schanche shot off the line at record pace but one-third up the hill he punctured. He had come so far for nothing – except for creating legends. He calmly drove the rest of the hill on the flat making third best time in the category, earning enough prize money in doing so to pay for his trip. Second quickest was Millen, his Mazda sounding superb as the driver committed his normally aspirated, underpowered car all the way, and fastest, to the relief of almost everyone was Michele.

Post-race reaction began to set in all round. Hardliners felt the Audi and the Escort assault had failed but it had been a close shave, something too worrying for peace of mind. It told them that Buffum's previous efforts had been no idle threat, that their beloved hill was no longer theirs by heritage. For Audi the message was what they wanted, maybe even they knew that to beat the record first-time out would devalue the achievement, and Michele was sure. Given half a chance – she would be back!

RIGHT
Martin Schanche and THAT wheel. The Revolution rim was virtually undamaged.

World Class Drivers

At the beginning of 1984 there were a total of 21 A-priority drivers (eight less than 1983), and 96 with priority B (45 less than 1983). A-priority drivers have gained their status through results as follows:

1 Being World Champion Driver in one of the three previous years.
2 Finishing 2nd or 3rd in a round of the World Rally Championship the previous year.
3 Winning a round of the World Rally Championship for either Manufacturers or Drivers during one of the preceding three years.
4 Winning the European Championship in one of the preceding three years.
5 Finishing in the first five in the preceding year's European Championship. (Drivers holding a FISA Grand Prix or Long Distance "super" licence who rally have the same priority).

B-priority drivers gain their status in one of five ways, as follows:

(a) Having been an A-priority driver the previous three years, and not having requalified for inclusion.
(b) Having finished either 4th, 5th or 6th on a World Championship for Drivers event in the previous year.
(c) Having finished either 1st or 2nd on a coefficient 3 or 4 round of the previous year's European Championship.
(d) Having finished 1st or 2nd on an African Championship event the previous year.
(e) Being nominated by the national club, such nomination being limited to three per country with the exception of West Germany, France, Great Britain and Italy, each of whom may nominate 5 drivers.

All drivers qualifying for A or B priority during 1984 commence such priority from 1 January 1985.

In this section are listed the performances of those drivers holding A-priority in 1984 in all world championship rallies entered, whether or not that driver finished the event in question, since the world championship began in 1973 until the end of the 1983 season.

B-priority drivers

A	Austria	George Fischer (**e**), Sepp Haider (**e**), Franz Wittmann (**a-1983**), Franz Wurz (**b**)
B	Belgium	Guy Colsoul (**a-1983**), Marc Duez (**a-1983**), Patrick Snyers (**c**)
BU	Burundi	Guy Collette (**d**)
CH	Switzerland	Jean-Pierre Balmer (**e**), Jean-Claude Bering (**e**)
CI	Ivory Coast	Alain Ambrosino (**b**), Samir Assef (**b**), Eugene Salim (**b**)
CY	Cyprus	Dino Maschias (**e**), Vahan Terzian (**c**)
D	West Germany	Harald Demuth (**c**), Jochi Kleint (**a-1982**), Achim Warmbold (**e**), Erwin Weber (**c**)
E	Spain	Eugenio Ortiz (**c**), Salvador Servia (**e**)
EAK	Kenya	Rob Collinge (**e**), John Hellier (**e**), Yasuhiro Iwase (**b**), Mike Kirkland (**a-1983**), Vic Preston Jnr (**a-1981**), Jayant Shah (**b**)
F	France	Jean-Claude Andruet (**a-1983**), Bernard Beguin (**a-1983**), Francois Chatriot (**c**), Maurice Chomat (**e**), Alain Coppier (**a-1981**), Jean-Pierre Nicolas (**a-1981**), Christian Rio (**e**), Bruno Saby (**b**), Jean-Luc Therier (**a-1983**), Francis Vincent (**e**), Philippe Wambergue (**e**)
GB	Great Britain	Russell Brookes (**b**), Simon Everett (**e**), Terry Kaby (**e**), Chris Lord (**e**), Tony Pond (**a-1982**), Darryl Weidner (**e**), Malcolm Wilson (**e**)
GR	Greece	George Moschous (**e**)
H	Hungary	Attila Ferjancz (**a-1982**)
I	Italy	'Lucky' Luigi Battistoli (**e**), Carlo Capone (**e**), Tony Carello (**a – 1981**), Dario Cerrato (**b**), Gianfranco Cunico (**e**), Antonella Mandelli (**c**), Sandro Munari (**e**), Mauro Pregliasco (**a – 1981**), Fabrizio Tabaton (**c**), Antonio Tognana (**c**), Antonio Zanussi (**a-1983**)
J	Japan	Yoshi Takaoka (**b**)
MC	Monaco	'Tchine' (Auguste Turuani) (**e**)
N	Norway	John Haugland (**e**)
NL	Netherlands	Renger Guliker (**e**), Paul Maaskant (**e**), Henk Vossen (**e**)
NZ	New Zealand	Peter Bourne (**e**), Reg Cook (**e**), Jim Donald (**b**), Malcolm Stewart (**b**)
P	Portugal	Jose Borges (**e**), Joaquim Santos (**e**)
PL	Poland	Marian Bublewicz (**e**), Blazej Krupa (**e**)
Q	Qatar	Saeed Al Hajri (**e**)
RA	Argentina	Carlos Celis (**e**), Jorge Recalde (**a-1982**), Carlos Reutemann (**a-1981**), Ernesto Soto (**e**)
RW	Rwanda	Mitraros (**d**), Robert (**d**)
S	Sweden	Ingvar Carlsson (**e**), Mikael Ericsson (**e**), Kalle Grundel (**b**), Mats Jonsson (**e**), Anders Kullang (**a-1983**)
SF	Finland	Rauno Aaltonen (**a-1982**), Pentti Airikkala (**a-1983**), Juha Kankkunen (**b**), Antero Laine (**e**), Mikael Sundstrom (**e**), Henri Toivonen (**a-1983**)
U	Uruguay	Domingo de Vitta (**a-1983**)
USA	United States	John Buffum (**b**), Rod Millen (**e**), Jon Woodner (**e**)
ZA	South Africa	Sarel van der Merwe (**d**)
ZAI	Zaire	Christian Brose (**d**)

Markku Alen (SF)

Born 15 February 1951 in Helsinki
First rally car Renault 8 Gordini in 1969

JT	=	Juhani Toivonen
IK	=	Ilkka Kivimaki
AA	=	Atso Aho
PW	=	Paul White

1973

SF	Volvo 142	JT 2nd
GB	Ford Escort RS1600	IK 3rd

1974

P	Fiat Abarth 124	IK 3rd
SF	Fiat Abarth 124	IK 3rd
I	Fiat Abarth 124	IK steering
CDN	Fiat Abarth 124	IK accident
USA	Fiat Abarth 124	AA 2nd
GB	Ford Escort RS1600	PW water pump
F	Fiat Abarth 124	IK excluded

1975

MC	Fiat Abarth 124	IK 3rd
S	Fiat Abarth 124	IK 6th
MA	Fiat Abarth 124	IK broken sump
P	Fiat Abarth 124	IK 1st
SF	Datsun Violet	IK accident
I	Fiat Abarth 124	IK gearbox
GB	Fiat Abarth 124	IK engine

1976

MC	Fiat Abarth 124	IK 6th
MA	Fiat Abarth 131	IK 12th
SF	Fiat Abarth 131	IK 1st
I	Fiat Abarth 131	IK accident
GB	Fiat Abarth 131	IK differential

1977

MC	Fiat Abarth 131	IK 54th
S	Fiat Abarth 131	IK electrics
P	Fiat Abarth 131	IK 1st
NZ	Fiat Abarth 131	IK 3rd
GR	Fiat Abarth 131	IK driveshaft
SF	Fiat Abarth 131	IK engine
CDN	Fiat Abarth 131	IK engine
GB	Fiat Abarth 131	IK piston

Markku Alen (SF)

Attilio Bettega (I)

1978

S	Fiat Abarth 131	IK 3rd
P	Fiat Abarth 131	IK 1st
GR	Fiat Abarth 131	IK 2nd
SF	Fiat Abarth 131	IK 1st
CDN	Fiat Abarth 131	IK 2nd
I	Lancia Stratos	IK 1st
GB	Lancia Stratos	IK gearbox

1st FIA Cup

1979

MC	Fiat Abarth 131	IK 3rd
S	Fiat Abarth 131	IK 4th
EAK	Fiat Abarth 131	IK 3rd
SF	Fiat Abarth 131	IK 1st
I	Fiat Abarth 131	IK 6th
GB	Lancia Stratos	IK 5th

3rd World Championship for Drivers

1980

MC	Fiat Abarth 131	IK accident
P	Fiat Abarth 131	IK 2nd
GR	Fiat Abarth 131	IK 3rd
RA	Fiat Abarth 131	IK broken sump
SF	Fiat Abarth 131	IK 1st
I	Fiat Abarth 131	IK engine

6th World Championship for Drivers

1981

MC	Fiat Abarth 131	IK 7th
P	Fiat Abarth 131	IK 1st
GR	Fiat Abarth 131	IK 2nd
SF	Fiat Abarth 131	IK 2nd
I	Fiat Abarth 131	IK 9th
GB	Lancia Stratos	IK accident

4th World Championship for Drivers

1982

F	Lancia Rally	IK 9th
GR	Lancia Rally	IK chassis
SF	Lancia Rally	IK engine
I	Lancia Rally	IK engine
GB	Lancia Rally	IK 4th

1983

MC	Lancia Rally	IK 2nd
P	Lancia Rally	IK 4th
F	Lancia Rally	IK 1st
GR	Lancia Rally	IK 2nd
RA	Lancia Rally	IK 5th
SF	Lancia Rally	IK 3rd
I	Lancia Rally	IK 1st

3rd World Championship for Drivers

Attilio Bettega (I)

Born 19 February 1953 in Trento
First rally car Fiat 128 Rallye in 1972

IT	=	Isabella Torghele
GV	=	Gianni Vacchetto
MP	=	Maurizio Perissinot
MM	=	Mario Mannucci
AB	=	Arnaldo Bernacchini

1978

I	Lancia Stratos	IT accident
F	Lancia Stratos	GV puncture

1979

MC	Fiat Ritmo 75	MP engine
I	Fiat Abarth 131	MP 3rd

1980

MC	Fiat Ritmo 75	MM 6th
P	Fiat Abarth 131	AB road accident
GR	Fiat Abarth 131	AB 8th
RA	Fiat Abarth 131	AB broken sump
I	Fiat Abarth 131	AB 6th
F	Fiat Abarth 131	AB accident

1981

MC	Fiat Ritmo 75	MP engine
P	Fiat Abarth 131	MP engine
GR	Fiat Abarth 131	MP 3rd
I	Fiat Abarth 131	MP accident

1982

F	Lancia Rally	MP accident

1983

F	Lancia Rally	MP 4th
GR	Lancia Rally	MP 5th
NZ	Lancia Rally	MP 3rd
I	Lancia Rally	MP 3rd

7th World Championship for Drivers

Massimo Biasion (I)

Massimo Biasion (I)

Born 29 January 1958 at Bassano del Grappa in Vicenza
First rally car Opel Kadett in 1979

TS	=	Tiziano Siviero

1980

I	Opel Ascona	TS differential

1981

I	Opel Ascona 400	TS 6th

1982

I	Opel Ascona 400	TS 8th

1983

I	Lancia Rally	TS 5th

European Champion

Stig Blomqvist (S)

Born 29 July 1946 in Orebro
First rally car Saab 96 in 1964

AH	=	Arne Hertz
HS	=	Hans Sylvan
'V'	=	'Vicki'
BC	=	Bjorn Cederberg

1973

S	Saab 96V4	AH 1st
SF	Saab 96V4	AH crankshaft
A	Saab 96V4	AH differential
GB	Saab 96V4	AH accident

1974

SF	Saab 96V4	HS 4th
GB	Saab 96V4	HS 2nd

1975

S	Saab 96V4	HS 2nd
SF	Saab 96V4	HS excluded
GB	Saab 96V4	HS engine

1976

S	Saab 96V4	HS 2nd
SF	Saab 99EMS	HS gearbox case
GB	Saab 99EMS	HS 2nd

1977

S	Saab 99EMS	HS 1st
SF	Saab 99EMS	HS distributor
GB	Saab 99EMS	HS transmission

1978

S	Lancia Stratos	HS 4th
CDN	Saab 99EMS	'V gearbox
GB	Saab 99 Turbo	HS driveshaft

Stig Blomqvist (S)

1979

S	Saab 99 Turbo	BC 1st
GB	Saab 99 Turbo	BC accident

Equal 10th World Championship for Drivers

1980

S	Saab 99 Turbo	BC 2nd
GB	Saab 99 Turbo	BC engine

1981

S	Saab 99 Turbo	BC 5th
SF	Talbot Sunbeam Lotus	BC 8th
GB	Talbot Sunbeam Lotus	BC 3rd

1982

S	Audi Quattro	BC 1st
SF	Audi Quattro	BC 2nd
I	Audi Quattro	BC 1st
GB	Talbot Sunbeam Lotus	BC 8th

4th World Championship for Drivers

1983

MC	Audi Quattro	BC 3rd
S	Audi 80 Quattro	BC 2nd
P	Audi Quattro	BC transmission
GR	Audi Quattro	BC 3rd
NZ	Audi Quattro	BC withdrawn
RA	Audi Quattro	BC 2nd
SF	Audi Quattro	BC 2nd
I	Audi Quattro	BC accident
GB	Audi Quattro	BC 1st

4th World Championship for Drivers

Bernard Darniche (F)

Born 28 March 1942 in Cenon
First rally car NSU 1000 in 1967

AM	=	Alain Mahe

1973

MC	Renault Alpine A110	AM 10th
S	Renault 12 Gordini	AM accident
P	Renault Alpine A110	AM differential
MA	Renault Alpine A110	AM 1st
GR	Renault Alpine A110	AM driver ill
A	Renault Alpine A110	AM 2nd
I	Renault Alpine A110	AM accident
F	Renault Alpine A110	AM differential

1974

EAK	Renault Alpine A110	AM engine/susp'n
USA	Renault 17 Gordini	AM 6th
F	Fiat Abarth 124	AM differential

1975

MC	Fiat Abarth 124	AM engine
MA	Fiat Abarth 124	AM wet electrics
F	Lancia Stratos	AM 1st

1976

MC	Lancia Stratos	AM 3rd
F	Lancia Stratos	AM 2nd

European Champion

Bernard Darniche (F)

1977

MC	Lancia Stratos	AM road accident
F	Fiat Abarth 131	AM 1st

European Champion

1978

MC	Fiat Abarth 131	AM 5th
P	Lancia Stratos	AM too late
F	Fiat Abarth 131	AM 1st

7th FIA Cup

1979

MC	Lancia Stratos	AM 1st
P	Lancia Stratos	AM electrics
GR	Lancia Stratos	AM rear susp'n
F	Lancia Stratos	AM 1st

6th World Championship for Drivers

1980

MC	Lancia Stratos	AM 2nd
P	Lancia Stratos	AM head gasket
GR	Lancia Stratos	AM steering
F	Fiat Abarth 131	AM accident

1981

MC	Lancia Stratos	AM 6th
F	Lancia Stratos	AM 1st

1982

F	BMW M1	AM oil pipe

1983

I	Audi Quattro	AM 9th

Per Eklund (S)

Born 26 June 1946 in Arvika
First rally car Volvo PV544 in 1964

RC	=	Rolf Carlsson
BC	=	Bjorn Cederberg
BR	=	Bo Reinicke
HS	=	Hans Sylvan
RS	=	Ragnar Spjuth
JB	=	Jan-Olaf Bohlin
DW	=	Dave Whittock

1973
S	Saab 96V4	RC 2nd
SF	Saab 96V4	BC driveshaft
A	Saab 96V4	BR 3rd
GB	Saab 96V4	BR suspension

1974
SF	Saab 96V4	BC accident
GB	Saab 96V4	BC differential

1975
S	Saab 96V4	BC 4th
SF	Saab 96V4	BC 4th
GB	Saab 96V4	BC engine

1976
S	Saab 96V4	BC 1st
SF	Saab 99EMS	BC piston
GB	Saab 99EMS	BC gearbox

1977
S	Saab 99EMS	BC piston
SF	Saab 99EMS	BC differential
GB	Saab 99EMS	BC 9th

1978
S	Saab 99EMS	BC engine
SF	Porsche 911	BC 4th
GB	Saab 99 Turbo	BC driveshaft

1979
MC	Fiat Ritmo 75	HS 89th
S	Saab 99 Turbo (Combi)	HS engine
SF	Triumph TR7V8	HS 8th
I	Triumph TR7V8	HS engine
GB	Triumph TR7V8	HS 13th

1980
MC	VW Golf GTI	HS 5th
S	Datsun 160J	HS 8th
P	Triumph TR7V8	HS fuel pump
SF	Triumph TR7V8	HS 3rd
GB	Triumph TR7V8	HS oil pipe
CI	Toyota Celica	HS 7th

Per Eklund (S)

1981
MC	VW Golf GTI	RS engine
S	Porsche 911SC	RS 9th
P	Toyota Celica	RS accident
F	Toyota Celica	JB 6th
GR	Toyota Celica	BC engine
SF	Porsche 911SC	RS engine
CI	Toyota Celica	RS 2nd
GB	Toyota Celica	RS 6th

10th World Championship for Drivers

1982
S	Saab 99 Turbo	RS 4th
P	Toyota Celica	RS 2nd
NZ	Toyota Celica	RS 2nd
SF	Porsche 911SC	RS trailing arm
I	VW Golf 16S	RS clutch
CI	Toyota Celica	RS 2nd
GB	Toyota Celica	DW 9th

5th World Championship for Drivers

1983
S	Saab 99 Turbo	RS engine
SF	Audi Quattro	RS 4th
CI	Toyota Celica TC Turbo	RS 3rd

10th World Championship for Drivers

Guy Frequelin (F)

Guy Frequelin (F)

Born 2 April 1945 in Langres
First rally car Renault 8 Gordini in 1967
JM = Jean Marcoup
PT = Pierre Thimonier
CD = Christian Delferrier
JD = Jacques Delaval
JT = Jean Todt
JF = Jean-Francois Fauchille

1973
F	Audi 80	JM engine

1974
F	Alfa Romeo Alfetta	PT 10th

1975
MC	Alfa Romeo 2000GTV	CD 8th

1976
MC	Porsche 911	JD 7th
F	Opel Kadett GT/E	JD transmission

1977
MC	Renault Alpine A310	JD accident
I	Renault 5 Alpine	JD electrics

1978
MC	Renault 5 Alpine	JD 3rd
CI	Renault 5 Alpine	JD 5th

1979
MC	Renault 5 Alpine	JD 8th

1980
MC	Talbot Sunbeam Lotus	JT accident
P	Talbot Sunbeam Lotus	JT 3rd
I	Talbot Sunbeam Lotus	JT 4th
F	Talbot Sunbeam Lotus	JT accident
GB	Talbot Sunbeam Lotus	JT 3rd

8th World Championship for Drivers

1981
MC	Talbot Sunbeam Lotus	JT 2nd
P	Talbot Sunbeam Lotus	JT 6th
EAK	Peugeot 504 Coupe V6	JT clutch
F	Talbot Sunbeam Lotus	JT 2nd
GR	Talbot Sunbeam Lotus	JT 4th
RA	Talbot Sunbeam Lotus	JT 1st
BR	Talbot Sunbeam Lotus	JT 2nd
I	Talbot Sunbeam Lotus	JT engine
CI	Peugeot 504 Coupe V6	JT 5th
GB	Talbot Sunbeam Lotus	JT accident

2nd World Championship for Drivers

1982
MC	Porsche 911SC	JF 4th
F	Porsche 911SC	JF 6th
GB	Talbot Sunbeam Lotus	JF 11th

1983
MC	Opel Ascona 400	JF accident
F	Opel Manta 400	JF engine

2nd European Championship

Lasse Lampi (SF)

Born 3 October 1951 in Piamio
First rally car Ford Escord 1600 in 1975
PK = Pentti Kuukkala
OH = Otto Harsch

Lasse Lampi (SF)

Shekhar Mehta (EAK)

1978
GB	Vaux. Chevette 2300HS	IM accident

1979
GB	Vaux. Chevette 2300HS	MN 12th

1980
GB	Vaux. Chevette 2300HS	MN accident

1981
GB	Opel Ascona 400	IG halfshaft

4th European Championship

1982
GR	Opel Ascona 400	IG 6th
GB	Opel Ascona 400	IG rear axle

2nd European Championship

1983
GR	Opel Manta 400	IG 8th
GB	Opel Manta 400	IG 3rd

4th European Championship

1977
SF	Ford Escort RS	PK 12th

1978
SF	Ford Escort RS	PK 11th
GB	Ford Escort RS	PK accident

1979
SF	Ford Escort RS	PK 6th

1980
SF	Ford Escort RS	PK 5th
GB	Ford Escort RS	PK head gasket

1981
S	Ford Escort RS	PK 7th
SF	Ford Escort RS	PK 7th
GB	Ford Escort RS	PK clutch

1982
S	Ford Escort RS	PK 6th
SF	Ford Escort RS	PK engine
GB	Audi Quattro	PK suspension

1983
S	Audi Quattro	PK 3rd
SF	Audi Quattro	PK 7th
CI	Audi Quattro	OH withdrawn
GB	Audi Quattro	PK 4th

8th World Championship for Drivers

Jimmy McRae (GB)

Born 28 October 1943 in Blackwood
First rally car Ford Lotus Cortina in 1974
IM = Ian Muir
MN = Mike Nicholson
IG = Ian Grindrod

1976
GB	Vaux. Magnum Coupe	IM 12th

1977
GB	Vaux. Magnum Coupe	IM engine

Jimmy McRae (GB)

Shekhar Mehta (EAK)

Born 20 June 1945 in Kampala (EAU)
First rally car BMW 1800 in 1966
LD = Lofty Drews
GP = Geraint Phillips
EM = Ensio Mikander
KW = Keith Wood
MD = Mike Doughty
MH = Martin Holmes
BB = Bob Bean
YP/YM = Yvonne Pratt/Mehta
HL = Henry Liddon
RC = Rob Combes

1973
EAK	Datsun 240Z	LD 1st
MA	Datsun 240Z	GP accident
SF	Datsun 240Z	EM oil pump
GB	Datsun Sunny	KW 37th

1974
EAK	Lancia Fulvia	MD 11th
I	Lancia Beta Coupe	MH 4th

1975
EAK	Lancia Beta Coupe	MD front susp'n
MA	Datsun Violet	BB 6th
P	Datsun Violet	YP 7th

1976
EAK	Datsun Violet	MD road accident
GR	Datsun Violet	HL 3rd

1977
EAK	Datsun Violet 1-cam	MD engine

1978
EAK	Datsun 160J	MD engine
GR	Datsun 160J	YM 3rd
CI	Opel Ascona	MD camshaft

1979
EAK	Datsun 160J	MD 1st

Equal 10th World Championship for Drivers

1980
EAK	Datsun 160J	MD 1st
GR	Opel Ascona 400	YM broken wheel
RA	Datsun 160J	YM 4th
CI	Datsun 160J	MD accident

9th World Championship for Drivers

1981
EAK	Datsun Violet GT	MD 1st
GR	Datsun 160J	YM 5th
RA	Datsun Violet GT	YM 2nd
BR	Datsun Violet GT	YM head gasket
CI	Datsun Violet GT	MD 3rd

5th World Championship for Drivers

1982
EAK	Nissan Violet GT	MD 1st
GR	Nissan Violet GT	YM 4th
NZ	Nissan Violet GT	YM engine
BR	Nissan Violet GTS	YM engine

8th World Championship for Drivers

1983

EAK	Nissan 240RS	RC engine
GR	Nissan 240RS	YM 6th
NZ	Nissan 240RS	YM 4th
RA	Audi Quattro	YM 4th

9th World Championship for Drivers

Hannu Mikkola (SF)

Hannu Mikkola (SF)

Born 24 May 1942 in Joensuu
First rally car Volvo PV544 in 1963

JP	=	Jim Porter
JD	=	John Davenport
AA	=	Atso Aho
ER	=	Erkki Rautanen
JT	=	Jean Todt
CB	=	Claes Billstam
AH	=	Arne Hertz
RG	=	Roland Gumpert

1973

MC	Ford Escort RS1600	JP 4th
EAK	Ford Escort RS1600	JD steering
MA	Peugeot 504	AA clutch
SF	Volvo 142	ER codriver ill
GB	Ford Escort RS1600	JD accident

1974

EAK	Peugeot 504	JT engine
SF	Ford Escort RS1600	JD 1st
GB	Ford Escort RS1600	JD wheel studs

1975

MC	Fiat Abarth 124	JT 2nd
S	Fiat Abarth 124	JT accident
EAK	Peugeot 504	JT accident
MA	Peugeot 504	JT 1st
P	Fiat Abarth 124	JT 2nd
SF	Toyota Corolla	AA 1st
GB	Toyota Celica	JT distributor

1976

MC	Opel Kadett GT/E	CB differential
P	Toyota Corolla	JT accident
EAK	Peugeot 504 Coupe V6	JT overheating
GR	Toyota Corolla	JT injector pump
MA	Peugeot 504 Coupe V6	JT driveshaft
SF	Toyota Celica	AH 3rd
F	Peugeot 104ZS	JT 10th
GB	Toyota Celica	JT differential

1977

S	Toyota Corolla	AH electrics
P	Toyota Celica	AH wheel studs
EAK	Peugeot 504	AH distributor
GR	Toyota Celica	AH differential
SF	Toyota Celica	AH flywheel
GB	Toyota Celica	AH 2nd

1978

S	Ford Escort RS	AH 2nd
P	Ford Escort RS	AH 2nd
SF	Ford Escort RS	AH distributor
GB	Ford Escort RS	AH 1st

3rd FIA Cup

1979

MC	Ford Escort RS	AH 5th
S	Ford Escort RS	AH 5th
P	Ford Escort RS	AH 1st
EAK	Merc. 450 SLC5.0	AH 2nd
GR	Ford Escort RS	AH engine
NZ	Ford Escort RS	AH 1st
SF	Ford Escort RS	AH head gasket
GB	Ford Escort RS	AH 1st
CI	Merc. 450 SLC5.0	AH 1st

2nd World Championship for Drivers

1980

MC	Porsche 911	AH driveshaft
S	Ford Escort RS	AH 4th
P	Ford Escort RS	AH accident
EAK	Merc. 450 SLC5.0	AH codriver ill
GR	Ford Escort RS	AH electrics
RA	Merc. 500 SLC	AH 2nd
SF	Toyota Celica	AH driveshaft
NZ	Merc. 500 SLC	AH 3rd
I	Ford Escort RS	AH 3rd
GB	Ford Escort RS	AH 2nd
CI	Merc. 500 SLC	AH withdrawn

2nd World Championship for Drivers

1981

MC	Audi Quattro	AH 91st
S	Audi Quattro	AH 1st
P	Audi Quattro	AH engine
F	Audi Quattro	AH piston
GR	Audi Quattro	AH excluded
SF	Audi Quattro	AH 3rd
I	Audi Quattro	AH 4th
GB	Audi Quattro	AH 1st

3rd World Championship for Drivers

Michele Mouton (F)

1982

MC	Audi Quattro	AH 2nd
S	Audi Quattro	AH 16th
P	Audi Quattro	AH accident
F	Audi Quattro	AH gearbox
GR	Audi Quattro	AH front susp'n
NZ	Audi Quattro	AH steering
BR	Audi Quattro	AH too late
SF	Audi Quattro	AH 1st
I	Audi Quattro	AH 2nd
CI	Audi Quattro	RG too late
GB	Audi Quattro	AH 1st

3rd World Championship for Drivers

1983

MC	Audi Quattro	AH 4th
S	Audi Quattro	AH 1st
P	Audi Quattro	AH 1st
EAK	Audi Quattro	AH 2nd
F	Audi Quattro	AH acc. damage
GR	Audi Quattro	AH oil loss/eng
NZ	Audi Quattro	AH injection
RA	Audi Quattro	AH 1st
SF	Audi Quattro	AH 1st
I	Audi Quattro	AH fire
CI	Audi Quattro	AH 2nd
GB	Audi Quattro	AH 2nd

World Champion

Michele Mouton (F)

Born 23 June 1951 in Grasse
First rally car Renault Alpine A110 in 1973

AA	=	Annie Arrii
FC	=	Francoise Conconi
'B	=	'Biche'
FP	=	Fabrizia Pons

1974

F	Renault Alpine A110	AA 12th

1975

F	Renault Alpine A110	FC 7th

1976

MC	Renault Alpine A110	FC 11th
I	Renault Alpine A310	'B radiator
F	Renault Alpine A310	FC differential

1977

MC	Autobianchi A112	FC 24th
F	Fiat Abarth 131	FC 8th

2nd European Championship

1978

MC	Lancia Stratos	FC 7th
F	Fiat Abarth 131	FC 5th

4th FIA Cup
5th European Championship

1979

MC	Fiat Abarth 131	FC 7th
F	Fiat Abarth 131	FC 5th

1980

MC	Fiat Abarth 131	AA 7th
F	Fiat Abarth 131	AA 5th

1981

MC	Audi Quattro	AA fuel blockage
P	Audi Quattro	FP 4th
F	Audi Quattro	FP camshaft
GR	Audi Quattro	FP excluded
SF	Audi Quattro	FP 13th
I	Audi Quattro	FP 1st
GB	Audi Quattro	FP accident

8th World Championship for Drivers

1982

MC	Audi Quattro	FP accident
S	Audi Quattro	FP 5th
P	Audi Quattro	FP 1st
F	Audi Quattro	FP 7th
GR	Audi Quattro	FP 1st
NZ	Audi Quattro	FP oil pipe
BR	Audi Quattro	FP 1st
SF	Audi Quattro	FP accident
I	Audi Quattro	FP 4th
CI	Audi Quattro	FP accident
GB	Audi Quattro	FP 2nd

2nd World Championship for Drivers

1983

MC	Audi Quattro	FP accident
S	Audi Quattro	FP 4th
P	Audi Quattro	FP 2nd
EAK	Audi Quattro	FP 3rd
F	Audi Quattro	FP fire
GR	Audi Quattro	FP accident
NZ	Audi Quattro	FP engine
RA	Audi Quattro	FP 3rd
SF	Audi Quattro	FP 16th
I	Audi Quattro	FP 7th
GB	Audi Quattro	FP accident

5th World Championship for Drivers

Jean Ragnotti (F)

Born 29 August 1945 in Carpentras
First rally car Renault 8 Gordini in 1967
JJ = Jacques Jaubert
PT = Pierre Thimonier
JA = Jean-Marc Andrie
MH = Martin Holmes

1973

MC	Renault 12 Gordini	JJ 15th

1975

MC	Renault Alpine A310	PT accident

1976

MC	Renault Alpine A310	JA 50th
P	Renault Alpine A310	JJ accident
GR	Renault Alpine A310	JJ rear susp'n
F	Renault Alpine A310	JJ 4th
GB	Renault Alpine A310	JJ differential

1977

MC	VW Golf GTI	JA 18th
I	Renault 5 Alpine	JA 7th
GB	Renault 5 Alpine	JA driveshaft

Jean Ragnotti (F)

1978

MC	Renault 5 Alpine	JA 2nd
CI	Renault 5 Alpine	JA 3rd

Equal 9th FIA Cup

1979

MC	Renault 5 Alpine	JA 11th
GR	Renault 5 Alpine	JA 4th
F	Renault 5 Alpine	JA 2nd

7th World Championship for Drivers

1980

F	Renault 5 Turbo	JA alternator

1981

MC	Renault 5 Turbo	JA 1st
F	Renault 5 Turbo	JA electrics
GB	Renault 5 Turbo	MH 5th

1982

F	Renault 5 Turbo	JA 1st
CI	Renault 5 Turbo	JA driver injury

10th World Championship for Drivers

1983

MC	Renault 5 Turbo	JA 7th
F	Renault 5 Turbo	JA acc. damage
GR	Renault 5 Turbo	JA wheel studs

Walter Rohrl (D)

Born 7 March 1947 in Regensburg
First rally car Fiat 850 Coupe in 1968
JB = Jochen Berger
CB = Claes Billstam
WP = Willi-Peter Pitz
CG = Christian Geistdorfer

1973

MC	Opel Commodore	JB 45th
A	Opel Ascona	JB differential
GB	Opel Ascona	JB oil pump

Equal 2nd European Championship

1974

P	Opel Ascona	JB engine
GB	Opel Ascona	JB 5th

European Champion

1975

MC	Opel Ascona	JB engine
GR	Opel Ascona	JB 1st
MA	Opel Ascona	JB front susp'n
P	Opel Ascona	JB electrics
I	Opel Kadett GT/E	JB prop. shaft
GB	Opel Kadett GT/E	JB transmission

1976

MC	Opel Kadett GT/E	JB 4th
P	Opel Kadett GT/E	CB transmission
EAK	Opel Kadett GT/E	CB road accident
I	Opel Kadett GT/E	WP engine
F	Opel Kadett GT/E	JB fanbelt
GB	Opel Kadett GT/E	JB rear axle

1977

MC	Opel Kadett GT/E	WP fanbelt/eng
GR	Opel Kadett GT/E	WP head gasket
CDN	Fiat Abarth 131	CG engine
I	Fiat Abarth 131	WP accident
GB	Opel Kadett GT/E	WP engine

1978

MC	Fiat Abarth 131	CG 4th
P	Fiat Abarth 131	CG clutch
GR	Fiat Abarth 131	CG 1st
CDN	Fiat Abarth 131	CG 1st
I	Fiat Abarth 131	CG accident
GB	Fiat Abarth 131	CG 6th

6th FIA Cup

1979

MC	Fiat Abarth 131	CG 83rd
EAK	Fiat Abarth 131	CG 8th
I	Fiat Abarth 131	CG 2nd
GB	Fiat Abarth 131	CG 8th

9th World Championship for Drivers

Walter Rohrl (D)

1980

MC	Fiat Abarth 131	CG 1st
P	Fiat Abarth 131	CG 1st
GR	Fiat Abarth 131	CG 5th
RA	Fiat Abarth 131	CG 1st
NZ	Fiat Abarth 131	CG 2nd
I	Fiat Abarth 131	CG 1st
F	Fiat Abarth 131	CG 2nd

World Champion

1981

I	Porsche 911SC	CG gearbox

1982

MC	Opel Ascona 400	CG 1st
S	Opel Ascona 400	CG 3rd
P	Opel Ascona 400	CG steering
EAK	Opel Ascona 400	CG 2nd
F	Opel Ascona 400	CG 4th
GR	Opel Ascona 400	CG 2nd
NZ	Opel Ascona 400	CG 3rd
BR	Opel Ascona 400	CG 2nd
I	Opel Ascona 400	CG 3rd
CI	Opel Ascona 400	CG 1st

World Champion

1983

MC	Lancia Rally	CG 1st
P	Lancia Rally	CG 3rd
F	Lancia Rally	CG 2nd
GR	Lancia Rally	CG 1st
NZ	Lancia Rally	CG 1st
I	Lancia Rally	CG 2nd

2nd World Championship for Drivers

Timo Salonen (SF)

Timo Salonen (SF)

Born 8 October 1951 in Helsinki
First rally car Datsun 1600SSS in 1970
SH = Seppo Harjanne
JM = Jaakko Markkula
EN = Erkki Nyman
SP = Stuart Pegg

1974

SF	Mazda 1300	SH 22nd

1975

SF	Datsun Violet	JM 6th

Ilia Tchubrikov (BG)

1976

SF	Datsun Violet	JM 6th

1977

SF	Fiat Abarth 131	JM 2nd
CDN	Fiat Abarth 131	JM 1st
GB	Fiat Abarth 131	JM accident

1978

S	Fiat Abarth 131	JM engine
SF	Fiat Abarth 131	EN 2nd
CDN	Fiat Abarth 131	EN differential

1979

GR	Datsun 160J	SH 2nd
NZ	Datsun 160J	SH excluded
SF	Datsun 160J	SH 5th
CDN	Datsun 160J	SH 2nd
I	Datsun 160J	SH engine valve
GB	Datsun 160J	SP 3rd

4th World Championship for Drivers

1980

S	Datsun 160J	SH 7th
P	Datsun 160J	SH road accident
GR	Datsun 160J	SH 2nd
SF	Datsun 160J	SH 6th
NZ	Datsun 160J	SH 1st
I	Datsun 160J	SH accident
F	Datsun 160J	SH accident
GB	Datsun 160J	SH crankshaft

7th World Championship for Drivers

1981

P	Datsun Violet GT	SH headgasket
EAK	Datsun Silvia	SH 4th
F	Datsun Violet GT	SH fuel starv'n
GR	Datsun Violet GT	SH engine
RA	Datsun Violet GT	SH transmission
SF	Datsun Violet GT	SH 4th
I	Datsun Violet GT	SH 12th
CI	Datsun Violet GT	SH 1st
GB	Datsun Violet GT	SH engine

6th World Championship for Drivers

1982

P	Nissan Violet GTS	SH rear susp'n
EAK	Nissan Violet GTS	SH withdrawn
GR	Nissan Violet GTS	SH differential
NZ	Nissan Violet GTS	SH 4th
SF	Nissan Silvia Turbo	SH 4th
GB	Nissan Violet GTS	SH accident

1983

MC	Nissan 240RS	SH 14th
P	Nissan 240RS	SH gearbox
EAK	Nissan 240RS	SH engine
GR	Nissan 240RS	SH gearbox
NZ	Nissan 240RS	SH 2nd
SF	Nissan 240RS	SH 8th
GB	Nissan 240RS	SH accident

Ilia Tchubrikov (BG)

Born 8 January 1935 at Gabrovo
First rally car Bulgareno (Renault) 8 in 1967

1983

5th European Championship
No World Championship Rallies entered

'Tony' Fassina (I)

Born 26 July 1945 in Treviso
First rally car Renault 8 Gordini in 1970
MM = Mauro Mannini
'R = 'Rudy'

1976

I	Lancia Stratos	MM 4th

1977

I	Fiat Abarth 131	MM 3rd

1979

I	Lancia Stratos	MM 1st

Equal 10th World Championship for Drivers

1980

I	Opel Ascona 400	'R brakes

1981

I	Opel Ascona 400	'R 3rd

5th European Championship

1982

European Champion

'Tony' Fassina (I)

Ari Vatanen (SF)

Ari Vatanen (SF)

Born 27 April 1952 in Joensuu
First rally car Opel Ascona in 1970
AK = Alf Krogell
GP = Geraint Phillips
PB = Peter Bryant
AA = Atso Aho
JS = Jim Scott
DR = David Richards
TH = Terry Harryman

1974
SF	Opel Ascona	AK lost wheel

1975
SF	Ford Escort RS1600	GP accident
GB	Ford Escort RS1800	PB accident

1976
SF	Ford Escort RS1800	AA accident
GB	Ford Escort RS1800	PB valve spring

1977
P	Ford Escort RS1800	PB accident
EAK	Ford Escort RS1800	AA halfshaft
NZ	Ford Escort RS1800	JS 2nd
GR	Ford Escort RS1800	AA accident
SF	Ford Escort RS1800	AA clutch
CDN	Ford Escort RS1800	AA ignition
I	Ford Escort RS1800	PB accident
GB	Ford Escort RS1800	PB driver ill

3rd European Championship

1978
S	Ford Escort RS	AA 5th
P	Ford Escort RS	PB halfshaft
SF	Ford Escort RS	AA oil pipe
GB	Ford Escort RS	PB excluded

8th FIA Cup

1979
MC	Ford Fiesta 1600	DR 10th
S	Ford Escort RS	DR head gasket
P	Ford Escort RS	PB driver ill
NZ	Ford Escort RS	DR 3rd
SF	Ford Escort RS	DR 2nd
CDN	Ford Escort RS	DR 3rd
GB	Ford Escort RS	DR 4th

5th World Championship for Drivers

1980
MC	Ford Escort RS	DR accident
P	Ford Escort RS	DR accident
GR	Ford Escort RS	DR 1st
SF	Ford Escort RS	DR 2nd
I	Ford Escort RS	DR 2.1
GB	Ford Escort RS	DR accident

4th World Championship for Drivers
4th European Championship

1981
MC	Ford Escort RS	DR engine
S	Ford Escort RS	DR 2nd
P	Ford Escort RS	DR accident
GR	Ford Escort RS	DR 1st
RA	Ford Escort RS	DR accident
BR	Ford Escort RS	DR 1st
SF	Ford Escort RS	DR 1st
I	Ford Escort RS	DR 7th
CI	Ford Escort RS	DR 9th
GB	Ford Escort RS	DR 2nd

World Champion

1982
S	Ford Escort RS	TH 2nd
SF	Ford Escort RS	TH engine
GB	Opel Ascona 400	TH accident

1983
MC	Opel Ascona 400	TH 5th
S	Opel Ascona 400	TH 6th
EAK	Opel Ascona 400	TH 1st
GR	Opel Manta 400	TH 4th
SF	Opel Manta 400	TH halfshaft
I	Opel Manta 400	TH accident
GB	Opel Manta 400	TH head gasket

6th World Championship for Drivers

Adartico Vudafieri (I)

Born 11 October 1950 in Castelfranco
Veneto (Treviso)
First rally car Simca Rallye 2 in 1973
MB = Marco Bonaga
MM = Mauro Mannini (1978)
BS = Bruno Scabini
MM = Mario Mannucci (1979)
FP = Fabio Penariol
AB = Arnaldo Bernacchini
MP = Maurizio Perissinot
LP = Luigi Pirollo

1974
I	Porsche Carrera	MB accident

1978
I	Lancia Stratos	MM accident
F	Lancia Stratos	BS accident

1979
I	Fiat Abarth 131	MM accident

1980
I	Fiat Abarth 131	FP gearbox

3rd European Championship

1981
I	Fiat Abarth 131	AB accident

European Champion

1982
GR	Lancia Rally	MP supercharger
CI	Lancia Rally	MP engine

1983
P	Lancia Rally	MP 5th
F	Lancia Rally	LP 3rd
RA	Lancia Rally	MP accident
I	Lancia Rally	LP accident

Adartico Vudafieri (I)

Bjorn Waldegard (S)

Born 12 November 1943 in Ro
First rally car VW1200 in 1962
HT = Hans Thorszelius
FS = Fergus Sager
AH = Arne Hertz
CA = Claes-Goran Andersson
CB = Claes Billstam
RS = Ragnar Spjuth

1973
MC	Fiat Abarth 124	HT accident
S	VW1303S	HT 6th
P	Fiat Abarth 124	HT accident
EAK	Porsche 911	HT engine
MA	Fiat Abarth 124	FS 6th
GR	BMW2002	HT head gasket
A	BMW2002	HT 4th
I	BMW2002	HT 51st
GB	BMW2002	HT 7th

1974
P	Toyota Celica	HT electrics
EAK	Porsche 911	HT 2nd
SF	Opel Ascona	AH 10th
GB	Toyota Corolla	HT 4th

1975
S	Lancia Stratos	HT 1st
EAK	Lancia Stratos	HT 3rd
GR	Lancia Stratos	HT electrics
MA	Fiat Abarth 124	CA transmission
P	Toyota Corolla	HT gearbox
I	Lancia Stratos	HT 1st
GB	Lancia Stratos	HT excluded

1976

MC	Lancia Stratos	HT 2nd
S	Lancia Stratos	HT accident
EAK	Lancia Stratos	HT starter
GR	Lancia Stratos	HT oil pipe
I	Lancia Stratos	HT 1st
GB	Ford Escort RS1800	HT 3rd

1977

P	Ford Escort RS1800	HT 2nd
EAK	Ford Escort RS1800	HT 1st
GR	Ford Escort RS1800	HT 1st
SF	Ford Escort RS1800	CB 3rd
I	Ford Escort RS1800	HT 5th
GB	Ford Escort RS1800	HT 1st

1978

S	Ford Escort RS	HT 1st
EAK	Porsche 911	HT 4th
P	Ford Escort RS	HT halfshaft
GB	Ford Escort RS	HT 2nd

Bjorn Waldegard (S)

1979

MC	Ford Escort RS	HT 2nd
S	Ford Escort RS	HT 2nd
P	Ford Escort RS	HT 2nd
EAK	Merc.450 SLC5.0	HT 6th
GR	Ford Escort RS	HT 1st
SF	Ford Escort RS	CB 3rd
CDN	Ford Escort RS	HT 1st
GB	Ford Escort RS	HT 9th
CI	Merc.450 SLC5.0	HT 2nd

World Champion

1980

MC	Fiat Abarth 131	HT 3rd
S	Fiat Abarth 131	HT 3rd
P	Merc.450 SLC5.0	HT 4th
EAK	Merc.450 SLC5.0	HT 10th
GR	Merc.450 SLC5.0	HT head gasket
RA	Merc.500 SLC	HT driveshaft
NZ	Merc.500 SLC	HT 5th
GB	Toyota Celica	HT oil filter
CI	Merc.500 SLC	HT 1st

3rd World Championship for Drivers

1981

MC	Ford Escort RS	HT 8th
P	Toyota Celica	HT 3rd
F	Toyota Celica	HT differential
GR	Toyota Celica	HT differential
SF	Toyota Celica	HT 9th
CI	Toyota Celica	HT engine
GB	Toyota Celica	HT rear susp'n

1982

MC	Porsche 911SC	HT 92nd
P	Toyota Celica	HT differential
NZ	Toyota Celica	HT 1st
CI	Toyota Celica	HT 3rd
GB	Toyota Celica	RS 7th

6th World Championship for Drivers

1983

SF	Toyota Celica TC Turbo	HT 12th
I	Ferrari 308GTB	CB engine
CI	Toyota Celica TC Turbo	HT 1st
GB	Toyota Celica TC Turbo	HT accident

Antonio Zanini (E)

Antonio Zanini (E)

Born 9 February 1948 in Barcelona
First rally car Simca 1000 in 1970
JP = Juan Petisco
VS = Victor Sabater

1976

| MC | SEAT 1430/1800 | JP 12th |

2nd European Championship

1977

| MC | SEAT 124 Especial | JP 3rd |

1979

2nd European Championship

1980

European Champion

1983

| P | Talbot Sunbeam Lotus | VS 6th |

3rd European Championship

LEFT
Successful Audi Sport team drivers.
(left to right) Mikkola, Rohrl,
Blomqvist, Geistdorfer, Cederberg,
Hertz.

Monaco

1984 1 1984 RALLYE MONTE-CARLO

... Walter Rohrl gains his Monte Carlo hat trick and his fourth win in as many attempts – all with different makes of car

* * *

... Audi prove four-wheel drive technology in wintry conditions. Not only do they take the top three places, but groups A and N and also the Pirelli challenge for the best studless driver

* * *

... Talbot Sambas are an ideal clubmen's car. They take the top three places in the Promotion category

* * *

... Lancias do not like the mixed conditions and are unlucky

* * *

HOLMES

ABOVE

All the others ever saw – the back of a Quattro. Walter Rohrl descends the icy track towards the finish of stage 14 on the Wednesday morning.

It was the Walter Rohrl Rally! His achievements in rallying, till now, had always struck a ring of credibility, but now the German did something nobody thought he could achieve: to win a world rally first-time out in an Audi Quattro in wintry conditions, beating Stig Blomqvist. It was shattering proof of his adaptability in rallying that he could win so consistently on the rally which is one of the most highly-pressured in the season. Not only his ability but his sense of timing was impeccable, moving from Lancia to Audi just in time for Audi to succeed in snowy weather!

There were three teams in the running. Audi hoped for wintry weather, Lancia preferred clear conditions and Renault

for what they called "soup" – a mixture, preferably everything in each stage. After years of confusion Audi came to Monte Carlo prepared and calm. Lancia were aware of the limitations of two-wheel drive but were full of ideas how to counter their deficiencies. They learned from their efforts when they changed tyres in mid-stage last year and longed for a chance to repeat the process. Renault had finally tuned their engines to the 300bhp level and reckoned their strength lay where everyone had to drive on the wrong type of tyres. Monte Carlo is a rally where a car will never have the optimum tyres for each corner. The fastest crew will have the tyres which perform to the least disadvantage in

these conditions, and Renault reckoned in this way they would be better than Lancia and Audi. Both Audi and Lancia reckoned their respective chances would be equated if there was 30% of snow.

The rally changed its form; for the first time in many years most of the competitive sections would be over by the time the cars first reached the principality. Cars assembled after the concentration run at Aix-les-Bains where the weather got steadily wetter and colder,

38

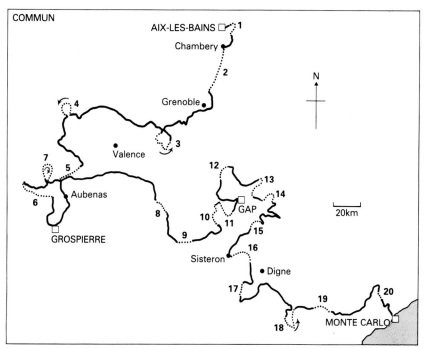

COMMUN

AIX-LES-BAINS 1
Chambery
2
Grenoble
4
3
Valence
7
5
Aubenas
6
8
GROSPIERRE
9
12
13
14
10
GAP
11
15
16
Sisteron
Digne
17
19
20
18
MONTE CARLO

20km

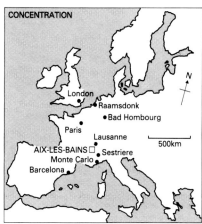

CONCENTRATION

London
Raamsdonk
Bad Hombourg
Paris
Lausanne
AIX-LES-BAINS
Sestriere
Monte Carlo
Barcelona

500km

dashed on stage five. They had decided to risk some racing tyres but the stage was delayed twenty minutes in which time the snow started falling – and the cars were trapped at the start, unable to change their wheels. So Audi gained a considerable lead, Therier was the best two-wheel driver four minutes behind and the best Lancia was over six and a half minutes behind – after only four stages had counted.

The Common run to Monte Carlo

ABOVE

Michelin have made considerable advances in their snow tyre design; this tyre was new for Monte Carlo, and by the next event (the Swedish) they had proved to be quicker than locally made tyres.

which could mean only one thing – snow in the mountains higher up. On the rally which began in earnest that evening the conditions were mostly wet snow but it gave the Audis the lead they hoped for. Blomqvist was quickest Mikkola second and Rohrl, finding his Quattro feet and delayed by failing turbo pressure, third. Walter was gradually gaining his confidence, as were Lancia who found to their delight the conditions on stage three were ideal for a quick tyre-change. They changed Alen's and Bettega's tyres in three-quarters of a minute and the Finn made best time on the stage. Later the stage was stopped because of an accident and the timing was cancelled.

Lancia's plans were then further

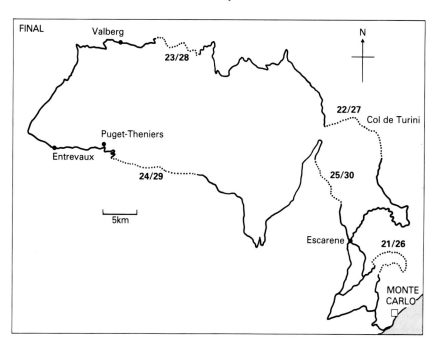

FINAL

Valberg
23/28
22/27
Col de Turini
Puget-Theniers
24/29
25/30
Entrevaux
Escarene
21/26
MONTE CARLO

5km

the penalty for arriving late at Gap, a happy thing for Biasion who had slid off the road on the stage for some time. . .

The next morning was one of the most beautiful you could want. Fresh snow, blue skies and bright sunlight greeted the drivers, more ideal Audi territory. Therier's fourth place at Gap had been almost eleven minutes' distant. By the time the cars reached Monte Carlo he was eighteen minutes behind. Blomqvist and Rohrl had outstretched Mikkola who was nearly seven minutes behind. Rohrl got the better of the Swede on the way down to Monte Carlo. As the stages went southwards the snow was less to be seen, but already the German had beaten the Swede even on some of the snowiest sections. The Swede made no excuses, but it was obvious he had been delayed on many stages having to pass slower drivers, something even more difficult than having to drive on stages with virgin snow.

ABOVE

Some drivers never seem to lose their flair. Jean-Luc Therier drove a works-specification Renault 5 Turbo for a dealer's team and came fourth, the best non A-seeded driver.

was punctuated by two six-hour halts at Grospierre and Gap. After the first halt came the stages at La Souche and then Burzet, the latter run in the complete loop last used in 1973 – the year when the blizzard trapped drivers and led to endless exclusions. This year there was again a blizzard, so bad that Alen went off the road unable to tell where the road was. Rohrl running first on the road arrived at the end of the 44km Burzet stage five minutes before the next driver, causing considerable alarm among the waiting team personnel! Between the two halts before Gap there were six stages and the weather was progressively worsening. The final stage before Gap was so bad for the later numbers that there were many blockages. The timing was cancelled – as was

RIGHT

Rain in Monte Carlo means snow in the hills – and Audi Quattro conditions! Walter Rohrl and Christian Geistdorfer are happy to be dry inside their car.

Unusual to see Bernard Darniche driving a "class" car instead of fighting for overall places. This 80 Quattro was run from the factory and had been used by Blomqvist on the Swedish eleven months before. Note the studded tyres on dry asphalt, an indication of ice to follow later in the stage.

A filthy morning in the mountains, just the conditions for a reliable and nippy car like the Talbot Samba. This was the first appearance of the evolution version of the group B Samba Rally, and Jean-Pierre Rouget (seen here) won the privateers' Promotion category in front of two more Sambas. This category offers the same prize money as the overall awards, but is limited to drivers who own their cars and are not FISA-graded.

41

RIGHT

The American tyre company BF Goodrich could never understand why they had so much publicity from the Pirelli-shod Golf GTI of Kalle Grundel, until they saw the "TA" motif on the side! Grundel finished best front-drive car second in group A but unable to match the speed of Darniche.

BELOW

The ladies' prize at Monte Carlo is traditionally the second most important award after the outright winner. For Mazda the choice of Minna Sillankorva a 22 year-old Finn, gave them much more publicity than they ever expected. The car was entered as a Mazda 323 but in fact was a Mazda Familia Turbo which developed 180bhp in 1500cc front-drive form.

WEYENS

The final night was a formality, Blomqvist not pressuring Rohrl even though Rohrl had some trouble with his car. Two times (both at the low-lying Col de la Madone stages) the Lancias were quickest – each time with Bettega. Lancia lost the services of Andruet who was excluded for opening the bonnet of his car in parc ferme, even though he had been given permission to do this. The "race" for the best conventional car was won by Timo Salonen's Nissan 240RS after Salvador Servia had gone off the road in his Manta 400. Apart from Andruet there were no official retirements in the top twenty starters – never had world championship cars been so reliable. Lancia finally gained fifth, sixth and eighth places, a severe blow to their world championship hopes for 1984.

WEYENS

52nd Monte Carlo Rally

21–27 January 1984   Monaco

OVERALL RESULTS

	ENTRANT	DRIVER/CODRIVER	NAT.	COMP NO.	CAR	GROUP	REG NO.	TOTAL PENALTY
1st	Audi Sport	WALTER ROHRL/Christian Geistdorfer	D	1	Audi Quattro	B	IN-NX47 (D)	8h.52m.29s.
2nd	Audi Sport	STIG BLOMQVIST/Bjorn Cederberg	S	7	Audi Quattro	B	IN-NR64 (D)	8h.53m.42s.
3rd	Audi Sport	HANNU MIKKOLA/Arne Hertz	SF/S	4	Audi Quattro	B	IN-NV83 (D)	9h.05m.09s.
4th	-	Jean-Luc Therier/Michel Vial	F	6	Renault 5 Turbo	B	21QV28 (F)	9h.16m.53s.
5th	Martini Racing	ATTILIO BETTEGA/Maurizio Perissinot	I	8	Lancia Rally	B	TOW67783 (I)	9h.21m.41s.
6th	Jolly Club	MASSIMO BIASION/Tiziano Siviero	I	9	Lancia Rally	B	TOW67773 (I)	9h.29m.49s.
7th	Yacco S.A.	BERNARD DARNICHE/Alain Mahe	F	10	Audi 80 Quattro	A	IN-NJ41 (D)	9h.32m.39s.
8th	Martini Racing	MARKKU ALEN/Ilkka Kivimaki	SF	2	Lancia Rally	B	TOW67785 (I)	9h.36m.05s.
9th	Volkswagen Motorsport	Kalle Grundel/Peter Diekmann	S/D	17	VW Golf GTI	A	WOB-VZ8 (D)	9h.44m.53s.
10th	Nissan Motor Co.	TIMO SALONEN/Seppo Harjanne	SF	3	Nissan 240RS	B	FIW6903 (GB)	9h.44m.54s.
14th	Takaoka Yoshio	SHEKHAR MEHTA/Yvonne Mehta	EAK	11	Subaru EAB5	A	GM58NI127 (J)	10h.18m.36s.
19th	-	Pierre Bos/Jean-Claude Leuvrey	F	44	Audi 80 Quattro	N	BDK027 (B)	10h.34m.57s.
22nd	Mazda R.T. (Europe)	Minna Sillankorva/Johanna Nieminen	SF	28	Mazda 323 Turbo	A	BLL604 (B)	10h.40m.46s.*

209 starters. 120 finishers. 75 completed route. *Ladies' winner. 9 A-PRIORITY DRIVERS. Winner's average speed over stages 81.35kph.

Positions in World Championship for Rallies after Round 1
Audi 18 points, Renault 12, Lancia 10, VW 9, Nissan 2.

Positions in World Championship for Drivers after Round 1
Rohrl 20 points, Blomqvist 15, Mikkola 12, Therier 10, Bettega 8, Biasion 6, Darniche 4, Alen 3, Grundel 2, Salonen 1.

LEADING RETIREMENTS

ENTRANT	DRIVER/CODRIVER	NAT.	COMP NO.	CAR	GROUP	REG NO.	CAUSE	STAGES COMPLETED
Martini Racing	Jean-Claude Andruet/Sergio Cresto	F/USA	5	Lancia Rally	B	TOW67772 (I)	excluded	25

Rally Leaders
Blomqvist stages 1–7, Rohrl 8, Blomqvist 9–16, Rohrl 17–30.

LEADING SPECIAL STAGE POSITIONS (including stages 3 and 11)

	1ST	2ND	3RD	4TH	5TH	6TH		1ST	2ND	3RD	4TH	5TH	6TH		1ST	2ND	3RD	4TH	5TH	6TH
Rohrl	15	6	5	-	1	-	Alen	1	4	5	3	3	5	Biasion	-	1	-	-	4	3
Blomqvist	10	11	3	2	-	1	Mikkola	-	6	11	3	2	2	Darniche	-	-	1	-	3	3
Bettega	2	-	4	4	2	5	Therier	-	1	1	8	2	5	Salonen	-	-	1	1	-	1

THE ROUTE

		SPECIAL STAGES	TOTAL DISTANCE	CREWS RUNNING
"Concentration"	8 starting towns (Saturday morning) – Aix-les-Bains (Sunday morning)	–	Average 1214km	204
"Commun" (1,2,4–10, 14–20)	Aix-les-Bains (Monday 2005) – Grospierre – Gap – Monte Carlo (Wednesday 1819)	16 asphalt-509km	1579km	121
"Final" (21–30)	Monte Carlo (Thursday 2000) – Monte Carlo – Monte Carlo (Friday 1407)	10 asphalt-213km	706km	75
		26 stages – 722km	Average 3499km	

Stage 3 cancelled after leading drivers had driven through because of accident; stage 11 cancelled because of extreme weather conditions when all cars had passed through; stages 12 and 13 never held – roads blocked by blizzards. All stages covered with ice, wet or dry snow to greater or lesser extent. Some falling snow or rain. 14 stages held in darkness.

RECENT WINNERS

1974 not held
1975 Sandro Munari/Mario Mannucci Lancia Stratos
1976 Sandro Munari/Silvio Maiga Lancia Stratos
1977 Sandro Munari/Silvio Maiga Lancia Stratos
1978 Jean-Pierre Nicolas/Vincent Laverne Porsche 911
1979 Bernard Darniche/Alain Mahe Lancia Stratos
1980 Walter Rohrl/Christian Geistdorfer Fiat Abarth 131
1981 Jean Ragnotti/Jean-Marc Andrie Renault 5 Turbo
1982 Walter Rohrl/Christian Geistdorfer Opel Ascona 400
1983 Walter Rohrl/Christian Geistdorfer Lancia Rally

Sweden

Stig Blomqvist will one day give up his claim to the throne of Swedish rallying but there was no hint of this at Karlstad in 1984. If ever there was proof that success is self-generating it was this. Being a round only of the drivers' series the only world championship team to compete was Audi, but then they were the only team who had a car capable of winning. On only one stage all rally did another driver get ahead of a Quattro (Stromberg's group A Saab on the first); the first and second best times on every stage were made by four-wheel drive Audis.

The form of the rally had changed little. Local people noted with delight that the snowbanks were higher than in recent years. Ideal conditions to them are temperatures around the minus ten degrees mark, with the snow stiff enough to enable drivers to bounce their cars along the stage. Most of the rally was in daylight; this year the event went a little further north, where conditions were expected to be more arctic than in previous years. Sensing that their entry numbers would be poor (less than half the year before – Swedish privateers normally use cars no longer recognised by FISA) the organisers invited other countries to enter junior teams. Britain was the only team to accept; the Swedes won the competition as expected but the British drivers gained a class win (group A, 1600cc) for Louise Aitken's Ford Escort RS1600i while Dean Senior had a second in class in his Toyota Corolla. It was the second consecutive world rally a British driver had won a class – Graham Newby took the 1300cc group A class in Monte Carlo.

The Swedish has its own challenge, so strong that Michele Mouton chose to

ABOVE
Stig Blomqvist slides his four-wheel drive Quattro round an artificial bend, run on a frozen lake at Torsby.

FACING PAGE TOP
King of Sweden! Nobody had won the same world championship rally more often than when Stig Blomqvist won the Swedish for the seventh time.

FACING PAGE BOTTOM
Best performance ever by an individually-run Quattro? Per Eklund was actually in the lead in the early sections in this works-loaned Audi. He lost time off the road but still finished third, as Lampi had done the year before.

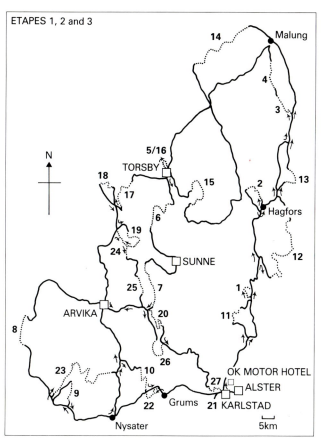

ETAPES 1, 2 and 3

STIG BLOMQVIST O+

TAYLOR

miss Monte Carlo (her "local" world rally, on which she felt she could not significantly improve her ability) and came instead to Sweden. Ironically 1984 was the first really snowy Monte Carlo since the Quattros arrived! The main interest in the Swedish was how the privately-run cars of Eklund and Lampi would fare. Eklund passionately wanted to do well on this event, and knew that only a Quattro could help him. He was immensely relieved when the factory lent him a car, even if the car must have been one of the oldest in Ingolstadt. He also had the chance of running Michelins, which this year were the best to have.

In the fine, clear conditions Audi had miscalculated how fast the rally would be. Blomqvist reported his car was undergeared – and Mouton would have done the same had she not been preoccupied with steering trouble. It was just the moment Eklund had been waiting for. By evening Blomqvist had been given a longer gear ratio and was pulling away from Eklund, Michele was third

and Lampi had retired with gearbox trouble. Eklund never gives up a fight but it was to no avail. He caught a snowbank at an awkward angle and his car was pulled off the road and straddled a bank, far away from spectators. From second he fell to twentieth position. With the two HB Audi cars now in the lead, this was the end of the rally as we knew it. The only thing in the drivers' minds was the chance of coming third, one of few opportunities to get A-priority rating this year if you did not drive a supercar. The trouble was that Eklund had already spotted that opportunity as well.

If the race for the lead was losing its interest, the battle for group A – the formula the Swedes wanted for world championship rallying – was very exciting. The fastest car was Stromberg's Saab. He had been the best non-Quattro right through to the start of the second day, when tyre troubles intervened. On the same stage Grundel, this time driving a locally prepared Golf, retired with

suddenly, out from the blue Eklund had passed them all! After stage 22 the group B Quattro had been seventh, two stages later it was third.

The Swedish holds a tenuous place in the world series. It is the shortest round in the series – because to make it longer would lead to inordinate tyre costs. For the past three years it has been an Audi benefit, though this will doubtless be challenged in the future, but it is also one of the best organised in the series. Maybe the advent of more four-wheel drive cars in the world series will give the Swedish a greater consequence.

LEFT
Back with works cars in rallies after 17 years were Volvo. There were three water-injection group A evolution cars on the Swedish, but only this one reached the end, driven by the girl Susanne Kottulinsky.

BELOW
Some people were disenchanted with so much publicity going to unproven youngsters. This was Stromberg's revenge . . .

engine trouble, after lying second in the group. With Eklund off the road at the same time, the rally really livened up! Bjorn Johansson went up to third place overall in his group A Ascona while Stromberg fell further back when he had to stop and change a tyre in a stage. By now the group B Ascona 400 of Mats Jonsson and the group A Ascona of Torph were also ahead of the Saab, so when he then had a broken driveshaft and the engine failed the driver sensed this was not to be his day.

Another group A contender entered the scene, Mikael Ericsson with an 80 Quattro. He passed Torph and on the final étape began exorably catching Johansson. In the final hours of darkness the group A battle became all the more intense. Johansson later explained that as soon as the 80 Quattro set off on the long stage 23 the four-wheel drive acceleration would have carried Ericsson into third place, but he never knew it. He went off the road, and presumably handed the group win and the third place to the Opel. But shortly afterwards Johansson's engine went off-song and he slowed. In the course of one stage, the 80 Quattro was out, Johansson had been passed by Jonsson's group B car and Torph's group A Ascona – and

Swedish Senior
Rally
team

34th Swedish Rally

10–12 February 1984   Sweden

OVERALL RESULTS

	ENTRANT	DRIVER/CODRIVER	NAT.	COMP NO.	CAR	GROUP	REG NO.	TOTAL PENALTY
1st	Audi Sport	STIG BLOMQVIST/Bjorn Cederberg	S	1	Audi Quattro	B	IN-NR64 (D)	4h.16m.45s.
2nd	Audi Sport	MICHELE MOUTON/Fabrizia Pons	F/I	3	Audi Quattro	B	IN-NV3 (D)	4h.24m.12s.*
3rd	Clarion	PER EKLUND/Dave Whittock	S/GB	2	Audi Quattro	B	IN-NN17 (D)	4h.33m.27s.
4th	Opel Team Sweden	Mats Jonsson/Ake Gustavsson	S	6	Opel Ascona 400	B	JLC173 (S)	4h.35m.25s.
5th	-	Lars-Erik Torph/Jan Sandstrom	S	21	Opel Ascona	A	CWH138 (S)	4h.36m.46s.
6th	-	Bjorn Johansson/Anders Olsson	S	17	Opel Ascona	A	GPB493 (S)	4h.37m.10s.
7th	-	Kenneth Eriksson/Lennart Larsson	S	24	Opel Kadett GT/E	A	LHK321 (S)	4h.41m.01s.
8th	-	Stig Andervang/Ove Lindell	S	15	Ford Escort RS	B	YCD988T (GB)	4h.42m.18s.
9th	-	Gunnar Pettersson/Arne Pettersson	S	20	Audi 80 Coupe	A	KOB173 (S)	4h.43m.02s.
10th	-	Jerry Ahlin/Urban Karlsson	S	23	Opel Ascona	A	CBH737 (S)	4h.45m.44s.
30th	-	Christian Dussert/Bernard Faure	F	81	Talbot Samba	N	2142WL38 (F)	5h.50m.35s.

66 starters. 41 finishers. *Ladies' winner. 4 A-PRIORITY DRIVERS. Winner's average speed over stages 105.16kph.

Leading positions in World Championship for Drivers after Round 2
Blomqvist 35 points, Rohrl 20, Mouton 15, Mikkola and Eklund 12, Therier and Jonsson 10, Bettega and Torph 8, Biasion and Johansson 6, etc.

Leading positions in European Championship after Round 4 (coefficient 4)
Blomqvist 80 points, Eklund 72, Mouton 60, Ericsson 50, Wittmann, Laine, Capone and Jonsson 40, Torph 32, Wurz and Pond 30, etc.

LEADING RETIREMENTS

ENTRANT	DRIVER/CODRIVER	NAT.	COMP NO.	CAR	GROUP	REG NO.	CAUSE	STAGES COMPLETED
-	LASSE LAMPI/Pentti Kuukkala	SF	4	Audi Quattro	B	LYV5X (GB)	gearbox	6
-	Anders Kullang/Lars-Ove Larsson	S	7	Volvo 240 Turbo	A	EHR056 (S)	head gasket	6
Team VAG Sweden	Kalle Grundel/Peter Diekmann	S/D	8	VW Golf GTI	A	GKL863 (S)	engine	10
-	Ola Stromberg/Per Carlsson	S	16	Saab 99 Turbo	A	BTP103 (S)	engine	18
Team VAG Sweden	Mikael Ericsson/Rolf Melleroth	S	9	Audi 80 Quattro	A	EHJ733 (S)	accident	23

Rally Leaders
Eklund stage 1, Blomqvist 2, Eklund 3–5, Blomqvist 6–27.

LEADING SPECIAL STAGE POSITIONS

	1ST	2ND	3RD	4TH	5TH	6TH		1ST	2ND	3RD	4TH	5TH	6TH		1ST	2ND	3RD	4TH	5TH	6TH
Eklund	14	9	2	-	-	-	Lampi	-	1	1	2	-	-	Jonsson	-	-	1	3	2	2
Blomqvist	13	11	2	1	-	-	Ericsson	-	1	-	7	3	4	Johansson	-	-	1	2	5	6
Mouton	-	6	18	2	1	-	Stromberg	-	-	1	6	4	-	Torph	-	-	-	4	4	3

THE ROUTE

		SPECIAL STAGES	TOTAL DISTANCE	CREWS RUNNING
Etape 1 (1–10)	Karlstad (Friday 0800) – Sunne – Alster (Friday 2220)	10 gravel – 139km	678km	54
Etape 2 (11–21)	Alster (Saturday 0700) – Torsby – Alster (Saturday 2130)	11 gravel – 210km	682km	44
Etape 3 (22–27)	Alster (Sunday 0200) – Arvika – OK Motor Hotel (Sunday 1000)	6 gravel – 101km	343km	41
		27 stages – 450km	1703km	

Dry throughout, some fog, all stages snow covered. 13 stages held in darkness.

RECENT WINNERS

1974 not held
1975 Bjorn Waldegard/Hans Thorszelius Lancia Stratos
1976 Per Eklund/Bjorn Cederberg Saab 96V4
1977 Stig Blomqvist/Bjorn Cedeberg Saab 99 Turbo
1978 Bjorn Waldegard/Hans Thorszelius Ford Escort RS
1979 Stig Blomqvist/Bjorn Cederberg Saab 99 Turbo Sedan
1980 Anders Kullang/Bruno Berglund Opel Ascona 400
1981 Hannu Mikkola/Arne Hertz Audi Quattro
1982 Stig Blomqvist/Bjorn Cederberg Audi Quattro
1983 Hannu Mikkola/Arne Hertz Audi Quattro

Portugal

. . . Audi just make it, hard-pressed by Lancia

* * *

. . . Four Lancias are entered from Italy, all four drivers held the lead

* * *

. . . fine run by Grundel gives VW its first group A win of the year

* * *

. . . Both Rohrl and Blomqvist overturn, but their tactics probably enabled Mikkola to win

* * *

Markku Alen never gave up. Right to the end he pressed Hannu Mikkola as hard as he could, hoping that something – even just a puncture, would give him the chance of another Portugal victory. It was a fantastic event, the first time both Audi and Lancia used brain power in their efforts, and if anything Audi showed greater aptitude in this connection. . . The 1984 Rally of Portugal was a classic Audi versus Lancia battle, the former enjoying a new-found reliability and a better team spirit. Lancia were using their long-established cleverness, their second-evolution 037 only being marginally better than last year's car, and not good enough to bridge the traction gap created by the Audis. Lancia were still far better on asphalt; but there was so much more gravel their advantage was not sufficient. The asphalt came first after which the rally cars would be reclassified before the gravel began, but all the tricks in the world would only delay an eventual Audi win.

Henri Toivonen was a fresh face at Lancia. Despite losing his A-seeding at the end of 1983, nobody could deny the Finn's speed behind the steering wheel, one only hoped that a fresh team would

BELOW
Jean Ragnotti rushes downhill on stage 26. At long last Renault were becoming happy with the handling of the group B version of their 5 Turbo.

HOLMES

were busy preparing for the Safari and New Zealand at the same time. Then came Renault on their first official outing since Acropolis 1983 and another appearance for the low-budget VW team; it was quite a remarkable entry, a complete contrast to Sweden.

How long could Lancia keep the lead? Obviously they should be two minutes ahead by Povoa at the end of the asphalt; could they keep the lead on the return

LEFT

Hannu Mikkola, after the last long Arganil stage, when victory was almost assured.

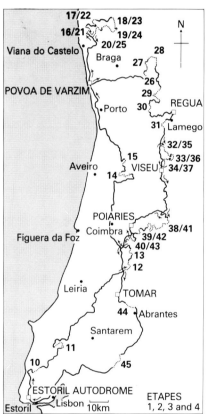

inject new wisdom. He suited Lancia's purpose, they sensed that Toivonen would keep Alen on his toes. After a disappointing Monte Carlo and an even less successful Swedish, Nissan hoped for better but Timo Salonen was invalided during training with back trouble, and they were lucky to find in Erkki Pitkanen a replacement driver who spoke Finnish and could use Salonen's notes! Portugal also saw the first appearance of the season for Toyota, who

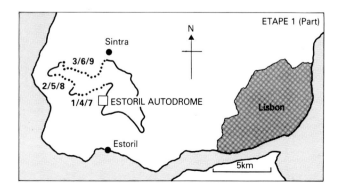

AUTOPRESSE

LEFT
Lancia decided to take Toivonen into their team to motivate their number one driver Markku Alen. The ploy did not work – as witness this scene in the Sintra stage. Alen said he had never lost control of a Rally in his life (till then!), his fellow Finn had done this on his first outing.

BELOW
Alen motivation method number two; during the long Arganil stage near the end of the event, Lancia wanted Alen to keep up the pressure on Mikkola, and their helicopter ordered emergency service crews to hold up pit signals. Eventually it seemed Alen was always told he was three seconds ahead of Mikkola. . .

to Povoa – and run first on the road on the way down to Viseu? Would the rally be dusty? If it were wet, Lancia might stop dreaming there and then. Initially the quickest Lancia driver, surprise surprise, was Toivonen. More than once Toivonen has gone well on these sections, but this time he also needed to find out how the Lancia worked. He discovered on stage six. Audi also lost a car on the opening sections – Sarel van der Merwe, the South African champion. Things were even newer for him, and when they turned up his boost it was an invitation to disaster. But more dramatic so far as the rally went was Rohrl's delay. He clipped a rock after a flying finish and broke a strut, losing seven minutes' road penalty. After the first nine stages the rally headed up-country at night, Alen losing his lead with a puncture and reaching Povoa in third place behind Biasion and Bettega. Mikkola was fourth, nearly 2½ minutes behind Biasion but, more relevantly only 45 seconds behind Alen. The race was on!

There was plenty of dust, what Audi would do about it was the question. Rohrl was the worst-hit, restarting in 12th place. Slower drivers in front were happy to swap places with him in control areas, but the organisers were furious when they realised this meant he got a two-minute clear run. Rule books were reached for, fines were imposed on him

BERRINO

ABOVE
Hannu Mikkola and Arne Hertz burst out of a corner at Candosa stage, accelerating out of a slow corner being ideal Quattro conditions.

BELOW
Markku Alen and Ilkka Kivimaki head for the evening in the far north of Portugal. Later that evening they inherited the lead but the next day Mikkola got in front for good.

(and Kankkunen) for "obstruction". Rohrl however was in fifth place when the rally went back to Povoa but Kankkunen (driving faster than Waldegard) fell back because of brake failure. The positions were now very clear; Lancia were one-two-three (with Alen now leading); Audi four-five-six. Mikkola was still one minute behind.

Running first on the road on the Povoa-Viseu étape was no joke. Alen was frequently afraid of the spectators in the road and could not force himself to go flat out. Audi were on the attack. Mikkola regained that one-minute in three stages, but with Mikkola, Rohrl and Blomqvist running in that order there was scope for initiative. It did not take long for Rohrl and Geistdorfer to see what they could do, particularly after losing time on a stage when their car caught fire. There was more to this incident than usual for the car had tipped on its side and the crew could not move it. Blomqvist soon arrived and nudged it back on to its wheels with the front of his car, but then the fire started. They even asked their helicopter to blow out the flames. Finally they got going. They lost no time at the next control, and

still very dusty. Lancia then played the Audi game, and Bettega and Biasion manoeuvred themselves so Alen had a six-minute clear run. It was to no avail. With a little help from his friends, Mikkola had won the rally and Lancia went home disappointed. They had needed a win in Portugal to restore their Monte Carlo defeat.

Behind Mikkola and the Lancias came Ragnotti. Both group B Toyotas retired but a local 16-valve Corolla was second in group A and was the best conventional car to finish. Toyota seemed to be all at sea, different sorts of problems afflicting them. This made what was to happen at the Safari all the more incredible.

LEFT

Like it really was! Walter Rohrl tells Portuguese journalist Fernando Petronilho how he tipped his Quattro on its side, during the rest halt at Regua.

BELOW

Scoring world championship points for the second time in three makes' championship rallies was Vauxhall, this time with the 23 year-old Welsh driver Russell Gooding – considered at the time not to be promising enough for the British Junior Team!

they deliberately clocked in early – in front of Mikkola. Mikkola therefore had to start one minute later than his ideal time, and immediately Rohrl started the stage he pulled over to stop, giving his Finnish teammate the benefit of running with two minutes of clear air. Lancia went mad, upset at not having thought of this sort of thing themselves!

This ploy helped Mikkola but was the downfall for Blomqvist. He found he had to drive with the dust of two cars running within a minute in front of him, and very soon he misjudged a bend and went off the road to retire. The Audi-Lancia battle was resolving itself, Mikkola started the last morning 43 seconds in front of Alen, but on the first section a differential mounting came loose. He nursed the car to the end, but his lead was suddenly down to 11 seconds. He pulled away again, even though the cars were running at two-minute intervals the final stages were

17th Port Wine Rally of Portugal

7–10 March 1984   Portugal

OVERALL RESULTS

	ENTRANT	DRIVER/CODRIVER	NAT.	COMP NO.	CAR	GROUP	REG NO.	TOTAL PENALTY
1st	Audi Sport	HANNU MIKKOLA/Arne Hertz	SF/S	1	Audi Quattro	B	IN-NE8 (D)	7h.35m.32s.
2nd	Martini Racing	MARKKU ALEN/Ilkka Kivimaki	SF	2	Lancia Rally	B	TOW67771 (I)	7h.35m.59s.
3rd	Martini Racing	ATTILIO BETTEGA/Maurizio Perissinot	I	5	Lancia Rally	B	TOW67775 (I)	7h.58m.21s.
4th	Jolly Club	MASSIMO BIASION/Tiziano Siviero	I	8	Lancia Rally	B	TOW67784 (I)	7h.59m.22s.
5th	Renault Portuguese	JEAN RAGNOTTI/Pierre Thimonier	F	9	Renault 5 Turbo	B	1465XD91 (F)	8h.13m.42s.
6th	Audi Sport	WALTER ROHRL/Christian Geistdorfer	D	4	Audi Quattro	B	IN-NX47 (D)	8h.21m.22s.
7th	Volkswagen Motorsport	Kalle Grundel/Peter Diekmann	S/D	17	VW Golf GTI	A	WOB-VZ8 (D)	8h.39m.00s.
8th	Traffic-S. Caetano	Jorge Ortigao/Joao Batista	P	22	Toyota Corolla 16-valve	A	TN-72-97 (P)	9h.19m.44s.
9th	-	Christian Dorche/Gilles Thimonier	F	27	Citroen Visa Chrono	B	13HM93 (F)	9h.25m.03s.
10th	-	Russell Gooding/Roger Jenkins	GB	20	Vauxhall Chevette 2300HSR	B	DEB507V (GB)	9h.35m.07s.
13th	Vasp-Guerin	Manuel Mello Breyner/Miguel Vilar	P	24	Audi 80 Quattro	N	83/15429 (B)	9h.51m.43s.

70 starters. 20 finishers. No Ladies' starters. 8 A-PRIORITY DRIVERS. Winner's average speed over stages 90.09kph.

Positions in World Championship for Rallies after Round 2
Audi 36 points, Lancia 26, Renault 22, VW 21, Toyota 10, Citroen 4, Nissan and Vauxhall 2.

Leading positions in World Championship for Drivers after Round 3
Blomqvist 35 points, Mikkola 32, Rohrl 26, Bettega 20, Alen 18, Biasion 16, Mouton 15, Eklund 12, Therier and Jonsson 10, etc.

LEADING RETIREMENTS

ENTRANT	DRIVER/CODRIVER	NAT.	COMP NO.	CAR	GROUP	REG NO.	CAUSE	STAGES COMPLETED
Audi Sport	Sarel van der Merwe/Franz Boshoff	ZA	12	Audi Quattro	B	IN-YA34 (D)	accident	4
Martini Racing	Henri Toivonen/Juha Piironen	SF	10	Lancia Rally	B	TOW67770 (I)	accident	5
Team Nissan Europe	Erkki Pitkanen/Seppo Harjanne	SF	6	Nissan 240RS	B	DXI918 (GB)	differential	15
Team Gaiss	Antonio Rodriguez/Jose Cotter	P	19	Lancia Rally	B	TOY09060 (I)	withdrawn	15
Diabolique Motorsport	Joaquim Santos/Miguel Oliveira	P	14	Ford Escort RS	B	GU-82-90 (P)	withdrawn	25
Toyota Team Europe	Juha Kankkunen/Fred Gallagher	SF/GB	11	Toyota Celica Twincam Turbo	B	K-UT433 (D)	steering	28
Toyota Team Europe	BJORN WALDEGARD/Hans Thorszelius	S	3	Toyota Celica Twincam Turbo	B	K-LV607 (D)	propshaft	30
Audi Sport	STIG BLOMQVIST/Bjorn Cederberg	S	7	Audi Quattro	B	IN-YD29 (D)	accident	33

Rally Leaders
Toivonen stages 1–5, Alen 6–11, Biasion 12–15, Biasion and Bettega 16, Bettega 17–23, Alen 24–27, Mikkola 28–45.

LEADING SPECIAL STAGE POSITIONS

	1ST	2ND	3RD	4TH	5TH	6TH		1ST	2ND	3RD	4TH	5TH	6TH		1ST	2ND	3RD	4TH	5TH	6TH
Mikkola	13	9	6	5	4	2	Bettega	5	7	9	8	10	5	Toivonen	5	-	-	-	-	-
Alen	12	13	14	4	-	-	Blomqvist	5	6	1	4	4	4	Rodriguez	-	1	1	-	-	2
Rohrl	6	7	7	10	9	3	Biasion	5	4	6	7	8	9	Kankkunen	-	1	-	1	1	2

THE ROUTE

		SPECIAL STAGES	TOTAL DISTANCE	CREWS RUNNING
Etape 1 (1–15)	Estoril Autodrome (Wednesday 0900) – Estoril Autodrome – Povoa de Varzim (Thursday 0500)	15 asphalt–137km	744km	52
Etape 2 (16–25)	Povoa de Varzim (Thursday 1430) Povoa de Varzim (Thursday 2400)	10 gravel – 166km	422km	38
Etape 3 (26–37)	Povoa de Varzim (Friday 0915) Regua Viseu (Friday 2045)	12 gravel – 205km	487km	22
Etape 4 (38–45)	Viseu (Saturday 0500) Poiares – Tomar – Estoril Autodrome (Saturday 2230)	8 gravel – 176km	747km	20
		45 stages – 684km	2400km	

Dry throughout. 16 stages held in darkness.

RECENT WINNERS

1974 Rafaelle Pinto/Arnaldo Bernacchini Fiat Abarth 131
1975 Markku Alen/Ilkka Kivimaki Fiat Abarth 124
1976 Sandro Munari/Silvio Maiga Lancia Stratos
1977 Markku Alen/Ilkka Kivimaki Fiat Abarth 131
1978 Markku Alen/Ilkka Kivimaki Fiat Abarth 131
1979 Hannu Mikkola/Arne Hertz Ford Escort RS
1980 Walter Rohrl/Christian Geistdorfer Fiat Abarth 131
1981 Markku Alen/Ilkka Kivimaki Fiat Abarth 131
1982 Michele Mouton/Fabrizia Pons Audi Quattro
1983 Hannu Mikkola/Arne Hertz Audi Quattro

Kenya

... Toyota win Safari, only the second team to win on their first appearance. They are also the first team to win with a turbocharged car

* * *

... Eight works teams enter this event. A class win at the debut for Citroen's group B four-wheel drive Visa 1000 Pistes

* * *

... Never has one driver led a Safari for so long and won

* * *

... Blomqvist retires for the second rally running

* * *

There was a saying that no team could win in Africa the first time. Mitsubishi killed the rumour ten years before, but the difficulty remains. Toyota had considerable Ivory Coast distance behind them, a rally which demands similar endurance qualities but which lacks the extra dimension of Kenya – the effect of considerable changes in altitude. Toyota Team Europe also came to Kenya with a considerable handicap – lack of time. Even in the days before the start the cars were still being readied. They possessed one particular feature which was expected to enable them to succeed – their turbocharger. Never had a turbo car won this event, which has a greater height variation than any other event in the world series. They also had Bjorn Waldegard, a driver whose capabilities on a tough event like this are almost incomparable. He had won the Safari for Ford, come second for Porsche, third for Lancia.

Opel had limited their 1984 programme to just the Safari and Ivory Coast, but spent considerable efforts trying to win a second year running. Last year Vatanen was first, coming from behind; this year they believed that their improved reliability should let them win from the front. They knew the Manta 400 had not improved as much over last year's model as other teams' cars had done. They had also noted that cars were becoming increasingly more reliable. Audi entered this event as the final rally before the Sport Quattro arrived, and hoped their new-found reliability would carry them through, but the most reliable cars of all – the Lancia Rallys – were in Kenya for the first

TAYLOR

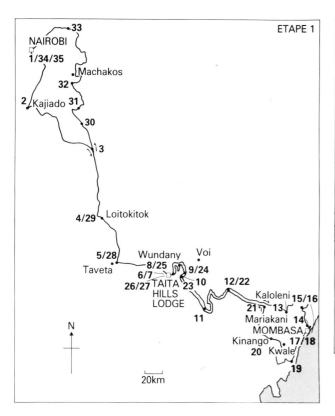

ETAPE 1

33
NAIROBI
1/34/35
2 Kajiado 31
32
Machakos
30
13
4/29 Loitokitok
5/28 Wundany 8/25 Voi
Taveta 9/24
6/7 10 12/22
26/27 TAITA 23 Kaloleni
HILLS 21 13 15/16
LODGE 11 Mariakani 14
MOMBASA
Kinango 17/18
20 Kwale
19

N

20km

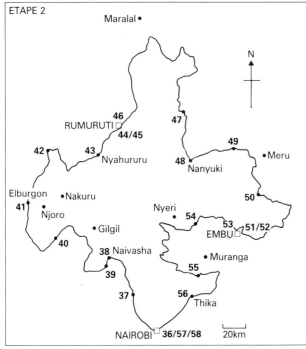

ETAPE 2

Maralal

N

46
RUMURUTI 47
44/45
42 43 49
Nyahururu 48 Meru
Elburgon Nakuru Nanyuki
41 Njoro 50
Gilgil Nyeri 54
40 53 51/52
38 Naivasha EMBU
39 Muranga
55
37 56
Thika
NAIROBI 36/57/58

20km

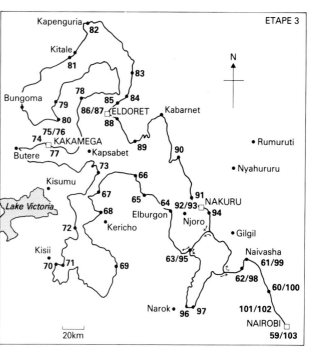

ETAPE 3

Kapenguria 82
Kitale
81 83
78
Bungoma 79 85 84
86/87 ELDORET Kabarnet
80 88 Rumuruti
75/76
74 KAKAMEGA 89 Nyahururu
Butere 77 Kapsabet 90
73
Kisumu 66
Lake 67 65 91
Victoria 68 64 92/93 NAKURU
72 Elburgon 94
Kericho Njoro Gilgil
Kisii 63/95 Naivasha
70 71 69 61/99
62/98 60/100
Narok 101/102
96 97 NAIROBI
59/103

N

20km

BELOW
People emerge from apparently nowhere to watch the Safari. This corner was nowhere near any village. . . Note the bent wing which flapped in the wind.

FACING PAGE

Twenty-first time – unlucky. Rauno Aaltonen finished the Safari in second place, for the fourth time in his career.

Flat across the main road! Everything in Kenya gives way for the Safari Rally. This is Waldegard winning in a Toyota Celica Twincam Turbo, on the team's first entry on the rally.

Shekhar Mehta was delayed when his Nissan hit a matatu (seen behind) in the Machakos Hills at the end of the first étape. The impact broke the propeller shaft but a spare was taken from Kirkland's retired rally car, which was then being used as a supervision car.

time. Lancia had not been to the Safari for eight years, their associated Fiat team for five. These four teams were expected to make the running. As long-odds teams came Nissan, four-times winners in consecutive years, but the 240RS was well out-performed and had suspect reliability; Citroen (their rally cars not arriving until two days before the start, their new four-wheel drive model never having been rallied in group B form – what a debut!), Subaru (well experienced at the Safari with group 1 and group 2 cars, now in Africa for the first time with group A) – and Daihatsu. They entered Charades in normal as well as one-litre turbocharged form.

Under Mike Doughty the character of the Safari has been considerably improved in details: it is aimed to be the sort of event a competitor can enjoy to the full, rather than an endurance test for its own sake. The opening sections were run at a competitive pace, the leading drivers losing only occasional minutes. Waldegard ran behind his teammate Eklund, and when the latter hit a bridge and was delayed, Waldegard could run with two-minutes' dust-free air in front of him. On the first day Audi were in trouble. Both Mouton and Blomqvist had trouble, the lady driver with a broken screen then a rotor arm which stopped the engine suddenly – and broke the turbo. The Swede had a broken oil pump. The two crippled Quattros met in the bush, and bush-mechanic Blomqvist cobbled up one of

First time in Kenya for the Lancia Rally, a car which demonstrated its legendary reliability. This is Markku Alen shortly before arriving at Embu on Saturday morning.

them so it could continue – his one! Nissan lost Kirkland in a bizarre accident, knocked down by a hit-and-run driver at a service point in his home town Mombasa and broke a leg. Next morning Mehta lost nearly an hour when he collided with a matatu (a locally built minibus), but at the head of the event only the odd minute separated Waldegard, Mikkola and Alen with Aaltonen close behind. Four makes in the top ten. So far the rally had been dry. With Easter so late it was confidently expected that the rain would soon come.

Waldegard arrived at Nairobi with his turbocharger hanging off, but this was repaired before the second étape got under way. Waldegard started first on the road, a situation which meant he could control the event and pull out occasional minutes on his rivals. Through the second night little happened, but Salonen was delayed the next morning with axle trouble. No more leading drivers retired, Aaltonen got ahead of Alen into third place and was only two minutes behind Mikkola. This was classic Aaltonen Safari driving, getting progressively faster through the event. In group A the Audi 80 Quattro of Criticos got ahead of the Subarus, while Chomat's

Visa 1000 Pistes was still running without problem and leading its class. The rally was still dry, how long could the drivers keep up the pace?

Toyota lost their second car, which had been rented to Munari, at the start of the final leg after long electrical trouble, but despite endless small delays with misfiring and driving in dust Alen still continued. Aaltonen was up to second when Mikkola stopped to change a differential but Waldegard kept on going. He used his legendary concentration to withstand the pressure and drive no faster than circumstances demanded. The final night arrived; last year the eventual winner, Vatanen, at this point in the rally was lying sixth. This year the positions never changed. Waldegard's car kept on going and going, the engine valves closed up a little, but there was never anything more serious. Mikkola finished third, small consolation after all Audi's trouble in the gruelling tracks of Kenya while it was apparent

Present-day engine tuner at work. Gerd Dicks changes microchips in the Toyota computer.

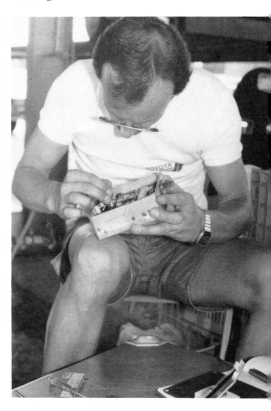

59

that Aaltonen's Opel had been defeated
by inadequacy of design rather than the
efforts of the team. Both Lancias reached
the finish, the rains never fell, and it had
been the fastest Safari in history.

The Safari had always been a great
leveller, Nissans could win here, if
nowhere else, Opels could use experience and anticipate troubles, Subarus
would always get a high placing. Citroen
beat all but one of the Subarus – light-
weight had never previously been
deemed a Safari expedience. So many
theories had been upturned at the 1984
Safari that it seemed the rallying revolution which had begun in Europe now
affected the whole world. The rally itself
was getting so professional, but still
African politics remained. The organisers
announced that no driver who competed
in future in South Africa would be allowed to start the Safari, and the Kenya-
licenced driver Rob Collinge had already
been told to stay away for this reason.
Rallying is the only international motor
sport where these threats have been
aired. Let's hope these dark clouds drift
away. The only clouds the Safari wants
are in the sky!

32nd Marlboro Safari Rally

19–23 April 1984   Kenya

OVERALL RESULTS

	ENTRANT	DRIVER/CODRIVER	NAT.	COMP NO.	CAR	GROUP	REG NO.	TOTAL PENALTY
1st	Westlands Motors	BJORN WALDEGARD/Hans Thorszelius	S	5	Toyota Celica Twincam Turbo B		K-UM210 (D)	2h.02m.
2nd	Opel Euro Team	Rauno Aaltonen/Lofty Drews	SF/EAK	10	Opel Manta 400	B	GG-CU261 (D)	2h.11m.
3rd	Audi Sport	HANNU MIKKOLA/Arne Hertz	SF/S	1	Audi Quattro	B	IN-NE8 (D)	2h.25m.
4th	Martini Racing	MARKKU ALEN/Ilkka Kivimaki	SF	7	Lancia Rally	B	TOW67787 (I)	3h.08m.
5th	D.T. Dobie & Co Ltd	SHEKHAR MEHTA/Rob Combes	EAK	2	Nissan 240RS	B	KNY59YA203 (J)	3h.35m.
6th	Martini Racing	Vic Preston Jnr/John Lyall	EAK	17	Lancia Rally	B	TOW67788 (I)	4h.14m.
7th	D.T. Dobie & Co Ltd	TIMO SALONEN/Seppo Harjanne	SF	9	Nissan 240RS	B	KNY59YA204 (J)	5h.52m.
8th	-	Franz Wittmann/Peter Diekmann	A/D	12	Audi Quattro	B	N.471573 (A)	7h.37m.
9th	-	Yoshio Iwashita/Yoshimasa Nakahara	J	29	Nissan 240RS	B	TKA33TA9762 (J)	7h.56m.
10th	-	Basil Criticos/John Rose	EAK	28	Audi 80 Quattro	A	KWO473 (EAK)	9h.53m.

76 starters. 25 finishers. No group N starters. No Ladies' finishers. 9 A-PRIORITY DRIVERS.

Positions in World Championship for Rallies after Round 3
Audi 50 points, Lancia 38, Toyota 28, Renault 22, VW 21, Opel 16, Nissan 12, Citroen 4, Vauxhall 2.

Leading positions in World Championship for Drivers after Round 4
Mikkola 44 points, Blomqvist 35, Alen 28, Rohrl 26, Bettega and Waldegard 20, Biasion 16, Mouton and Aaltonen 15, Eklund 12, etc.

LEADING RETIREMENTS

ENTRANT	DRIVER/CODRIVER	NAT.	COMP NO.	CAR	GROUP	REG NO.	CAUSE	CONTROLS VISITED
-	Franz Wurz/Gerald Brandstetter	A	15	Audi Quattro	B	W.595393 (A)	engine	3
Audi Sport	MICHELE MOUTON/Fabrizia Pons	F/I	3	Audi Quattro	B	IN-YD6 (D)	turbo	11
Westlands Motors	PER EKLUND/Dave Whittock	S/GB	4	Toyota Celica Twincam Turbo B		K-HT127 (D)	accident	12
D.T. Dobie & Co Ltd	Mike Kirkland/Anton Levitan	EAK	11	Nissan 240RS	B	KNY58SO6293 (J)	driver injury	16
-	Jayant Shah/Aslam Khan	EAK	20	Nissan 240RS	B	KUP090 (EAK)	engine	29
Davies Motor Corp.	Christian Rio/Jean-Bernard Vieu	F	21	Citroen Visa 1000 Pistes	B	8424ME92 (F)	front suspension	29
Opel Euro Team	GUY FREQUELIN/Bruno Berglund	F/S	6	Opel Manta 400	B	GG-CT310 (D)	engine	63
International Casino	Sandro Munari/Ian Street	I/EAK	18	Toyota Celica Twincam Turbo B		K-AL4949 (D)	alternator/overheating	63
Audi Sport	STIG BLOMQVIST/Bjorn Cederberg	S	8	Audi Quattro	B	IN-YJ81 (D)	engine	67

Rally Leaders
Many drivers without penalty controls 1–8, Waldegard and Blomqvist 9–11, Waldegard 12–14, Mikkola 15–19, Mikkola, Waldegard and Alen 20, Mikkola 21–24, Mikkola and Waldegard 25–29, Waldegard 30–105.

THE ROUTE

		CONTROLS	TOTAL DISTANCE	CREWS RUNNING
Etape 1 (1–35)	Nairobi (Thursday 1000) – Taita Hills – Mombasa – Taita Hills – Nairobi (Friday 1031)	35	1718km	46
Etape 2 (36–58)	Nairobi (Friday 1800) – Rumuruti – Embu Nairobi (Saturday 1529)	23	1353km	37
Etape 3 (59–105)	Nairobi (Sunday 0400) – Timborua – Kakamega – Eldoret – Nakuru – Nairobi (Monday 1525)	47	2183km	25
		105 controls	5254km	

RECENT WINNERS

1974 Joginder Singh/David Doig Mitsubishi Colt Lancer
1975 Ove Andersson/Arne Hertz Peugeot 504
1976 Joginder Singh/David Doig Mitsubishi Colt Lancer
1977 Bjorn Waldegard/Hans Thorszelius Ford Escort RS1800
1978 Jean-Pierre Nicolas/Jean-Claude Lefebvre Peugeot 504 Coupe V6
1979 Shekhar Mehta/Mike Doughty Datsun 160J
1980 Shekhar Mehta/Mike Doughty Datsun 160J
1981 Shekhar Mehta/Mike Doughty Datsun Violet GT
1982 Shekhar Mehta/Mike Doughty Datsun Violet GT
1983 Ari Vatanen/Terry Harryman Opel Ascona 400

Dry and dusty throughout with very few showers. Total scheduled time 49h.33m., the winner taking 51h.35m. Of the 105 controls only 25 could not be covered within the time limit allowed. No special stages. 48 controls held in darkness.

France

XXVIIIᵉ TOUR DE CORSE
RALLYE DE FRANCE

HOLMES

. . . Alen wins again, but Peugeot are the stars

* * *

. . . rain gives four-wheel drives their first chance to demonstrate advantage on an asphalt world championship rally

* * *

. . . debut not only for the Peugeot 205 Turbo 16 but also the Audi Sport Quattro

* * *

. . . Frequelin ninth – the first conventional car, his Opel Manta 400 hopelessly outclassed

* * *

One senses that even Peugeot did not really believe things would go so well on their debut. It has always taken time to strike a winning pace, and nowadays things are so much more sophisticated. Peugeot had never competed with a top-line car before, few of the team members had ever worked together, Vatanen had come back from the cold and his teammate Nicolas – from retirement. And yet after eight stages they were lying in first and second positions. And all they had really wanted was to get to the finish.

Corsica could not boast as many teams as the Safari did; like the Swedish it is an event for which many types of car are completely unsuitable. Lancia were on a hiding to nothing. After failing to win any rallies so far this year they knew

that if anything went wrong here they might as well forget everything – except their still-secret new car. They, like everyone else, were keenly interested to see what the Peugeot would be like. Their new car had been conceived on similar though more dramatic lines, yet no car had ever proved the formula on a rally till now. If they were going to suffer a reverse, it HAD to be at the hands of Peugeot.

The roads of Corsica present a unique challenge for asphalt driving, even if pressure groups in France find commercially it would be more profitable to take the rally to mainland France. The rally is remarkably slow – even the winners can barely average 80kph, which shows how the new rules are counteracting the advances in suspensions and

62

FACING PAGE
*Markku Alen scored his second
consecutive win on the all-asphalt Tour
de Corse, taking over the lead early on
the final day.*

ABOVE
*In the hills above the Golfe de Sagone
the Corsican driver Yves Loubet passes
with his group A winning Alfa Romeo
GTV6.*

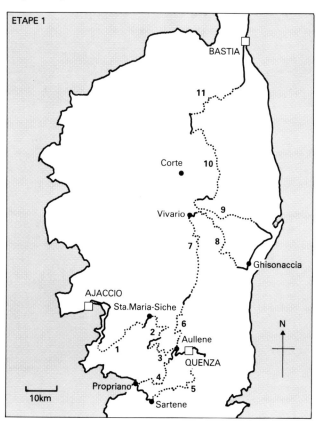

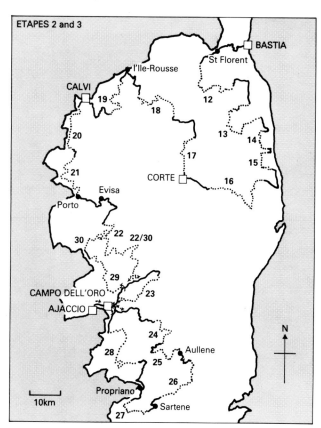

tyre designs. Whereas rallies on gravel get faster by spectacular bounds, asphalt rallies remain constant year to year. This year, for the first time in ages, it was wet. It was difficult to decide whether the Sport Quattro was a good thing or not. Certainly the engine was the thing the old cars had always needed; but what was the purpose of the short chassis? Official policy dictated this was necessary to make the car more competitive on narrow roads, and of course the missing bodywork saved weight. But overheating denied Rohrl the chance to make any useful analysis as to its handling. Also the engine had not been sufficiently developed and gave too much power too high up.

Lancia came in style with five cars whereas Audi had two team cars (one new and one old) and an old-type car for Darniche. At first sight one would assume that only Renault could match Lancia's speed. It had been a long struggle to get the 5 Turbo right but now things were going better for them. They even had 300bhp engines, so the only car in the top runners with less was Frequelin's Opel. Only two of the Lancias were official Martini cars, Biasion and Vudafieri had Jolly Club/

Totip cars and Andruet a Total Chardonnet car.

Bettega shot into the lead. Remembering his terrible accident in Corsica two years ago on the Lancia's debut and his nervous return to rallying here last year, it was good to see him go so well. He had already had another misfortune the week before at the Costa Smeralda Rally when he hospitalised his faithful codriver Maurizio Perissinot in an accident. Bettega came to Corsica with a completely new codriver, the Italian resident American Sergio Cresto, who read Perissinot's notes. Even by the second stage Vatanen was showing the speed of the new Peugeot by making fastest time, but Bettega was striking out. Alen arrived at the service point after stage 7 solemnly studying the broken front of his car – the first incident he had had in two years of 037 activity.

ABOVE

The sensation of the event was the speed of the Peugeots. At every possible occasion team chief Jean Todt (right) checked with the Finn to see if he was dreaming. When the Finn finally crashed, there were no recriminations; the team had done far better than anyone had expected.

BELOW

The Sport Quattro was overheating right from the start, and retired with engine failure as a result. Rohrl was still quicker than Blomqvist with a "long" car, but the Swede had never been to Corsica before.

irretrievable while Darniche could only regain the route after a big diversion. At Calvi Vatanen was 107 seconds in front. It was hard to tell if Lancia were happy or sad. Blomqvist was doing his best as the last Audi left, lying in sixth place and eyeing the places in front.

Vatanen crashed out of the event on the first stage of the last day, losing control on a pool of water, overturning and the car started to burn till there was little left. Even Alen had no idea what had happened a minute before. Lancias were first and second, but Biasion was in a bad way physically, twice nearing

LEFT

No fuss, no bother – quite unlike the Vatanen we used to know. How long it will be before the Peugeots have to be driven in anger remains to be seen.

It was a moment of anxiety. The following stage was going to be decisive, the roads were too wet for dry weather tyres but not wet enough for wets. Most of the leaders went on slicks, the Lancias having a miserable time but the four-wheel drive cars suffering much less. In the stage there was also fog, and here Bettega hit a rock which punctured two tyres. There was confusion all round. Spare tyres came from other competitors and even their helicopter, and eventually all the cars emerged from the stage, late but intact, though Bettega's Lancia never really handled properly again all rally.

Peugeot now led, but Nicolas lost time when he had a puncture. When the rally reached Bastia Vatanen led Alen by almost five minutes, was six and a half in front of Biasion and Ragnotti was fourth nearly seven behind. Bettega, despite losing 25 minutes, was thirteenth. The next day was wet, but on the first stage it was Vatanen who had the wrong tyres and Alen fought back. His pressure worked for on stage 16 Vatanen had to stop and change a flat tyre, which put Alen only 80 seconds behind. Both Lancia and Audi lost a car at the same treacherous place; Vudafieri's being

RIGHT

Off the road was Darniche, seen in wet weather on the second day. This was a factory car painted for use in French championship events.

collapsing at a service point. He recovered and Lancia planned their strategy. With Vatanen out, Blomqvist was fifth, pressing hard for fourth and it was worth a lot of Lancia's effort to stop Blomqvist catching Nicolas in front. So they made a pact with Peugeot, who they saw as an ally in the fight against the Germans. They gave Peugeot every help, even the use of their helicopter, to make sure there were no more tyre choice errors. It paid off, coupled with Nicolas' detailed knowledge of the last few stages, and so the German threat was averted.

Grundel had various suspension troubles and fell behind the Alfa of Loubet in group A, and not far behind them were the leading group N cars. The new Renault 11 Turbos took first and second place, after a long battle which involved a Fiat Abarth 130, a BMW 323i and an Alfa Romeo GTV6.

RIGHT
Never short of well-meaning advice! Markku Alen just before the finish, with Lancia team manager Cesare Fiorio and team co-ordinator Ninni Russo (right).

BELOW
Third place went to Jean Ragnotti, the end of a famine of good results for a group B 5 Turbo.

LINEAR

28th Tour de Corse Rally

3–5 May 1984   France

OVERALL RESULTS

	ENTRANT	DRIVER/CODRIVER	NAT.	COMP NO.	CAR	GROUP	REG NO.	TOTAL PENALTY
1st	Martini Racing	MARKKU ALEN/Ilkka Kivimaki	SF	5	Lancia Rally	B	TOW67785 (I)	13h.24m.56s.
2nd	Jolly Club	MASSIMO BIASION/Tiziano Siviero	I	9	Lancia Rally	B	TOW67784 (I)	13h.29m.11s.
3rd	Equipe Renault Elf	JEAN RAGNOTTI/Pierre Thimonier	F	10	Renault 5 Turbo	B	1465XD91 (F)	13h.33m.16s.
4th	Peugeot-Talbot Sport	Jean-Pierre Nicolas/Charley Pasquier	F	12	Peugeot 205 Turbo 16	B	697EXC75 (F)	13h.44m.50s.
5th	Audi Sport	STIG BLOMQVIST/Bjorn Cederberg	S	6	Audi Quattro	B	IN-NJ5 (D)	13h.45m.55s.
6th	Total Chardonnet	Jean-Claude Andruet/Martine Rick	F	11	Lancia Rally	B	7235HX93 (F)	13h.48m.07s.
7th	Martini Racing	ATTILIO BETTEGA/Sergio Cresto	I/USA	1	Lancia Rally	B	TOW67783 (I)	13h.55m.40s.
8th	Diac Societe	Francois Chatriot/Moel Perin	F	15	Renault 5 Turbo	B	38EHN75 (F)	13h.57m.25s.
9th	Opel Euro Team	GUY FREQUELIN/'Tilber'	F	3	Opel Manta 400	B	GG-CT361 (D)	14h.08m.53s.
10th	-	Yves Loubet/Patricia Trivero	F	19	Alfa Romeo GTV6	A	2888US06 (F)	14h.48m.11s.
17th	-	Jean-Pierre Deriu/Joel Mariani	F	121	Renault 11 Turbo	N	110EK2B (F)	15h.29m.30s.

155 starters. 58 finishers. No Ladies' starters. 10 A-PRIORITY DRIVERS. Winner's average speed over stages 82.98kph.

Positions in World Championship for Rallies after Round 4
Audi 60 points, Lancia 56, Renault 36, Toyota 28, VW 21, Opel 18, Peugeot and Nissan 12, Alfa Romeo 9, Citroen 4, Vauxhall 2.

Leading positions in World Championship for Drivers after Round 5
Alen 48 points, Mikkola 44, Blomqvist 43, Biasion 31, Rohrl 26, Bettega 24, Waldegard and Ragnotti 20, Mouton and Aaltonen 15, etc.

LEADING RETIREMENTS

ENTRANT	DRIVER/CODRIVER	NAT.	COMP NO.	CAR	GROUP	REG NO.	CAUSE	STAGES COMPLETED
Audi Sport	WALTER ROHRL/Christian Geistdorfer	D	2	Audi Sport Quattro	B	IN-NC46 (D)	engine	7
Jolly Club	ADARTICO VUDAFIERI/Luigi Pirollo	I	7	Lancia Rally	B	TOW67772 (I)	accident	15
Yacco S.A.	BERNARD DARNICHE/Alain Mahe	F	8	Audi Quattro	B	IN-NL1 (D)	accident	17
Peugeot-Talbot Sport	ARI VATANEN/Terry Harryman	SF/GB	4	Peugeot 205 Turbo 16	B	323EXA75 (F)	accident	19
Philips Auto Radio	Bruno Saby/Jean-Francois Fauchille	F	16	Renault 5 Turbo	B	572WG38 (F)	accident	21

Rally Leaders
Bettega stages 1–7, Vatanen 8–19, Alen 20–30.

LEADING SPECIAL STAGE POSITIONS

	1ST	2ND	3RD	4TH	5TH	6TH		1ST	2ND	3RD	4TH	5TH	6TH		1ST	2ND	3RD	4TH	5TH	6TH
Bettega	12	2	3	3	2	3	Ragnotti	3	4	2	3	5	7	Vudafieri	1	3	4	1	1	-
Vatanen	7	5	1	3	1	1	Nicolas	2	3	4	3	1	3	Andruet	-	1	3	4	3	6
Alen	5	5	8	3	6	-	Biasion	1	9	5	4	2	2	Darniche	-	-	2	-	-	1

THE ROUTE

			SPECIAL STAGES	TOTAL DISTANCE	CREWS RUNNING
Etape 1 (1–11)	Ajaccio (Thursday 0900) – Quenza – Bastia (Thursday 2100)		11 asphalt – 425km	581km	102
Etape 2 (12–19)	Bastia (Friday 0900) – Corte – Calvi (Friday 1745)		8 asphalt – 265km	408km	76
Etape 3 (20–30)	Calvi (Saturday 0500) – Ajaccio – Ajaccio (Saturday 1715)		11 asphalt – 423km	629km	58
			30 stages – 1113km	1618km	

Mostly damp with some fog. 2 stages held in darkness.

RECENT WINNERS

1974 Jean-Claude Andruet/'Biche' Lancia Stratos
1975 Bernard Darniche/Alain Mahe Lancia Stratos
1976 Sandro Munari/Silvio Maiga Lancia Stratos
1977 Bernard Darniche/Alain Mahe Fiat Abarth 131
1978 Bernard Darniche/Alain Mahe Fiat Abarth 131
1979 Bernard Darniche/Alain Mahe Lancia Stratos
1980 Jean-Luc Therier/Michel Vial Porsche 911SC
1981 Bernard Darniche/Alain Mahe Lancia Stratos
1982 Jean Ragnotti/Jean-Marc Andrie Renault 5 Turbo
1983 Markku Alen/Ilkka Kivimaki Lancia Rally

Greece

6
ROTHMANS
31 ACROPOLIS RALLY

. . . Blomqvist wins his third world rally of the season and takes on the role of heir apparent to the championship

* * *

. . . Lancia are outclassed, their hopes destroyed by unexpected tyre troubles

* * *

. . . Peugeot impresses on gravel, the Sport Quattro goes better

* * *

. . . encouraging ninth place on Mazda's group B debut

* * *

Lancia's hopes gradually faded away. They went to Greece knowing their world championship chances needed luck not only that everything should be right but also that things should go wrong for others – but it did not happen that way. Not only were the two old Quattros reliable (both the Sport Quattros retiring) but they themselves were cruelly struck by tyre trouble. It was visibly the end of the two-wheel drive era. Four-wheel drive cars (Audis or Peugeot) were so much faster; only eight times all rally did a two-wheel drive car make a fastest time, and then it was always a Lancia. When Peugeot showed their pace in conditions where they were obviously well suited the Lancia Rally,

which only last season had been the champion car, suddenly looked like a vehicle from a bygone age.

Audi came with four works cars, two four-valve short-chassis cars and two two-valve, long-chassis models. In addition John Buffum drove a private car – one of the older cars fitted with the slightly bigger engines. It was a big team, but the rally is always popular so that

BELOW

Third time lucky: after two world championship rallies ending in retirement and a poor showing in Corsica, Stig Blomqvist and Bjorn Cederberg were back and winning.

TAYLOR

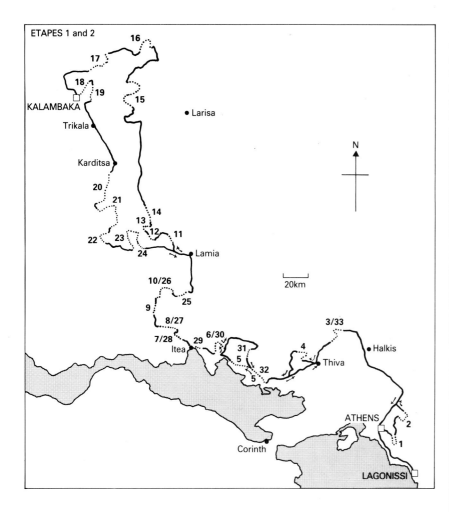

ETAPES 1 and 2

KALAMBAKA
Trikala
Karditsa
Larisa
Lamia
Itea
Halkis
Thiva
ATHENS
Corinth
LAGONISSI

20km

N

Early on the second day, Blomqvist got into the lead for good, though Mikkola was always close behind. He and co-driver Cederberg (left) pause while racing tyres are fitted for the asphalt hillclimb stage outside Itea.

Audi team manager Roland Gumpert did not want to say no to his drivers. For Buffum it was an eye-opener. "Roughness takes on a new meaning", he exclaimed and BF Goodrich rubbed their hands with glee, hoping the legendary toughness of their tyres would keep John going when others lost air in their more sophisticated ones. But it was Peugeot which attracted the greatest attention. The 205 Turbo 16s had proved so good on the asphalt roads of Corsica, conditions there were not so immediately advantageous, that on the gravel tracks in Greece it was expected they would murder the opposition, while they lasted. The cars looked so right. They seemed to float over the rough parts, the drivers could turn the car into corners in rear-wheel drive slides, they had none of the brute-force which the heavy, big Quattros demanded.

If the Lancias seemed like museum pieces in comparison, what of the conventional front-engined, rear-drive cars? The miracle of Datsun/Nissan in Greece

had been their reliability,and how they hung-on even when progressively out-classed. They won on their first attempt

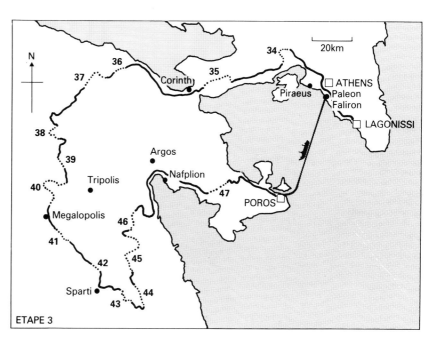

ETAPE 3

N

Corinth
ATHENS
Piraeus
Paleon Faliron
LAGONISSI
Argos
Nafplion
Tripolis
POROS
Megalopolis
Sparti

20km

engine broke, leaving behind a trail of oil. Punctures soon dictated the competition. Rohrl lost a minute on the first stage, Mouton lost time as well, Bettega had two on the same stage. Lancia soon realised the worst, that the special Pirellis made for this event were vulnerable in the heat. In the dusty conditions, the front runners strengthened their grip on the event but the normally reliable Quattros of the leaders Mikkola and Blomqvist both struck trouble near the end of the first leg, because of overheated electrics. Rohrl was most surprised to hold the lead at the Kalambaka halt – but not for long. His car then suffered electrical trouble the next morning, stopping for help from his team's helicopter in mid-stage and dropping back. This misfortune gave Peugeot their moment of glory.

LEFT
Second rally out, second time leading. Ari Vatanen had already lost his chances of victory when this picture was taken, but the message had been clearly written.

BELOW
Lancia Good Boy. Markku Alen did not usually drive so sideways, his Pirelli tyres at this event being unable to take the strain, but he drove his heart out and finished third, an incredible achievement in the circumstances.

at the Acropolis in 1976 (an amazing achievement) but have finished in worse positions ever since. This year they could only manage seventh. But then came Mazda with their rotary-engined RX7 group B car, the most powerful normally aspirated works rally car. This car possessed a better natural balance and its engine developed a softness of power without the tyre-destroying violence of two-wheel drive cars of similar power. With four-wheel drive to come in a year or so, it was time for Mazda to start their group B programme.

Five works teams in group B were an endorsement of the importance of the Acropolis, even though few expected anyone other than Audi to win. The Sport Quattros started overheating as soon as the day grew hot. Rohrl was forced to drive with the heater on having forever to lift off when the oil got too hot. Mouton had similar troubles, and towards the end of the first day the

TAYLOR

ABOVE

Lancia Bad Boy. Henri Toivonen seems to leave every grain of accumulated sense and experience behind when he is in the company of other Finns – and losing. This incident was not much appreciated by the Lancia team, who were already pre-occupied overcoming their tyre troubles.

RIGHT

Big surprise was the consistency and intelligence of John Buffum, the American champion who finished fifth in this private, David Sutton-run, BF Goodrich sponsored Audi Quattro. BF Goodrich gain many of their competition successes in off-road events, where their tyres (tires?) spend a long time off the ground!

this time on a stage. He tried to drive on but the engine failed. As the rally returned towards Athens Lancia lost Toivonen in his second accident in as many rallies with the team, and Mazda lost Carlsson with differential failure. Three Quattros led two Lancias and Nicolas' Peugeot, but both Nicolas and Warmbold were lucky to be able to carry on, both having been stranded on the road section after the final stage of that étape, when their service cars had already headed southwards.

Nicolas did not last much longer. He had been troubled with stones damaging the rear brakes and this time it was terminal. The third étape was shorter than in previous years, and by breaking the event into three étapes of similar length the rally had found a most popular format. Audi lost Rohrl three stages from the end when the car stopped with clutch failure, which allowed a struggling Alen up to third place. The effect on the Lancia team would normally have been very depressing, seeing their winning car in 1983 so outclassed twelve months later. But the team were not downhearted, they knew their misfortune would not afflict them for long. They expected to start testing the 038 shortly, and if their buoyancy was any guide, that was going to put the record straight in very little time.

ABOVE
First time in group B, manager of Mazda Rallye Team Europe Achim Warmbold finished ninth, despite being stopped for half an hour with a broken differential at the end of the second étape.

RIGHT
Seaside rallying. Greece is such an attractive place it is a pity you always have to be on the move. On the first day, Ari Vatanen is seen clocking-in at Itea, while Michele Mouton and Attilio Bettega wait behind the control area board for their turn.

Vatanen had been closing on the leaders and suddenly the Peugeot was in the lead, but only for two stages. Then an oil pump drive belt failed on a road section, but when the driver suddenly switched off the engine, the turbo broke as well. He reached the next time control four minutes late, and Blomqvist was back in the lead on the rally and first on the road. Vatanen carried on, but later he had the same trouble again,

31st Acropolis Rally

28–31 May 1984   Greece

OVERALL RESULTS

	ENTRANT	DRIVER/CODRIVER	NAT.	COMP NO.	CAR	GROUP	REG NO.	TOTAL PENALTY
1st	Audi Sport	STIG BLOMQVIST/Bjorn Cederberg	S	10	Audi Quattro	B	IN-YD29 (D)	10h.41m.51s.
2nd	Audi Sport	HANNU MIKKOLA/Arne Hertz	SF/S	7	Audi Quattro	B	IN-NL1 (D)	10h.44m.58s.
3rd	Martini Racing	MARKKU ALEN/Ilkka Kivimaki	SF	2	Lancia Rally	B	TOW67771 (I)	10h.56m.01s.
4th	Martini Racing	ATTILIO BETTEGA/Sergio Cresto	I/USA	6	Lancia Rally	B	TOW67774 (I)	11h.03m.49s.
5th	BF Goodrich Motorsport	John Buffum/Fred Gallagher	USA/GB	14	Audi Quattro	B	WMN44 (GBM)	11h.22m.10s.
6th	N.J. Theocarakis S.A.	TIMO SALONEN/Seppo Harjanne	SF	5	Nissan 240RS	B	17356 (GR)	11h.26m.29s.
7th	N.J. Theocarakis S.A.	SHEKHAR MEHTA/Yvonne Mehta	EAK	8	Nissan 240RS	B	17357 (GR)	11h.33m.57s.
8th	N.J. Theocarakis S.A.	George Moschous/Alexis Constantakatos	GR	16	Nissan 240RS	B	17355 (GR)	11h.47m.45s.
9th	Mazda R.T. (Europe)	Achim Warmbold/"Biche"	D/F	17	Mazda RX7	B	CRJ130 (B)	12h.06m.38s.
10th	-	Yoshio Iwashita/Yoshimasa Nakahara	J	40	Nissan 240RS	B	TKA33TA9762 (J)	12h.36m.23s.
13th	N. Kioleidis S.A.	Manolis Halivelakis/Costas Exarchos	GR	35	Toyota Corolla	A	DOK914 (GR)	13h.22m.27s.

104 starters. 32 finishers. No group N starters. No Ladies' finishers. 10 A-PRIORITY DRIVERS. Winner's average speed over stages (corrected to allow for 30s. penalty for one minute late at time control) 74.71kph.

Positions in World Championship for Rallies after Round 5
Audi 78 points, Lancia 70, Renault 36, Toyota 28, VW 21, Nissan 20, Opel 18, Peugeot 12, Alfa Romeo 9, Citroen 4, Vauxhall and Mazda 2.

Leading positions in World Championship for Drivers after Round 6
Blomqvist 63 points, Alen 60, Mikkola 59, Bettega 34, Biasion 31, Rohrl 26, Waldegard and Ragnotti 20, Mouton and Aaltonen 15, etc.

LEADING RETIREMENTS

ENTRANT	DRIVER/CODRIVER	NAT.	COMP NO.	CAR	GROUP	REG NO.	CAUSE	STAGES COMPLETED
West R.T.	Carlo Capone/Paolo Spollon	I	15	Lancia Rally	B	TOW67787 (I)	differential	0
Audi Sport	MICHELE MOUTON/Fabrizia Pons	F/I	4	Audi Sport Quattro	B	IN-NL2 (D)	engine	14
Mazda R.T. (Europe)	Ingvar Carlsson/Benny Melander	S	20	Mazda RX7	B	CJH710 (B)	differential	16
Martini Racing	Henri Toivonen/Juha Piironen	SF	11	Lancia Rally	B	TOW67770 (I)	accident	24
Rothmans Porsche R.T.	Saeed Al Hajri/John Spiller	Q/GB	18	Porsche 911SC RS	B	A815CCF (GB)	gearbox	24
Peugeot-Talbot Sport	ARI VATANEN/Terry Harryman	SF/GB	3	Peugeot 205 Turbo 16	B	716EXC75 (F)	engine	31
Peugeot-Talbot Sport	Jean-Pierre Nicolas/Charley Pasquier	F	12	Peugeot 205 Turbo 16	B	709EXC75 (F)	hub	37
Jolly Club	MASSIMO BIASION/Tiziano Siviero	I	9	Lancia Rally	B	TOW67784 (I)	driveshaft	40
Audi Sport	WALTER ROHRL/Christian Geistdorfer	D	1	Audi Sport Quattro	B	IN-NC46 (D)	clutch/electrics	44

Rally Leaders
Blomqvist stages 1–3, Mikkola 4, Blomqvist 5–16, Rohrl 17, Vatanen 18–19, Blomqvist 20–47.

LEADING SPECIAL STAGE POSITIONS

	1ST	2ND	3RD	4TH	5TH	6TH		1ST	2ND	3RD	4TH	5TH	6TH		1ST	2ND	3RD	4TH	5TH	6TH
Blomqvist	12	11	8	4	5	4	Rohrl	8	9	8	8	2	4	Mouton	2	-	1	2	1	-
Vatanen	11	6	4	4	2	2	Alen	5	5	3	8	9	4	Toivonen	1	-	3	6	6	4
Mikkola	8	10	11	9	5	1	Bettega	2	3	5	6	4	6	Nicolas	-	2	1	1	2	5

THE ROUTE

		SPECIAL STAGES	TOTAL DISTANCE	CREWS RUNNING
Etape 1 (1–17)	Athens (Monday 0930) – Kalambaka (Monday 2344)	17 gravel – 281km	809km	69
Etape 2 (18–33)	Kalambaka (Tuesday 1000) – Lagonissi (Wednesday 0021)	15 gravel – 274km 1 asphalt – 7km	749km	44
Etape 3 (34–47)	Lagonissi (Wednesday 2100) – Poros – then by boat to Paleon Faliron – Athens (Thursday 1730)	12 gravel – 215km 2 asphalt – 21km	707km	36
		47 stages – 798km	2265km	

Hot, dry and dusty throughout. 10 stages held in darkness.

RECENT WINNERS
1974 rally not held
1975 Walter Rohrl/Jochen Berger Opel Ascona
1976 Harry Kallstrom/Claes-Goran Andersson Datsun Violet
1977 Bjorn Waldegard/Hans Thorszelius Ford Escort RS1800
1978 Walter Rohrl/Christian Geistdorfer Fiat Abarth 131
1979 Bjorn Waldegard/Hans Thorszelius Ford Escort RS
1980 Ari Vatanen/David Richards Ford Escort RS
1981 Ari Vatanen/David Richards Ford Escort RS
1982 Michele Mouton/Fabrizia Pons Audi Quattro
1983 Walter Rohrl/Christian Geistdorfer Lancia Rally

73

New Zealand

. . . Blomqvist's third win of the season, good compensation for his frustration the year before

* * *

. . . Four works teams enter group B cars, all finishing in the top five places

* * *

. . . this year's rally run without the controversies which had marred previous events

* * *

. . . Alen again does everything he can, but is powerless against drivers with more suitable cars

* * *

Finally it looked as if the New Zealand Rally had broken its run of bad luck. Now devoid of the unsettling problems of earlier years the event was a great success, a worthy justification of FISA's policy of spreading the world championship round the globe. As a qualifying round of the world championships, however, it only served to tell us what we already knew, that Audi were un-catchable – when they used their old cars. Audi had previously decided to run only two-valve cars on this event, to reduce the logistic difficulties of running two types of car so far from home. Blomqvist drove cannily, never being worried if Mikkola got ahead of him, and in the end his problems were re-moved when Mikkola overturned and lost time.

The Acropolis had been happy to have five works teams in group B – but New Zealand had four. The event is popular with drivers, and the only factor which daunts the teams is the sheer distance from the rest of the world. It is always more expensive if teams decide, like Lancia, only to enter at the last

FACING PAGE
No point trying any more. Markku Alen once again drove splendidly but second place was no use. There would be no point in going to Argentina after this.

BELOW
However hard Stig Blomqvist tried, he could not match Rohrl's speed in the opening stages. He was driving at his limit and sometimes beyond.

HOLMES

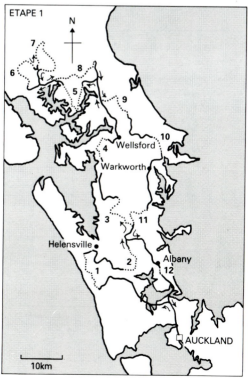

ETAPE 1

N

7
6
8
5
9
Wellsford 10
4
Warkworth
3 11
Helensville
Albany
1 2 12
AUCKLAND

10km

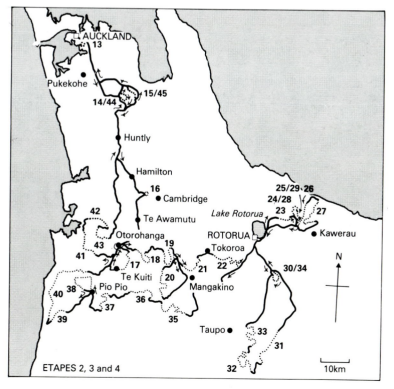

AUCKLAND
13

Pukekohe
15/45
14/44

Huntly

Hamilton
16
Cambridge
42
Te Awamutu
25/29 26
24/28
Lake Rotorua 23 27
Otorohanga 19
43 ROTORUA
41 Tokoroa Kawerau
18 22 N
17 21 30/34
Te Kuiti 20
40 38 Pio Pio Mangakino
36
37 35
39
Taupo 33
31
32

ETAPES 2, 3 and 4

10km

Stig Blomqvist poses on his arrival at Rotorua in the middle of the third étape, just after Mikkola had fallen back.

moment, and for the German-based Toyota team it had been the end of a difficult first half year, when at the same time they had prepared cars for Portugal, Safari and New Zealand. Nissan (and also their associated company Subaru) worked more easily, preparing cars in Japan instead of Europe. The event is undamaging on cars to a remarkable degree. Last year's record of a puncture-free rally was broken by a dangerously placed pile of rocks on the very first stage, but this had been in a forest, the type of stage which does not have the same character as the closed public road sections.

Audi have been to New Zealand twice before, had on each occasion led the event but never managing to finish; the Italians three times, twice scoring victory through reliability. Nissan scored a surprise win on one occasion, and had always been well placed while Toyota fondly remembered their unexpected win the previous time they were there. So whichever way you looked, it seemed it was Audi's turn to win! They were already in a winning groove, having

won four of the previous six rallies in this year's series, and the decision to leave behind their undeveloped four-valve car was obviously sensible.

The rally ran true to predictions. Only Audi held the lead, each of the three HB team drivers holding it at one point or another, but there was one quite unexpected thing – the speed of Rohrl. Driving at number one on a rally

in New Zealand is a Bad Thing! The roads are covered with loose gravel, and the fastest times are normally put up by drivers when previous cars have cleared the surface. But nobody told Rohrl that he should not drive too fast. He knew the problems for himself, and simply said afterwards the challenge had "motivated" him. Just how incredibly well he went can be judged by the stage times. Four seconds fastest over 32.26kms on the first stage, finishing the stage with a flat tyre, another deflating and the brakes jammed after hitting the rocks. He was then fastest on the second despite differential trouble, sixth fastest on each of the next two stages, despite driving with the rear differential broken, fastest on the next four stages despite intermittent electrical trouble, caused by a failing Motronic unit. On the next stage the car stopped for good.

Rohrl was disappointed that an "old" Quattro had let him down and even more that he (one of the most reliable drivers ever in world championship rallying) had retired three rallies running.

Timo Salonen has long enjoyed good results in New Zealand, and this year he came fourth, driving the highest placed car of orthodox design. He is seen on the first stage, one of the forest sections which generally were not as popular as the gravel public road stages.

Mikkola was proving the faster but Blomqvist was steadier. The Swede eased his pace on the night stages (not running first on the road till the third étape), and was catching up in daylight. And Markku Alen gradually lost ground behind them in third place. It was on stage 27 that the rally suddenly came alive. Toyotas were already in trouble. They were hard pressed to stay ahead of Salonen's Nissan. Kankkunen had just lost road penalties because the fuel tank had been punctured at a service point, and Waldegard lost stage time and road

RIGHT

A long and winding road. Bjorn Waldegard did not have a happy time, the Toyota being well outclassed by the Audis and Lancias and beaten by Salonen's consistency.

BELOW

Best placed New Zealander in the early stages was Neill Allport, who (save for this occasion!) drove with commendable neatness. He retired with engine failure, leaving Reg Cook to take the local honours.

Not Mikkola's year. After Blomqvist and Rohrl had put their cars on the roof in Portugal, Mikkola did the same in New Zealand. Team manager Roland Gumpert uses his feet to help straighten the roof, as Hertz and Cederberg look on.

penalties when a fuel line came adrift, coming up to this section. Then on the stage itself Allport stopped with piston trouble, having got ahead of Reg Cook for the honour of being the best local driver, and accidents befell Mikkola, Salonen and Kankkunen. All three went on their roofs, Salonen losing very little time (finishing third quickest on the stage) but Mikkola lost twelve minutes and Kankkunen's car took some hours to retrieve. Mikkola was unlucky that his car was jammed upside down against a bank, but lucky his team manager and chief mechanic saw what happened from their helicopter, landed and were able to help right the car and extinguish the inevitable fire.

Mikkola then began the long chase of second placed Alen, making a series of fastest times as he tried to make good the necessary second-per-kilometre deficit. For some time it seemed he would make it, but it was only by virtue of unacceptable risk to Audi. They wanted Mikkola to finish and eventually he settled for third place. Japanese cars scored an amazing success in group A. The works Subarus were first and second, other places taken by Toyota Starlet or Corolla 16-valve cars, Nissan with a Bluebird Turbo (all three winning their classes) and Mitsubishi. The New Zealand Rally was an event in which everyone proved something, but most of all the organisers. This was an event which put the organisation of many European classics to shame.

Peter "Possum" Bourne won group A in a four-wheel drive Subaru for the second year running. The loose stones are a feature of New Zealand rallying; they are small enough not to cause punctures but slippery enough to make great demands on driving skills.

14th Sanyo Rally of New Zealand

23–26 June 1984   New Zealand

OVERALL RESULTS

	ENTRANT	DRIVER/CODRIVER	NAT.	COMP NO.	CAR	GROUP	REG NO.	TOTAL PENALTY
1st	Audi Sport	STIG BLOMQVIST/Bjorn Cederberg	S	3	Audi Quattro	B	IN-NJ5 (D)	10h.40m.41s.
2nd	Martini Racing	MARKKU ALEN/Ilkka Kivimaki	SF	6	Lancia Rally	B	TOW67772 (I)	10h.45m.28s.
3rd	Audi Sport	HANNU MIKKOLA/Arne Hertz	SF/S	4	Audi Quattro	B	IN-YD29 (D)	10h.48m.10s.
4th	Dealer Team Nissan	TIMO SALONEN/Seppo Harjanne	SF	5	Nissan 240RS	B	LO4674 (NZ)	11h.05m.29s.
5th	Toyota NZ Ltd	BJORN WALDEGARD/Hans Thorszelius	S	2	Toyota Celica Twincam Turbo	B	K-DS940 (D)	11h.35m.58s.
6th	Dealer Team Nissan	Reg Cook/Wayne Jones	NZ	10	Nissan 240RS	B	LA5832 (NZ)	11h.44m.20s.
7th	-	Malcolm Stewart/Doug Parkhill	NZ	11	Ford Escort RS	B	JX780 (NZ)	11h.46m.00s.
8th	Motor Holdings	"Possum" Bourne/Michael Eggleton	NZ	31	Subaru Leone 4WD	A	LA1785 (NZ)	12h.04m.46s.
9th	Subaru Motor Sports	Tony Teesdale/Gary Smith	NZ	36	Subaru Leone 4WD	A	TKN58MU4755 (J)	12h.21m.01s.
10th	Heatway	Blair Robson/Don Campbell	NZ	15	Mitsubishi Lancer Turbo	B	KN8700 (NZ)	12h.25m.08s.

63 starters. 35 finishers. No group N starters. No Ladies' finishers. 6 A-PRIORITY DRIVERS. Winner's average speed over stages 97.80kph.

Positions in World Championship for Rallies after Round 6
Audi 96 points, Lancia 86, Toyota 38, Renault 36, Nissan 32, VW 21, Opel 18, Peugeot 12, Subaru 11, Alfa Romeo 9, Citroen 4, Vauxhall, Mazda and Mitsubishi 2.

Leading positions in World Championship for Drivers after Round 7
Blomqvist 83 points, Alen 75, Mikkola 71, Bettega 34, Biasion 31, Waldegard 28, Rohrl 26, Salonen 21, Ragnotti 20, Mouton and Aaltonen 15, etc.

LEADING RETIREMENTS

ENTRANT	DRIVER/CODRIVER	NAT.	COMP NO.	CAR	GROUP	REG NO.	CAUSE	STAGES COMPLETED
Toyota NZ Ltd	Paul Adams/Jim Scott	NZ	32	Toyota Corolla	A	LP1600 (NZ)	oil pump	5
Audi Sport	WALTER ROHRL/Christian Geistdorfer	D	1	Audi Quattro	B	IN-YD6 (D)	ignition	8
Tulloch Transport	Ian Tulloch/Wade Peterson	NZ	18	Ford Escort RS	B	IF780 (NZ)	accident	11
-	Franz Wittmann/Peter Diekmann	A/D	9	Audi Quattro	B	N511.005 (A)	engine	21
Toyota NZ Ltd	Juha Kankkunen/Fred Gallagher	SF/GB	8	Toyota Celica Twincam Turbo	B	K-MT779 (D)	accident	26
-	Neill Allport/Roger Freeth	NZ	12	Ford Escort RS	B	JX3553 (NZ)	engine	26

Rally Leaders
Rohrl stages1–2, Blomqvist 3–4, Rohrl 5–8, Blomqvist 9–11, Mikkola 12–15, Blomqvist 16–45.

LEADING SPECIAL STAGE POSITIONS

	1ST	2ND	3RD	4TH	5TH	6TH		1ST	2ND	3RD	4TH	5TH	6TH		1ST	2ND	3RD	4TH	5TH	6TH
Mikkola	21	18	4	-	1	-	Rohrl	6	-	-	-	1	1	Salonen	-	-	1	13	16	5
Blomqvist	13	18	11	1	1	-	Waldegard	-	3	2	14	14	4	Wittman	-	-	-	5	1	5
Alen	7	7	24	6	1	-	Kankkunen	-	1	1	4	6	8	Stewart	-	-	-	1	3	8

THE ROUTE

		SPECIAL STAGES	TOTAL DISTANCE	CREWS RUNNING
Etape 1 (1–12)	Auckland (Saturday 1005) – Auckland (Saturday 2214)	12 gravel – 247km	599km	54
Etape 2 (13–22)	Auckland (Sunday 1000) – Rotorua (Sunday 2212)	1 asphalt – 2km 9 gravel – 197km	633km	45
Etape 3 (23–34)	Rotorua (Monday 0900) – Rotorua – Rotorua (Monday 2241)	12 gravel – 280km	797km	38
Etape 4 (35–45)	Rotorua (Tuesday 0700) – Auckland (Tuesday 2100)	11 gravel – 318km	597km	37
		45 stages – 1044km	2626km	

All rally held in dry conditions. 13 stages held in darkness.

RECENT WINNERS

1974 not held
1975 Mike Marshall/Arthur McWatt Ford Escort RS1800
1976 Andrew Cowan/Jim Scott Hillman Avenger
1977 Fulvio Bacchelli/Francesco Rossetti Fiat Abarth 131
1978 Russell Brookes/Chris Porter Ford Escort RS
1979 Hannu Mikkola/Arne Hertz Ford Escort RS
1980 Timo Salonen/Seppo Harjanne Datsun 160J
1981 Jim Donald/Kevin Lancaster Ford Escort RS
1982 Bjorn Waldegard/Hans Thorszelius Toyota Celica
1983 Walter Rohrl/Christian Geistdorfer Lancia Rally

Argentina

. . . Stig Blomqvist becomes the first man to win three world championship rallies in succession

* * *

. . . The long-chassis Audi Quattro wins its twenty-first world event, equalling the Ford Escort as the most successful rally car in history – but the opposition was minimal

* * *

. . . Jorge Recalde takes advantage of his works Audi drive to become the first South American to lead a world championship rally

* * *

. . . the move to Cordoba takes away the grandeur of the Andes but provides a well-run and popular event. Gone also are the high-speed stages of previous years

* * *

Blomqvist was in charge again! The chosen king of 1984 repaid Audi's trust in him with his third successive victory and headed a one-two-three domination of the only South American round in the series. Backed up by a subservient Hannu Mikkola who had to forego his chances in the British Open championship simply to run as Blomqvist's number two on this event, Blomqvist brought home maximum points both for himself and for Audi. Lancia did not enter. . .

LEFT
Happiness is . . . winning in Argentina. Stig Blomqvist finds company in Cordoba.

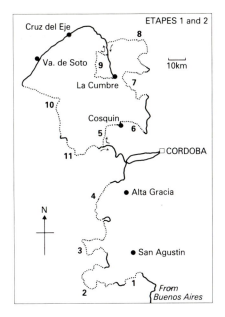

For a rally which is organised with such enthusiasm it was a shame that only Audi took works cars down from Europe. The event moved this year to Cordoba, centre of Argentina's motor industry and hub of the rallying, away from the spectacular mountains of Tucuman and the lonely roads of Bariloche, but into far easier organisational territory – and into the land of race-bred enthusiasts. It was the best-supported, non-European world rally ever, even discounting the large numbers of non-homologated cars which were also allowed to compete, yet the local drivers

BELOW
Watersplash at dawn on Wednesday for Mario and Daniel Stillo with their group A winning Renault 12.

were denied a chance of matching their skills purposefully against the foreigners. Audi, mindful that the only justification for coming was to gain points, held back their drivers on the strictest possible rein.

Against Audi were two local works teams, Renault and Peugeot. The former (for whom Recalde normally drives) used 18GTX models, and had promised their champion a 5 Turbo for this event, but anticipated help from France fell through for lack of service. This gave the driver from nearby Mina Clavero the chance of driving something even more exciting! The Marlboro-sponsored Renaults were similar to those seen at Bariloche the year before, but Peugeot had a newer version of the 504, called the GR TN. The only other important entry came from Kenya for Iwase who had acquired an ex-works Ascona 400 and Marlboro support. From Uruguay came the popular team of Escort RS2000s, but the remaining local interest was centred on a fourth Quattro, for di Palma. Last year di Palma, who races Volkswagen touring cars for the local factory, had entered a Quattro but crashed, and this year he competed again, his works-loaned car liberally covered with the stickers of sponsors.

For ever more one can argue that Recalde was "allowed" to win the first special stage by the courtesy of the other

ABOVE
Stig Blomqvist and Bjorn Cederberg passing the outskirts of San Marcos on stage nine.

BELOW
Jorge Recalde created excitement wherever he went, and after hearing he had actually been leading the spectators were ecstatic.

Quattro drivers, but it made good publicity for the team – so long as Recalde clearly understood that this was no licence for freedom on the other stages. As a works entry so far away, it was a very low-key operation. In a reverse situation to 1983 Blomqvist made the pacenotes which Mikkola's co-driver Hertz then copied and translated for their own use. With birthdays for both Blomqvist and Cederberg falling in their stay in Argentina, it was obviously a time for relaxation as well. Mikkola, mindful of the need to act as Blomqvist's understudy, claimed he made his training on the golf course! But experienced men such as these can take such liberties with impunity. For others there were pitfalls. Both Iwase and the Uruguayan team leader de Vitta had already acquired massive penalties through arriving at the pre-rally parc ferme too late.

With di Palma stranded by the roadside on the way from Buenos Aires to the first stage Audi had only three Quattros left, but inevitably they dominated the event. On every stage in the rally they were to take the top three stages times except once, first thing Monday morning, when Soto beat Mikkola who seemed a little sleepy. After four stages Soto was lying fourth, twelve minutes behind the German four-wheelers, who were all running within a half-minute of each other. It had been an awful event for the others. Two of the Uruguayan Escorts and one of the works Renaults were out already, behind the leaders the only non-Renaults were the two official Peugeots.

INFORMACION DEL RALLY.
~~~~~~~~~~~~~~~~~~~~~~
POR ROTURA DE LA CAJA DE VEL.
DEBIO ABANDONAR LA PRUEBA EL
PILOTO DE V.DOLORES E.SOTO CON
RENAULT 18 ÚLTIMA MAQUINA DEL
EQUIPO OFICIAL DE LA CITADA
MARCA.

STEWAR - WARNER   AUTOTROL

ABOVE

Luis di Palma left Buenos Aires in high hopes but later that night his engine expired on the road out to the first stage.

LEFT

Cordoba's World Cup football stadium made a splendid headquarters for the event. It was spacious, well equipped for the media and the scoreboard could tell everything that went on. Soto's retirement in the last remaining works Renault is being announced.

The top fourteen group A cars were Renaults – the Peugeots running in group B.

The carnage was to continue on the Monday. At the end of that day no works Peugeot or Renault cars and none of the Uruguayans were left, and the best non-Audi was Chiavarolle's private Renault 18GTX which was almost three-quarters of an hour behind Blomqvist. Recalde had a moment of anxiety when the injection failed at a service point, and was only discovered when it was time for him to leave for the next stage. Iwase was still paying heavily for his earlier error having to run well down the field but on Monday night he was eighth overall, hoping hard for the last two days. On the Tuesday Blomqvist

with local man Recalde in action even this did not worry the enthusiasts. It was quite a day for nearby Villa Carlos Paz, a resort town close to Cordoba where many of the journalists and VIPs were staying. This had been a staging post on the old Gran Premio round-Argentina road race the year when the Swedish girl Ewy Rosqvist was the winner. Plus ça change . . .

LEFT
Heartbreak. Chiavarolle broke down eighteen kilometres before the end of the final stage, the last remaining Renault 18GTX after all three works group A cars had retired, when he had hoped to gain an unexpected group win.

BELOW
This is a Fiat 128 Super Europa! When non-homologated cars were allowed to run in the middle of the rally proper, FISA's officials were not pleased but it was good publicity for Fiat.

had his puncture, ironically about the most interesting thing which happened to the works Audis all event! This upset the status quo, Mikkola having to slow down to let the Swede take back the lead the Finn had mistakenly acquired. Last year's champion made a show of it, pausing and waving to friends and journalists he spotted en route. When the tyre went down Blomqvist could not make up his mind what to do. He radioed team manager Gumpert and chief mechanic Harsch, flying behind in a helicopter, but they were too far back to help, so Blomqvist and Cederberg had to change the wheel themselves. Still the Quattros took one-two-three even on this stage. At the end of Tuesday Chiavarolle was more than an hour behind but still leading group A, Iwase was up to seventh.

The final day was essentially a re-run of stages held the previous Saturday, though the final stage was abandoned following the masses of spectators who had been there before. The Audis cruised through to victory but there was disaster for Chiavarolle whose Renault was stuck in the last stage. Iwase came through to fifth place and another week of Argentine motor sport was over. Cordoba had been a great success in every aspect except the excitement of the event, but

5th Marlboro Rally of Argentina YPF Cordoba

27 July–1 August 1984   Argentina

OVERALL RESULTS

	ENTRANT	DRIVER/CODRIVER	NAT.	COMP NO.	CAR	GROUP	REG NO.	TOTAL PENALTY
1st	Audi Sport	STIG BLOMQVIST/Bjorn Cederberg	S	1	Audi Quattro	B	IN-NC59 (D)	10h.33m.38s.
2nd	Audi Sport	HANNU MIKKOLA/Arne Hertz	SF/S	2	Audi Quattro	B	IN-NJ5 (D)	10h.36m.54s.
3rd	Audi Sport	Jorge Recalde/Jorge Del Buono	RA	3	Audi Quattro	B	IN-NE8 (D)	10h.38m.48s.
4th	-	Mario Stillo/Daniel Stillo	RA	19	Renault 12	A	C/I 151102 (RA)	12h.12m.20s.
5th	-	Yasuhiro Iwase/Surinder Thatthi	EAK	4	Opel Ascona 400	B	KWC269 (EAK)	12h.18m.24s.
6th	-	Miguel Torras/Fernando Stella	RA	20	Renault 12	A	N064843 (RA)	12h.20m.57s.
7th	-	Carlos Bassi/Roberto Syriani	RA	32	Peugeot 504	B	KKW639 (RA)	12h.56m.23s.
8th	-	Hugo Hernandez/Adolfo Coggiola	RA	25	Peugeot 504 TN	B	R069968 (RA)	13h.09m.12s.
-	-	Omar De Giovanni/Roque Perez	RA	119	Fiat 128 SE 1500	-	DAL4085 (RA)	13h.16m.30s.*
9th	-	Monnenmacher Perez/Enrique Marongiu	RA	38	Peugeot 504	B	Z012331 (RA)	13h.37m.56s.
10th	-	Walter D'Agostini/Cesar Romero	RA	80	Renault 12	A	X465322 (RA)	13h.51m.19s.

105 starters (plus 58 non-homologated cars). 21 finishers (plus 13 non-homologated*). No group N starters. No Ladies' finishers. 2 A-PRIORITY DRIVERS. Winner's average speed over stages 89.80kph.

Positions in World Championship for Rallies after Round 7
Audi 114 points, Lancia 86, Renault 51, Toyota 38, Nissan 32, Opel 29, VW 21, Peugeot 20, Subaru 11, Alfa Romeo 9, Ford 6, Citroen 4, Vauxhall, Mazda and Mitsubishi 2.

Leading positions in World Championship for Drivers after Round 6
Blomqvist 103 points, Mikkola 86, Alen 75, Bettega 34, Biasion 31, Waldegard 28, Rohrl 26, Salonen 21, Ragnotti 20, Mouton and Aaltonen 15, etc.

LEADING RETIREMENTS

ENTRANT	DRIVER/CODRIVER	NAT.	COMP NO.	CAR	GROUP	REG NO.	CAUSE	STAGES COMPLETED
-	Luis di Palma/Nestor Straimel	RA	24	Audi Quattro	B	IN-NX47 (D)	engine	0
-	Gustavo Trelles/Raul Ivetich	U	10	Ford Escort RS2000	B	11.940 (U)	gearbox	2
-	Paulo Lemos/Artur Cezar	BR	21	VW Voyage	A	BP0863 (BR)	driveshaft	2
-	Carlos Veronesi/Carlos Silva	RA	16	Renault 18GTX	A	X455047 (RA)	road accident	3
-	Luis Etchegoyen/Luis Borrallo	U	8	Ford Escort RS2000	B	235.134 (U)	halfshaft	4
Renault Argentina	Alejandro Moroni/Raul Campana	RA	15	Renault 18GTX	A	X487952 (RA)	engine	4
-	Federico West/Gregorio Asadourian	U	9	Ford Escort RS2000	B	714.468 (U)	accident/steering arm	6
-	Francisco Alcuaz/Daniel Muzio	RA/U	26	Peugeot 504GR TN	B	DAE.4083 (RA)	engine	7
Renault Argentina	Ernesto Soto/Martin Christie	RA	6	Renault 18GTX	A	X487953 (RA)	gearbox	8
-	Gabriel Raies/Ruben Quiros	RA	18	Renault 12	A	B/1 493022 (RA)	differential	8
-	Domingo de Vitta/Washington Antunez	U	5	Ford Escort RS2000	B	11.977 (U)	steering arm	9
-	Carlos Celis/Luis Oyola	RA	7	Renault 12	A	C/1 125705 (RA)	accident	9
-	Jorge Maggi/Hector Valles	RA	11	Peugeot 504 TN	B	B/1 477834 (RA)	accident	11
C. Concesionarios Sevel	Carlos Garro/Marcelo Tornqvist	RA	12	Peugeot 504GR TN	B	DAE.4082 (RA)	head gasket	14
-	Eduardo Chiavarolle/Piccioni Lopez	RA	17	Renault 18GTX	A	X481238 (RA)	gearbox	23

Rally Leaders
Recalde stage 1, Blomqvist 2–15, Mikkola 16, Blomqvist 17–23.

LEADING SPECIAL STAGE POSITIONS

	1ST	2ND	3RD	4TH	5TH	6TH		1ST	2ND	3RD	4TH	5TH	6TH		1ST	2ND	3RD	4TH	5TH	6TH
Blomqvist	11	6	6	-	-	-	Soto	-	-	1	5	1	-	Garro	-	-	-	2	7	1
Mikkola	6	9	7	1	-	-	Iwase	-	-	-	7	2	5	Torras	-	-	-	2	1	3
Recalde	6	8	9	-	-	-	Chiavarolle	-	-	-	5	7	-	Hernandez	-	-	-	1	-	-

THE ROUTE

		SPECIAL STAGES	TOTAL DISTANCE	CREWS RUNNING
Etape 1 (1–4)	Buenos Aires (Friday 2200) – Cordoba (Saturday 1432)	4 gravel – 173km	1109km	69
Etape 2 (5–11)	Cordoba (Monday 0600) – Cordoba (Monday 1706)	7 gravel – 320km	582km	34
Etape 3 (12–18)	Cordoba (Tuesday 0600) – Cordoba (Tuesday 1646)	7 gravel – 279km	526km	24
Etape 4 (19–23)	Cordoba (Wednesday 0600) – Cordoba (Wednesday 1403)	5 gravel – 176km	402km	21
		23 stages – 948km	2619km	

Stage 24 cancelled for reasons of security. Dry throughout. 4 stages held in darkness.

RECENT WINNERS

1979 Jean Guichet/Jean Todt Peugeot 504
1980 Walter Rohrl/Christian Geistdorfer Fiat Abarth 131
1981 Guy Frequelin/Jean Todt Talbot Sunbeam Lotus
1982 not held
1983 Hannu Mikkola/Arne Hertz Audi Quattro

Finland

9
OKOBANK OF FINLAND

. . . Peugeot's first win with a 205 Turbo 16 car with second and third places for Lancia suddenly puts Audi into the cold

*   *   *

. . . Best Audi performance is Blomqvist's fourth place with an old long-chassis car – but it is enough for the Germans to claim the world title

*   *   *

. . . Outclassed group A cars again fail to reach the top ten but Grundel's new VW is surprisingly fast. Rear-drive Opel Asconas take seven out of the top eight finishers

*   *   *

. . . Michele Mouton overturns for the second time in Finland in three years. It is just like her teammates have done on other events this year!

*   *   *

Interviewed before the start, Peugeot's competition boss Jean Todt said he thought Peugeot could win any of the world championship events from then on. Coolly, just like that – and how right he was! Ari Vatanen took a little time for the car to be adjusted to the uniquely undulating roads of his native Finland, but from then on he made all the running. Audi had started as pre-rally favourites, but they eventually gained only fourth place, just enough to clinch the world title. It was dismal to see the previous winners struggling like that. Suddenly our values had been changed, the Peugeot had upset our

views. It was astounding to realise that Audi had been so outclassed, not only by the winners, but also by the Lancia Rallys of Alen and Toivonen.

In the increasingly fast-changing technical environment of present-day rallying the old Audi could not have lasted much longer and after three years of rally winning the Quattro's day had to end. Having seen them winning so often earlier this season the victory of Peugeot came as an extra shock. Concentrating on so many different things had stretched Audi beyond their capabilities. With one eye on reliability which only the old car could offer they had to

run two types of car; wanting to win both the makes' and the drivers' championship in the same season meant they had not only mechanical problems to conquer – but also the challenge of making the right driver succeed as well. At least it was Blomqvist who was to score the points for them. But Blomqvist's fourth place was no result for a potential champion, especially as his greatest rival Markku Alen came second once again with a car that had never gone as well on this event before. Audi's disgrace was unbelievable. Lancia gained nineteen fastest times whereas Audi could only take six, and three of these

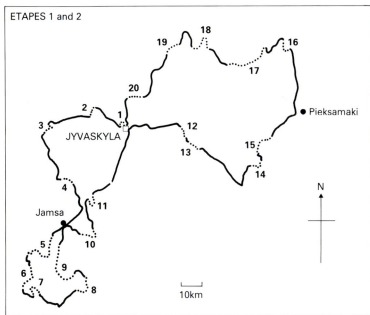

ETAPES 1 and 2

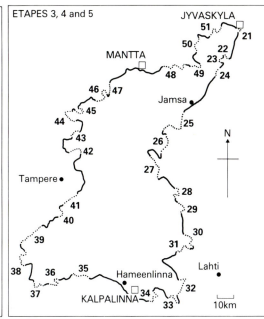

ETAPES 3, 4 and 5

FACING PAGE
Jumping down the Humulamaki stage is Ari Vatanen with the Peugeot 205 Turbo 16 on his way to an historic win.

BELOW
For the second year running a Nissan 240RS was the best normally aspirated car to finish the 1000 Lakes, but this time it was the "forgotten Finn" Erkki Pitkanen who gained the honour.

by Blomqvist in the old car. Except in the first three hours of the event, Audi never led the event at all.

The Peugeot looked so right. Vatanen grew angry when friends said how fit and well he looked, unlike the drivers of other cars who were exhausted during the rally. Spectators said the Audis were terrific to watch but the stopwatch rejected their opinions. In fact both Sport

Quattros retired, Mouton following an accident, and seven-times previous winner Mikkola when his steering broke. There was a frightening truth about the Peugeot, their's was a system which worked. Their pre-event confusion was not true to form. At the unique test-day before the start the car had handled badly, floating over the bumps in a disconcerting way. What worried the team

HOLMES

was not the problem but how they could have miscalculated things so wrongly. Midnight oil was burned and on the event things were progressively cured. On this event it was the only Peugeot turbocar but not the only group B car from this make. The importers were sponsoring a pick-up, but this was banned by the Police from competing as it counted as a commercial vehicle. The organsers let it run as course-opening car, and the driver gained much more publicity as a result!

The other important entries came from Toyota and Nissan. The former had shown their latest car in the world championship just twelve months before and had won two events in the meantime, but again Finland was not their scene. Theoretically it should have been as this is a good event for turbos and high power, but Toyota Team Europe are finding the Celica Twincam Turbo is becoming suitable only for endurance rallies. The Nissan 240RS has neither turbo nor high power and for this event they again lost their top driver Timo Salonen at short notice, through back trouble. He was replaced by Pentii Airikkala who had little opportunity for training, and the Nissan star was to be Erkki Pitkanen, who finished as driver of the best normally aspirated car.

The novelty of the event was Volkswagen, who finally appeared with their

ABOVE

A changed man! For Henri Toivonen it was a welcome change to escape the pressures of Rothmans and drive once more for Lancia. He was visibly at ease. Some say his steadiness showed a maturity they had not noticed in his driving for a long while.

long-chassis model, mysteriously called a "19" Golf GTI. Although fitted with the same engine the car was very different to the old square cars the team had been running since 1977, the longer wheelbase chassis giving far greater stability than before – something important on the 1000 Lakes. Grundel had strangely never competed on the 1000 Lakes before so a lacklustre performance would have been quite understandable, but in fact he drove with remarkable speed for the first eight stages. On the ninth he learned that the smallest departure from a chosen line can end your hopes. . . From then there was a battle between Ericsson with an 80 Quattro and Sundstrom with an Abarth 130, the Swede's Audi gradually pulling ahead, particularly when the Finn's Italian car suffered an oil leak, but on the same stage they both retired. The other group A cars were completely out of the overall picture.

Per Eklund was easily the best private driver, but as the leading drivers struck trouble others came along. The most impressive was Bruno Saby with a factory-specification Renault 5 Turbo. This

LEFT

Another second-timer! Per Eklund finished best privateer again, with an Audi Quattro.

RIGHT

Appliance of Science? Audi team manager Roland Gumpert gives vent to his feelings with a hammer after Michele Mouton rolled her Sport Quattro. Once again Finnish rules limited exposure for sponsors; note the way that the "HB" name has been taken away from the stickers.

BELOW

Mikael Sundstrom drove this Fiat Abarth 130 with gusto until the transmission failed on the second night, at the same time as his group A rival Mikael Ericsson also went out.

gave Renault more world points on an event where they have never done well before. After the retirement of two of the three works cars, Olivier Tabatoni won his class in a private Citroen Visa 1000 Pistes.

Vatanen's win was a new chapter in rallying, the first win by a purpose-built four-wheel drive rallycar. It was difficult to know what impressed the most, whether it was the speed with which a new team could win, or the foresight necessary to design a car at a time when nobody knew what the winning formula would be, and few had time even to know how the regulations would work. Rallying is full of teams who issue hopeful statements about their prospects but Peugeot were not like that at all. They had never said their car was good, only that they thought it would be. Their victory threw Audi into a frenzy. Testing for Sanremo now became an absolute priority, for they had announced the long Quattro would be pensioned off as soon as the makes' title was obtained. Maybe there had been a resignation that the Peugeot would be a natural winner, but the way the Lancias walked over Audi was something which hurt. And with the memory of last year's Sanremo defeat still in their minds it was time to fight back or give up. The Germans decided to fight.

ABOVE

Ari Vatanen rejects alcohol and enjoys the chance of promoting the product of a sponsor – milk! Terry Harryman (left) shares a drink but keeps the bottle of the real thing for later.

LEFT

Juha Kankkunen took fifth place with his Toyota Celica Twincam Turbo, the second time running he had a good run on this event when his team leader Waldegard struck problems.

34th 1000 Lakes Rally

26–28 August 1984   Finland

OVERALL RESULTS

	ENTRANT	DRIVER/CODRIVER	NAT.	COMP NO.	CAR	GROUP	REG NO.	TOTAL PENALTY
1st	Peugeot-Talbot Sport	ARI VATANEN/Terry Harryman	SF/GB	4	Peugeot 205 Turbo 16	B	704EXC75 (F)	4h.08m.49s.
2nd	Martini Racing	MARKKU ALEN/Ilkka Kivimaki	SF	2	Lancia Rally	B	TOW67785 (I)	4h.10m.49s.
3rd	Martini Racing	Henri Toivonen/Juha Piironen	SF	10	Lancia Rally	B	TOW67776 (I)	4h.12m.57s.
4th	Audi Sport	STIG BLOMQVIST/Bjorn Cederberg	S	3	Audi Quattro	B	IN-YJ81 (D)	4h.14m.01s.
5th	Toyota Team Europe	Juha Kankkunen/Fred Gallagher	SF/GB	11	Toyota Celica Twincam Turbo	B	K-AM6232 (D)	4h.19m.39s.
6th	Clarion	PER EKLUND/Dave Whittock	S/GB	6	Audi Quattro	B	IN-04209 (D)	4h.20m.18s.
7th	Team Nissan Finland	Erkki Pitkanen/Rolf Mesterton	SF	12	Nissan 240RS	B	X-1781 (SF)	4h.33m.58s.
8th	Philips Auto-Radio	Bruno Saby/Jean-Francois Fauchille	F	15	Renault 5 Turbo	B	6711WE38 (F)	4h.35m.26s.
9th	Fotolux-Hebert Oy/Akai	Jouko Poysti/Reijo Savolin	SF	23	Opel Ascona 400	B	XHX-400 (SF)	4h.36m.37s.
10th	Empty Pocket Racing Team	Kalevi Aho/Timo Hakala	SF	24	Opel Manta 400	B	U-4549 (SF)	4h.36m.51s.
16th	Turun Auto-Tarvike Oy	Timo Metsamaki/Juhani Isotalo	SF	58	Opel Ascona	A	NEL-23 (SF)	4h.52m.22s.
30th	Karin Auto Tarvike Oy	Carita Ekroos/Tuula Moilanen	SF	90	Ford Escort RS2000	B	UCR-633 (SF)	5h.08m.19s.*
37th	VV-Auto Oy	Matti Alamaula/Matti Hiltunen	SF	119	Audi 80 Quattro	N	VMT-299 (SF)	5h.19m.39s.

144 starters, 74 finishers. *Ladies' winner. 8 A-PRIORITY DRIVERS. Winner's average speed over stages 110.25kph.

Positions in World Championship for Rallies after Round 8
Audi (126) 116 points, Lancia 102, Renault 55, Toyota 48, Peugeot 40, Nissan 38, Opel 31, VW 21, Subaru 11, Alfa Romeo 9, Ford 6, Citroen 4, Vauxhall, Mazda and Mitsubishi 2.
Audi now Champion

Leading positions in World Championship for Drivers after Round 9
Blomqvist 113 points, Alen 90, Mikkola 86, Bettega 34, Biasion 31, Waldegard 28, Rohrl 26, Salonen 21, Ragnotti and Vatanen 20, etc.

LEADING RETIREMENTS

ENTRANT	DRIVER/CODRIVER	NAT.	COMP NO.	CAR	GROUP	REG NO.	CAUSE	STAGES COMPLETED
VV-Auto Oy	LASSE LAMPI/Pentti Kuukkala	SF	9	Audi Quattro	B	IN-NV35 (D)	engine	1
Citroen	Philippe Wambergue/Jean de Alexandris	F	16	Citroen Visa 1000 Pistes	B	8448ME92 (F)	transmission	4
Volkswagen Motorsport	Kalle Grundel/Peter Diekmann	S/D	20	VW 19 Golf GTI	A	WOB-AZ 754 (D)	accident	8
Citroen	Maurice Chomat/Didier Breton	F	17	Citroen Visa 1000 Pistes	B	8437ME92 (F)	transmission	9
Audi Sport	MICHELE MOUTON/Fabrizia Pons	F/I	7	Audi Sport Quattro	B	IN-NL2 (D)	accident damage	20
Team Nissan Europe	Pentti Airikkala/Seppo Harjanne	SF	8	Nissan 240RS	B	EXI7115 (GB)	gearbox	23
-	Antero Laine/Risto Virtanen	SF	13	Audi Quattro	B	U-4074 (SF)	driveshaft	23
Audi Sport	HANNU MIKKOLA/Arne Hertz	SF/S	1	Audi Sport Quattro	B	IN-NT2 (D)	steering	25
Toyota Team Europe	BJORN WALDEGARD/Hans Thorszelius	S	5	Toyota Celica Twincam Turbo	B	K-AM6321 (D)	engine	25
-	Mikael Ericsson/Rolf Melleroth	S	19	Audi 80 Quattro	A	EHJ 733 (S)	gear linkage	34
Autonovo Oy	Mikael Sundstrom/Voitto Silander	SF	21	Fiat Abarth 130	A	A-2216 (SF)	gearbox	34

Rally Leaders
Blomqvist stages 1+3, Alen 4–12, Vatanen 13–51.

LEADING SPECIAL STAGE POSITIONS (including stage 2)

	1ST	2ND	3RD	4TH	5TH	6TH		1ST	2ND	3RD	4TH	5TH	6TH		1ST	2ND	3RD	4TH	5TH	6TH
Vatanen	31	12	4	1	2	1	Blomqvist	3	9	9	18	8	4	Eklund	-	-	-	4	17	20
Alen	12	23	8	4	1	1	Mikkola	3	7	7	5	1	1	Laine	-	-	-	1	2	7
Toivonen	7	7	16	11	6	3	Kankkunen	-	-	-	10	13	13	Waldegard and Poysti	-	-	-	-	1	-

THE ROUTE

		SPECIAL STAGES	TOTAL DISTANCE	CREWS RUNNING
Etape 1 (1,3–11)	Jyvaskyla (Friday 1801) Jyvaskyla (Saturday 0052)	10 gravel – 113km	332km	122
Etape 2 (12–20)	Jyvaskyla (Saturday 0710) Jyvaskyla (Saturday 1320)	9 gravel – 76km	309km	106
Etape 3 (21–34)	Jyvaskyla (Saturday 1510) Kalpalinna (Saturday 2238)	13 gravel – 124km 1 asphalt – 2km	322km	86
Etape 4 (35–47)	Kalpalinna (Saturday 2350) Mantta (Sunday 0715)	13 gravel – 110km	344km	77
Etape 5 (48–51)	Mantta (Sunday 0750) Jyvaskyla (Sunday 1020)	4 gravel – 32km	113km	74
		50 stages – 457km	1420km	

Stage 2 cancelled – accident after leading competitors had passed. Mostly dry, some rain. 20 stages held in darkness.

RECENT WINNERS

1974 Hannu Mikkola/John Davenport Ford Escort RS1600
1975 Hannu Mikkola/Atso Aho Toyota Corolla
1976 Markku Alen/Ilkka Kivimaki Fiat Abarth 131
1977 Kyosti Hamalainen/Martti Tiukkanen Ford Escort RS1800
1978 Markku Alen/Ilkka Kivimaki Fiat Abarth 131
1979 Markku Alen/Ilkka Kivimaki Fiat Abarth 131
1980 Markku Alen/Ilkka Kivimaki Fiat Abarth 131
1981 Ari Vatanen/David Richards Ford Escort RS
1982 Hannu Mikkola/Arne Hertz Audi Quattro
1983 Hannu Mikkola/Arne Hertz Audi Quattro

Italy

. . . Blomqvist blows it! The Swede is offered the world championship but then his engine fails

*   *   *

. . . Markku Alen fights valiantly but his engine let him down

*   *   *

. . . Sixth place and group A win for Grundel's VW 19 Golf GTI

*   *   *

. . . Once more the Sport Quattros fail but they could not challenge Vatanen's winning Peugeot

*   *   *

If there was any prize for determination Markku Alen would earn it. All season nobody has tried so hard yet failed. Let down right at the wrong moment, Alen knew that Sanremo had been his last realistic chance to upset Audi's plans to win both the makes' and the drivers' championship. The former had already been won, but the decision to enter Stig Blomqvist in one of the unreliable Sport Quattros meant the latter was far from settled. Delayed by punctures early on Alen had fought back furiously, holding station behind Blomqvist and he knew he would have passed him on the asphalt stages at the end. Alen had not retired from a rally since this event two years before. . .

The Peugeot was untouchable once

more. After staying close to the leaders on the opening asphalt stages, Vatanen pulled out a lead immediately the rally came to gravel and cruised home to victory. Lancia were entered in strength but their leader Alen was delayed just when he should have made the running. A surprise on the opening stages was the speed of Rohrl in his Sport Quattro. A lot of work had been done on these cars since they last appeared, to good effect. Rohrl said they had come to Sanremo on target, having effectively shaken the bugs out of the car. Unfortunately the target had subsequently fallen short of the horizon. The Peugeot had pushed the barriers back.

A repeat win by Lancia was thwarted from the outset by Peugeot. The only

way either Audi or Lancia could score was by the French team's default. Apart from Alen the 037s were all driven by Italians, and this gave team manager Fiorio his only chance of fun. Bettega had a works car like Alen, Biasion and Vudafieri had Jolly Club cars which were almost the same. Biasion is a strong contender for the honour of being Italy's best rallyman. He is cool, reliable and approachable. By watching them react under pressure Fiorio gained a good insight into their real abilities.

Already there was a monotony about Peugeot's success! They had few problems, Ari's teammate Jean-Pierre Nicolas' worst (as with other competitors) was having to deal with indifferent officials, who on two occasions gave him

RIGHT

Giant-killer number one. Ari Vatanen and Terry Harryman win their second world rally running.

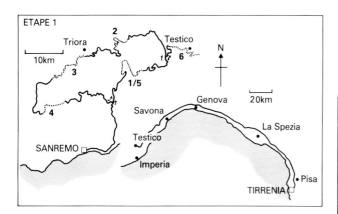

ABOVE

Michele Rayneri came second in group A and scored Fiat's first world championship points for 28 months.

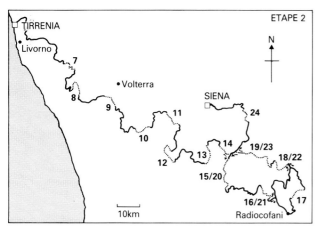

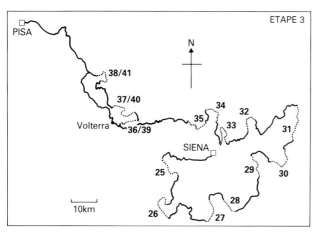

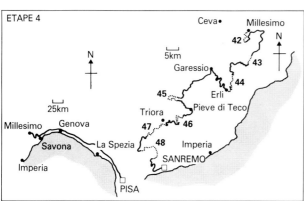

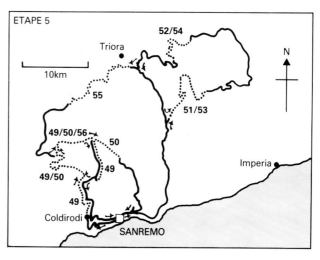

TAYLOR

road penalties he felt he never deserved. By analysing the Peugeots' performances it became obvious that a lack of power was their most important problem. Despite serious efforts, the weight of the car was still around the minimum weight for a three-litre class car, whereas they were running in the 2.5 litre cat-egory. They had difficulty in beating the 450bhp Sport Quattros on the wider asphalt stages where the inferior handling of the Audis was of less importance.

The rally was not clear-cut like 1983. With Vatanen entering the equation and Audis' new-found power bringing fresh variables, the two-wheel versus four-

ABOVE
The man who refused to give in. Markku Alen waits for his Lancia Rally to be serviced during the first evening on the rally, frustrated with having two punctures during the opening stages.

wheel formulae were confused. Lancia were probably one second a kilometre faster than the Quattros on asphalt, meaning they could pass a Quattro on the final two days even if they were four minutes behind them at the end of the gravel. With Peugeot still not being driven flat-out no real information about the French cars' capabilities was available. Blomqvist knew his real challenge was to pull sufficiently ahead of Alen on the gravel. Rohrl, although quicker, was available to help Blomqvist in any way he could, but it all depended on Blomqvist staying ahead of Alen.

Interest in the event evaporated when Alen blew up on stage 27. Stig therefore

LEFT
Giant-killer number two. Kalle Grundel won group A in the new long-chassis Golf GTI on his first time at Sànremo, despite overturning on the second stage.

ABOVE

With Alen out, spectators were ready to applaud Stig Blomqvist as the new world champion but the congratulations were premature.

stood to be champion so long as he could cruise home third, and he monitored the times of the battling Bettega and Biasion carefully. It was touch-and-go, but with luck he would do it. But then he let the side down! He hit a bump very hard, an oil pipe was damaged and the engine wrecked. Markku retained a chance to be champion if he could win both Ivory Coast and the RAC, with Blomqvist still failing to be well placed. But he was not alone, Mikkola had an equal opportunity. Lancia knew the form and announced it was over, they would not return to

RIGHT

Mind the Gap! Maurice Chomat (Citroen Visa 1000 Pistes) cautiously descends the Passi di Teglia during the first etape. This road is used as a liaison section between two asphalt special stages but there is no need to drive too quickly.

Africa, one of the Audi men would be champion.

On the final two etapes there was bad weather in the air. Rohrl was lying second over five minutes behind Vatanen before the final etape, and the weather was getting worse. He felt cushioned against the two Lancias who were four

minutes behind, but he knew they would be fighting against themselves like never before. The conditions were frightening. If there was no downpour rivers were streaming across the road, if the roads were merely damp there was fog. Drivers, already critical about the standard of organisation of one of the world's

95

Floodlights at two in the afternoon. After good weather for the gravel stages the previous two days, the last two etapes on asphalt were held in unpleasant weather. The biggest umbrellas belong to the HB publicity ladies.

most popular events, felt that people did not realise that today's rally cars are very different to those a few years ago. On the first stage Cerrato crashed heavily in his Manta 400, on the second it was potentially even more frightening. Since driving the same roads an hour earlier the weather had abated but suddenly the cars came across torrents of water. Vatanen, who had twice destroyed his Sanremo hopes in just this area, was first on the scene and spun helplessly but safely. Rohrl then arrived and his Sport Quattro went straight off the road, bounced off a wall and finally came to rest, on the track, some 150 metres from the impact.

With the various problems ahead Grundel started to climb up the field. Earlier on the group A lead was held by Loubet's Alfa Romeo but he went off and the Volkswagen drew comfortably ahead of the opposition. Behind him was Rayneri's Fiat and then, creeping

into the top ten, was Werner Grissmann's Audi 80 Quattro. Because of the "seven-best" rule Grissmann's efforts did nothing for Audi but they continued their record of finishing every event in the top ten in 1984, with or without works cars.

Vatanen scored his second victory in a row, but plans for a hattrick were upset when Peugeot announced they were not now entering Ivory Coast, preferring instead to go testing in Kenya at the same time. Audi were then left to deal with the Alen threat. Never short of objectives they decided that having Alen finish second in the championship was no good, and decided to take both Blomqvist and Mikkola down to Ivory Coast. This sounded fine for Audi until it started looking as if Blomqvist's original promise to be made champion was in doubt. There is no peace for the people at the top!

Ready for the final night fling. Attilio Bettega (left) and Massimo Biasion arrive at the storm-swept parc ferme in Sanremo prepared for battle. Two punctures dashed Biasion's hopes of beating the works driver.

26th Rallye Sanremo

30 September–5 October 1984   Italy

OVERALL RESULTS

	ENTRANT	DRIVER/CODRIVER	NAT.	COMP NO.	CAR	GROUP	REG NO.	TOTAL PENALTY
1st	Peugeot-Talbot Sport	ARI VATANEN/Terry Harryman	SF/GB	3	Peugeot 205 Turbo 16	B	128FBL75 (F)	8h.44m.34s.
2nd	Martini Racing	ATTILIO BETTEGA/Maurizio Perissinot	I	4	Lancia Rally	B	TOW67775 (I)	8h.50m.01s.
3rd	Jolly Club	MASSIMO BIASION/Tiziano Siviero	I	6	Lancia Rally	B	TOW67784 (I)	8h.53m.58s.
4th	Grifone	Fabrizio Tabaton/Luciano Tedeschini	I	11	Lancia Rally	B	GE941679 (I)	9h.07m.53s.
5th	Peugeot-Talbot Sport	Jean-Pierre Nicolas/Charley Pasquier	F	8	Peugeot 205 Turbo 16	B	123FBL75 (F)	9h.13m.16s.
6th	Volkswagen Motorsport	Kalle Grundel/Peter Diekmann	S/D	16	VW 19 Golf GTI	A	WOB-AZ754 (D)	9h.43m.30s.
7th	-	Massimo Ercolani/'Popi' Amati	RSM/I	22	Opel Ascona 400	B	Roma 61351D (I)	9h.50m.02s.
8th	-	Gerhard Kalnay/Franz Zehetner	A	31	Opel Ascona 400	B	VB-H401 (D)	9h.57m.47s.
9th	Jolly Club	Michele Rayneri/Ergy Bartolich	I	24	Fiat Abarth 130	A	TO18310A (I)	10h.05m.05s.
10th	-	Werner Grissmann/Jorg Pattermann	A	42	Audi 80 Quattro	A	T439.150 (A)	10h.13m.23s.
12th	Jolly Club	Stefano Fabbri/Luisa Bosco	I	86	Fiat Abarth 130	N	FO563717 (I)	10h.21m.48s.
19th	-	Paola Alberi/Anna Milano	I	40	Citroen Visa Chrono	B	MI43075S (I)	10h.54m.18s.*

100 starters. 35 finishers. * Ladies winner. 7 A-PRIORITY DRIVERS. Winner's average speed over stages 88.88kph.

Positions in World Championship for Rallies after Round 9
Audi (133) 116 points, Lancia (118) 108, Peugeot 56, Renault 55, Toyota 48, Nissan and Opel 38, VW 34, Subaru 11, Alfa Romeo and Fiat 9, Ford 6, Citroen 4, Vauxhall, Mazda and Mitsubishi 2.

Leading positions in World Championship for Drivers after Round 10
Blomqvist 113 points, Alen 90, Mikkola 86, Bettega 49, Biasion 43, Vatanen 40, Waldegard 28, Rohrl 26, Salonen 21, Ragnotti 20, etc.

LEADING RETIREMENTS

ENTRANT	DRIVER/CODRIVER	NAT.	COMP NO.	CAR	GROUP	REG NO.	CAUSE	STAGES COMPLETED
Citroen	Christian Rio/Jean-Bernard Vieu	F	14	Citroen Visa 1000 Pistes	B	8443ME92 (F)	accident	9
Conrero	Giovanni Del Zoppo/Betty Tognana	I	20	Talbot Samba Rallye	B	TOY79635 (I)	driveshaft	14
Jolly Club	ADARTICO VUDAFIERI/Luigi Pirollo	I	7	Lancia Rally	B	TOW67779 (I)	accident	18
Martini Racing	MARKKU ALEN/Ilkka Kivimaki	SF	1	Lancia Rally	B	TOW67769 (I)	engine	27
Citroen	Maurice Chomat/Didier Breton	F	12	Citroen Visa 1000 Pistes	B	8437ME92 (F)	engine	37
Audi Sport	STIG BLOMQVIST/Bjorn Cederberg	S	2	Audi Sport Quattro	B	IN-NL2 (D)	engine	41
Citroen	Philippe Wambergue/Vincent Laverne	F	15	Citroen Visa 1000 Pistes	B	8448ME92 (F)	transmission	44
Bologna Corse	Gianfranco Cunico/Max Sghedoni	I	9	Lancia Rally	B	TOY63867 (I)	accident	45
Conrero	Dario Cerrato/Giuseppe Cerri	I	10	Opel Manta 400	B	Roma 06277E (I)	accident	48
Audi Sport	WALTER ROHRL/Christian Geistdorfer	D	5	Audi Sport Quattro	B	IN-NY39 (D)	accident	49

Rally leaders
Biasion stages 1–3, Bettega 4–5, Biasion 6, 7 not held, Bettega 8, Vatanen 9–56.

LEADING SPECIAL STAGE POSITIONS (including stages 2, 31 and 49)

	1ST	2ND	3RD	4TH	5TH	6TH		1ST	2ND	3RD	4TH	5TH	6TH		1ST	2ND	3RD	4TH	5TH	6TH
Vatanen	31	9	3	4	4	1	Bettega	6	5	6	7	11	14	Vudafieri	1	1	-	1	5	1
Rohrl	7	19	12	5	2	-	Blomqvist	3	11	14	3	1	-	Tabaton	-	1	2	6	4	4
Biasion	7	5	7	13	13	4	Alen	1	4	5	11	-	-	Nicolas	-	-	1	4	9	9

THE ROUTE

		SPECIAL STAGES	TOTAL DISTANCE	CREWS RUNNING
Etape 1 (1–6)	Sanremo (Sunday 1401) – Tirrenia (Monday 0034)	6 asphalt – 85km	508km	86
Etape 2 (8–24)	Tirrenia (Monday 0601) – Radicofani – Siena (Monday 2200)	17 gravel – 245km	634km	62
Etape 3 (25, 27–41)	Siena (Tuesday 0801) – Volterra – Pisa (Tuesday 2235)	16 gravel-195km	551km	51
Etape 4 (42–48)	Pisa (Wednesday 1431) – Sanremo (Thursday 0206)	7 asphalt – 96km	506km	45
Etape 5 (49–56)	Sanremo (Thursday 2231) – Sanremo – Coldirodi – Sanremo (Friday 0926)	8 asphalt – 156km	377km	37
		54 stages – 777km	2576km	

Stages 7 and 26 not held, 2, 31 and 49 were interrupted after leading cars had passed. Crews who tackled these stages at non-competitive speeds were awarded the worst time from before the interruption. Very mixed weather. 21 stages held in darkness.

RECENT WINNERS

1974 Sandro Munari/Mario Mannucci Lancia Stratos
1975 Bjorn Waldegard/Hans Thorszelius Lancia Stratos
1976 Bjorn Waldegard/Hans Thorszelius Lancia Stratos
1977 Jean-Claude Andruet/Christian Delferrier Fiat Abarth 131
1978 Markku Alen/Ilkka Kivimaki Lancia Stratos
1979 'Tony'/Mauro Mannini Lancia Stratos
1980 Walter Rohrl/Christian Geistdorfer Fiat Abarth 131
1981 Michele Mouton/Fabrizia Pons Audi Quattro
1982 Stig Blomqvist/Bjorn Cederberg Audi Quattro
1983 Markku Alen/Ilkka Kivimaki Lancia Rally

Ivory Coast

. . . Blomqvist takes the title and the Sport Quattro finishes its first world event

* * *

. . . wet weather beforehand contributes to organisational problems during the rally

* * *

. . . Shekhar Mehta's forlorn hopes of victory in a 240RS are dashed by the Audis

* * *

. . . Once again, fifty starters are found and the event keeps its status for another year!

* * *

Stig Blomqvist earned the world title the hard way! Suggestions that he had things easy and that Audi "gave" him the title may be well founded but the memory of the Ivory Coast Rally will also make them unfair. He had to survive Ivory Coast to be champion, drive 4000km round a lonely route in a car which had never lasted that long before, against an entry which provided no opposition or stimulus. Ivory Coast is a long way from home to prove your point!

The determination of the Ivory Coast Rally to survive is one of modern rallying's miracles. There was a general expectation that it would pass away of its own accord, that the impossibility of raising the necessary fifty starters, all of whom this year had to comply with the new Appendix J rules, would rule out

any more events in the future. Such assumptions underestimated the determination of the organisers. This was again the year of the "taxi", cars which are in reality normal private road cars, on to which stickers have been affixed and used to make up the fifty-car minimum. This year another concession was offered, that towing eyes would not be necessary on group N cars, so immediately a lot of competitors changed their entry from group A to group N! The route out of Abidjan after the start was lined with cars stopped beside the road having their numbers taken off . . .

At the top end the field was very thin. Audi's entry was a Sport Quattro for Stig and his training car, an old long car, driven by Hannu Mikkola after a rebuild. Stig would make notes for both crews

ETAPE 1

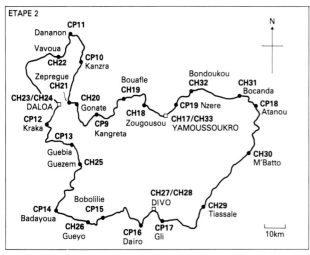

ETAPE 2

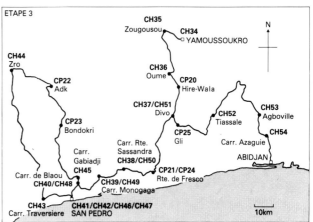

ETAPE 3

FACING PAGE

Stig Blomqvist at Speed! It didn't happen very often in Ivory Coast, but on this occasion he had hurriedly to retrace his steps after being given wrong route instructions after a re-route.

RIGHT

Mehta on the Move. Seen shortly after leaving Daloa, Shekhar races to catch up Ambrosino whom he had been following for the past two days.

ABOVE

Man of the Match. Dave Horsey gained the lead of the African championship twelve hours after the finish – when the organisers cancelled the Tai forest and finally let him qualify as a finisher.

LEFT

Hannu Mikkola's worst moment was a broken strut which caused some tyre torture. This Michelin TRX stayed inflated even in this condition.

BELOW

Taxi! These were some of the fifty cars which crossed the starting line. Most of them did not go much further down the route.

and allow Mikkola a few days golfing practice before the event. Against them were a Nissan 240RS for Shekhar Mehta, the Kenyan who had often been unlucky on this event (eight previous entries but had only finished once) and a works Opel Manta 400 lent to the local driver Alain Ambrosino. And perhaps the most interesting was another driver from Kenya, Dave Horsey. Horsey drives a Peugeot 504 pick-up, a model assembled in his country although officially a French car for homologation purposes, and he entered hoping for more points in the African championship. He had previously won the Zimbabwe Rally outright. Getting from Kenya to Ivory Coast was not as easy as the map might suggest – the car eventually had to be flown via Europe.

Things got difficult before the rally even started. This year's route was held in the green, jungle areas and never went into the fast open areas in the north of the country. This may have given a greater test for drivers but the roads were also much more susceptible to bad weather conditions, as drivers found during training. Stig Blomqvist never managed to drive right round the Forest of Tai, and had to ask Hannu to check some sections nearer Abidjan for him. On the organisers' part they had a wish not to cancel parts of the route in advance – especially if they might have been clear for the rally itself, but this reluctance led to further trouble. In many cases the route did have to be cancelled, and the organisers never had the chance to check alternative routes beforehand, and although the Forest of Tai section was in fact run the organisers did not spot errors in the roadbook which had been created by construction of new roads in the past year. This created uncertainty with the competitors and, as the rally developed, a lot of trouble.

Blomqvist's greatest problem was to know the right pace to set. He went charging off on the first gravel section to take a nine-minute lead, and then things settled down with him holding an advantage over Mikkola of about five. Mehta had a fanbelt problem on the first stretch of the rally, which lost him time but more importantly the opportunity to run in the clear air ahead of Ambrosino's Manta. The pre-rally rains had disappeared and the rally became

ABOVE

*Excitement in Lagota. Alain Ambrosino
arrives up the main street shortly before
the rest halt at Divo. He drove all rally
hoping one of the top three would fall
out, but they never did.*

BELOW

*The best moment is when it's all over.
Stig Blomqvist (left) celebrates in style,
but Bjorn Cederberg is a little concerned
for his friend Arne Hertz (right).*

HOLMES

surprisingly dry and dusty. With cars
being re-grouped at every rest halt
Mehta's problems got worse, for two
days he had to stay in the Opel's dust. It
got to a situation where he kept catching
the Opel and taking time off Ambrosino
so he actually led him on overall placings,
but physically he could not get the Nissan
in front. Eventually he did, but by then
the Audis were so far in front they were
uncatchable.

The professional cars were driven
round without problems and for two
days the rally was uneventful. In group
A the Toyota Celica of Molinie was
ahead of Thibaud's Mitsubishi and the
Italian Molino's Subaru, the latter two
retiring before returning to Yamoussoukro. The third and final étape was
the most different, however. Things
started badly. A controversial section
just outside Yamoussoukro was cancelled, but competitors were not given

ABOVE
The marvels of modern science.

the proper instructions as to how they should meet up again with the correct route. The two group B Mitsubishi drivers Assef and Salim knew the errors, made straight for the correct route – and missed a control point. This eventually led to some exchanges at the finish when they were excluded.

An even greater problem ahead was the six-hundred kilometre lap of Tai forest. Until the start of the rally nobody had been able to get round the route, but then came word that it was passable, the various broken bridges were mended, so the route would be run intact. It was bedlam. The only two drivers to go the correct way were Ambrosino and Mehta,

and one suspected the latter had waited for the former – and followed him all the way round! The two Audi drivers had helped each other, trees which had fallen in the first real storm of the whole event had blocked the route and Horsey went round and round in circles. Eventually all the cars were accounted for, but according to the original time schedules only the two Audis, the Nissan and the Opel were still eligible. The others continued except for Molinie who was too exhausted.

Blomqvist made it back to Abidjan, the Sport Quattro cruising all the way and the world title was his. The organisers eventually cancelled the whole Tai

section, so penalties were deleted and drivers who emerged too late were allowed to finish the event. The only loser had been Molinie. It had been an adventure, not a rally: questions kept on being asked why it was necessary to go there when it was so untypical of the rest of the championship. But through it all there was humour, as Blomqvist's codriver evidenced. "For me this rally has been not one journey but two; it has been both my first and my last trip to this place. . ."

16th Cote d'Ivoire Rallye

31 October–4 November 1984   Ivory Coast

OVERALL RESULTS

	ENTRANT	DRIVER/CODRIVER	NAT.	COMP NO.	CAR	GROUP	REG NO.	TOTAL PENALTY
1	Audi Sport	STIG BLOMQVIST/Bjorn Cederberg	S	1	Audi Sport Quattro	B	IN-NZ9 (D)	5h.24m.
2	Audi Sport	HANNU MIKKOLA/Arne Hertz	SF/S	3	Audi Quattro	B	IN-NX47 (D)	5h.46m.
3	-	SHEKHAR MEHTA/Rob Combes	EAK	2	Nissan 240RS	B	TKS57TE8013 (J)	6h.28m.
4	-	Alain Ambrosino/Daniel le Saux	CI	4	Opel Manta 400	B	GG-CN346 (D)	7h.03m.
5	-	Dave Horsey/David Williamson	EAK	11	Peugeot 504 Pickup	B	KWC860 (EAK)	13h.58m.
6	-	Patrick Tauziac/Lois Cournil	CI	18	Mitsubishi Colt	A	AC3753CI1 (CI)	24h.13m.

50 starters. 6 finishers. No group N finishers. No Ladies' finishers. 3 A-PRIORITY DRIVERS.

Leading positions in World Championship for Drivers after Round 11
Blomqvist (133) 125 points, Mikkola 101, Alen 90, Bettega 49, Biasion 43, Vatanen 40, Waldegard 28, Rohrl 26, Mehta 24, Salonen 21, etc.
Blomqvist now Champion.

LEADING RETIREMENTS

ENTRANT	DRIVER/CODRIVER	NAT.	COMP NO.	CAR	GROUP	REG NO.	CAUSE	CONTROLS VISITED
-	Surinder Thatti/Norman Main	EAK	8	Nissan 240RS	B	17357 (GR)	withdrawn	0
-	Claude Thibaud/Claude Papin	CI	14	Mitsubishi Turbo Lancer	A	Y9588CI1 (CI)	front suspension	28
-	Eugene Salim/Clement Konan	CI	5	Mitsubishi Turbo Lancer	B	4970TTACI (CI)	missed control	35
-	Samir Assef/Christian Boy	CI	6	Mitsubishi Turbo Lancer	B	5053TTACI (CI)	missed control	35
-	Michel Molinie/Marc Molinie	CI	15	Toyota Celica	A	4686TTACI (CI)	withdrawn	46

Rally Leaders
Blomqvist controls 1–55.

THE ROUTE

		SECTIONS	TOTAL DISTANCE	CREWS RUNNING
Etape 1 (1–16)	Abidjan (Wednesday 1700) – Bondoukou – Yamoussoukro (Thursday 1018)	14	1089km	14
Etape 2 (17–33)	Yamoussoukro (Friday 0000) – Daloa – Divo – Yamoussoukro (Friday 1645)	13	1188km	9
Etape 3 (34–55)	Yamoussoukro (Saturday 0900) – San Pedro – San Pedro – Abidjan (Sunday 1030)	19	1735km	8
		46 sections	4012km	

Penalties at Controls 36 and 45 were cancelled after the event. No special stages. Weather was mostly dry. 16 sections held in darkness.

RECENT WINNERS

1974 Timo Makinen/Henry Liddon Peugeot 504
1975 Bernard Consten/Gerard Flocon Peugeot 504
1976 Timo Makinen/Henry Liddon Peugeot 504 Coupe V6
1977 Andrew Cowan/Johnstone Syer Mitsubishi Lancer
1978 Jean-Pierre Nicolas/Michel Gamet Peugeot 504 Coupe V6
1979 Hannu Mikkola/Arne Hertz Mercedes-Benz 450SLC 5.0
1980 Bjorn Waldegard/Hans Thorszelius Mercedes-Benz 500SLC
1981 Timo Salonen/Seppo Harjanne Datsun Violet GT
1982 Walter Rohrl/Christian Geistdorfer Opel Ascona 400
1983 Bjorn Waldegard/Hans Thorszelius Toyota Celica Twincam Turbo

Great Britain

... so easy for Peugeot, their third world win in three outings, the first team to win the RAC Rally on their first attempt

* * *

... best rear-drive car was Eklund's third-placed Toyota, best normally aspirated was Brookes' fifth placed Opel

* * *

... Mikael Ericsson wins group A for the second time in three years

* * *

... there will be no British A-priority drivers in 1985

* * *

Ari Vatanen had one of the most leisurely victories of his career. His problem was how to drive at less than top speed, knowing that the Peugeot's four-wheel drive and special handling gave exactly the right ingredients for success on the only secret route event in the world championship. Lack of concentration led to an accident during the final night of the rally, the delay from which was soon recovered while other unforeseen dramas included a lost bonnet, leaking fire extinguisher and broken driveshaft. For an event in which every victory is described as "classic", this one was characterised as the easiest in memory – even though the final winning margin was one of the smallest.

With no pressures from the world championships it was a pleasant surprise how many teams came to the RAC Rally. The only major teams absent were Lancia and Renault, though Audi decided to stay away officially and leave David Sutton to maintain their interests, additionally running Mouton's Sport Quattro. In the days before the start it was announced that Stig Blomqvist would not take part so number one place was left vacant; Audi being keen to spend as much time as possible preparing for the Monte Carlo Rally, without knowing just how serious the problems between that event's organisers and FISA were becoming. Toyota were the only team to send three cars, this being Eklund's final event for Toyota Team Europe. Despite the relaxed nature of the event, no team took the opportunity of testing new, young drivers though

HOLMES

RIGHT
Vatanen and Harryman at the ford in Trentham Gardens at dusk on Sunday evening. Even by this time the Peugeot had already demonstrated its invincibility.

Britain's 1984 national champion Dai Llewellin was given a ride in Blydenstein's 240RS.

Based once again at Chester the RAC was again a five-day event, the first being run on stages local to the start with a heavy emphasis on spectator facilities. Much of the first étape was run on asphalt roads which made the immediate lead gained by Vatanen all the more impressive. The car even retained its normal gravel road torque split but was still nearly two seconds a mile quicker than the opposition. The first stage held at Knowsley held the same excitement as last year, for the second year running Mikkola went off the road, though this time not seriously, but the drama came from Tony Pond's works group A Rover. Televised from both in- and out-side the car, the accident caused retirement and led to great disappointment as this was Rover's first works entry on a world rally. Vatanen took fastest time on the first six stages, Waldegard on the seventh after the Peugeot made a miscalculation on the best tyres for the Oulton Park racetrack test.

Early on Monday morning the "real" RAC started, when the cars were sent first to make a two-day loop of the Lake District, the border country and then North Yorkshire. Starting with Grizedale at dawn, Kankkunen (then lying fourth), among others had punctures and Mouton broke a front differential. Waldegard then made another fastest time at Lowther Park stage, but on the next stage his Toyota's engine broke. Four-wheel drive cars held the top five placings until Malcolm Wilson had gearbox troubles and fell back. Vatanen was cruising ahead of Mikkola, Mouton and Buffum, while fifth now was Eklund in front of McRae.

FACING PAGE
Surprise turn of speed came from Waldegard's Toyota, which took two fastest times in the ten stages it completed. On the eleventh stage the engine blew up.

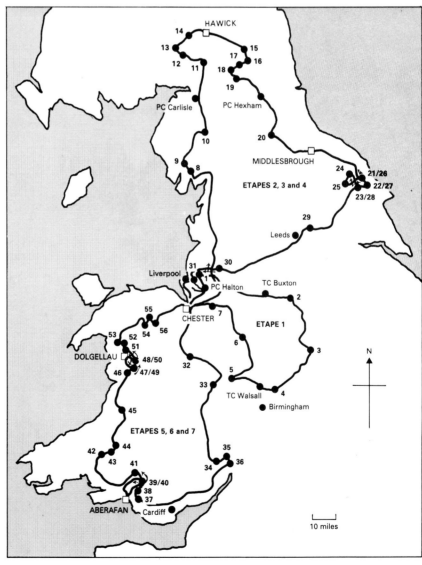

The Kielder stages were long, lonely and as unyielding as ever, though among the top runners there were few incidents. McRae momentarily fell behind Brookes after a puncture but then Brookes fell back to tenth after going off the road and rolling. The Mazda RX7s were continuing to have the rear axle problems they have suffered in recent rallies; last-minute replacement driver Wambergue retiring when losing a wheel and Carlsson only being able to continue in the event

LEFT
Michele Mouton was beaten by the determined Eklund, after she had to stop and change a punctured tyre on a stage.

BELOW
John Buffum retired when he left the road in the later stages, but earlier he made best time at Sutton Park using BF Goodrich street tyres.

enjoy this change of circumstance because almost immediately his steering broke and he crashed. After the Forest of Dean the rally headed for the Neath stages, which was where the excitement built up. Treacherous for drivers due to deceptive corners, these new-found stages have become some of the RAC Rally's most demanding. Kaby was going slowly, struggling with a jammed gearbox and both he and Mouton had to stop and change a puncture in mid-stage. Buffum was up to third place at the Aberafan rest halt while Kankkunen crashed heavily and was out.

After Aberafan the excitement mounted considerably as news came through that Vatanen had rolled and thrown away his lead to Mikkola, but then Audi realised they had lost Buffum, again by going off the road. Suddenly the face of the event had changed. Vatanen, for the first time, had a challenge though he regained his lead after only three more stages. Mouton was stuck behind Eklund and started a long process of trying to regain third place. The central Welsh stages had no more effect on the order, and when cars arrived at Dolgellau the order seemed stabilised. But life with Vatanen is

by refusing to stop when his car did likewise. Coming into the top ten was a great battle, between Nissan's team leader Salonen and the semi-works driver Terry Kaby, which was to continue into the final night when the British driver had gearbox problems. In the Yorkshire stages Buffum had to slow with gear problems and in group A the FISA champion Stromberg was pulling well ahead of Grundel, who was being pressed by Ericsson.

Four-wheel drive cars held the top four places, Eklund led McRae and Salonen, and after Kaby spun the Finn was now 61 seconds ahead of the British Nissan driver. In the surprisingly dry conditions, still the only top driver to have retired was Waldegard. The Welsh loop started on the Wednesday morning with Vatanen over four minutes in the lead, and Mikkola some eight in front of Mouton. Even before the first forest stage was tackled Stromberg was out, his Saab broke the clutch input shaft and the crowds were unable to push the car to the finish. But Grundel could not

ABOVE
Works driver Timo Salonen finished a fine sixth place, but for much of the rally was hounded by the British driver Terry Kaby driving a similar, but semi-official, Nissan 240RS

RIGHT
Early Monday morning at Grizedale, Mikael Ericsson charges off in pursuit of Stromberg and Grundel. His sponsor is the Swedish Post Office.

ABOVE
The first entry by Rover in a world championship rally did not last very long! Pond tried to emulate Mikkola's spectacular antics on the 1983 RAC Rally.

RIGHT
Ten years on and STILL he enjoys his accidents! Ari Vatanen poses beneath the lowered roofline of his Peugeot 205 Turbo 16 after winning his third world rally running.

always full of surprises. This time he had a broken driveshaft at the start of the two long Dovey stages and once again lost his lead to Mikkola! This time he took it back again after only one more stage and kept it to the finish. It had been an enjoyable RAC, everywhere something interesting was happening. Roger Clark came out of three year's retirement to drive a Porsche for Rothmans and came eleventh, while twelfth after many problems with the British Citroen Team's Visa 1000 Pistes was Mark Lovell.

33rd Lombard RAC Rally

25–29 November 1984   Great Britain

OVERALL RESULTS

	ENTRANT	DRIVER/CODRIVER	NAT.	COMP NO.	CAR	GROUP	REG NO.	TOTAL PENALTY
1st	Peugeot-Talbot Sport	ARI VATANEN/Terry Harryman	SF/GB	2	Peugeot 205 Turbo 16	B	128FBL75 (F)	9h.19m.48s.
2nd	Audi Sport UK	HANNU MIKKOLA/Arne Hertz	SF/S	3	Audi Quattro	B	44CMN (GBM)	9h.20m.29s.
3rd	Team Toyota GB	PER EKLUND/Dave Whittock	S/GB	8	Toyota Celica Twincam T	B	K-MT779 (D)	9h.37m.07s.
4th	Audi Sport	MICHELE MOUTON/Fabrizia Pons	F/I	6	Audi Sport Quattro	B	IN-NT2 (D)	9h.37m.28s.*
5th	Andrews Heat for Hire/GM D	Russell Brookes/Mike Broad	GB	16	Opel Manta 400	B	WIA9855 (GB)	9h.48m.06s.
6th	Team Nissan Europe/ Blydenstein Racing Ltd	TIMO SALONEN/Seppo Harjanne	SF	7	Nissan 240RS	B	FXI2372 (GB)	9h.49m.37s.
7th	GM Dealersport/AC Delco	JIMMY McRAE/Mike Nicholson	GB	4	Opel Manta 400	B	WIA5958 (GB)	10h.04m.20s.
8th	Team Nissan Europe/ Blydenstein Racing Ltd	SHEKHAR MEHTA/Yvonne Mehta	EAK	10	Nissan 240RS	B	FIW9463 (GB)	10h.07m.01s.
9th	GM Dealersport/Shell Gold Card	Bertie Fisher/Austin Frazer	GB	37	Opel Manta 400	B	DIl3307 (GB)	10h.14m.19s.
10th	GM Dealersport/SOS	Mikael Ericsson/Claes Billstam	S	22	Audi 80 Quattro	A	EHJ733 (S)	10h.15m.03s.
28th	-	Brian Wiggins/Tony Shepherd	GB	142	Vauxhall Astra GT/E	N	GTM420Y (GB)	11h.35m.23s.

120 starters. 52 finishers. *Ladies winner. 8 A-PRIORITY DRIVERS. Winner's average speed over stages 57.44mph.

Final positions in World Championship for Rallies after Round 10
Audi (149) 120 points, Lancia (118) 108, Peugeot 74, Toyota 62, Renault 55, Opel 48, Nissan 46, VW 34, Subaru 11, Alfa Romeo and Fiat 9, Ford 6, Citroen 4, Vauxhall, Mazda and Mitsubishi 2.

Final leading positions in World Championship for Drivers after Round 12
Blomqvist (133) 125 points. Mikkola (116) 104. Alen 90, Vatanen 60, Bettega 49, Biasion 43, Eklund 30, Waldegard 28, Salonen and Mehta 27, etc.

LEADING RETIREMENTS

ENTRANT	DRIVER/CODRIVER	NAT.	COMP NO.	CAR	GROUP	REG NO.	CAUSE	STAGES COMPLETED
Unipart Rallying with the Daily Mail	Tony Pond/Rob Arthur	GB	18	Austin Rover Vitesse	A	A478WOE (GB)	accident	1
Team Toyota GB	BJORN WALDEGARD/Hans Thorszelius	S	5	Toyota Celica Twincam T Turbo	B	K-AM6321 (D)	engine	10
Mazda R.T. Europe	Philippe Wambergue/Michel Vial	F	21	Mazda RX7	B	CRJ130 (B)	lost wheel	13
Top Gear	Malcolm Wilson/Nigel Harris	GB	14	Audi Quattro	B	MVV 44Y (GB)	engine	17
-	Ola Stromberg/Per Carlsson	S	42	Saab 99 Turbo	A	BTP103 (S)	clutch	32
VW Motorsport	Kalle Grundel/Peter Diekmann	S/D	20	VW 19 Golf GTI	A	WOB-AZ754 (D)	steering/accident	36
Team Toyota GB	Juha Kankkunen/Fred Gallagher	SF/GB	15	Toyota Celica Twincam T	B	K-AM6232 (D)	accident	38
BF Goodrich Motorsport	John Buffum/Neil Wilson	USA/GB	17	Audi Quattro	B	WMN44 (GBM)	accident	39
Mazda R.T. Europe	Ingvar Carlsson/Benny Melander	S	26	Mazda RX7	B	CJH710 (B)	rear axle	39
Team Nissan Europe	Terry Kaby/Kevin Gormley	GB	23	Nissan 240RS	B	EXI7316 (GB)	excluded	56

Rally leaders
Vatanen stages 1–39, Mikkola 40–42, Vatanen 43–49, Mikkola 50, Vatanen 51–56.

LEADING SPECIAL STAGE POSITIONS

	1ST	2ND	3RD	4TH	5TH	6TH		1ST	2ND	3RD	4TH	5TH	6TH		1ST	2ND	3RD	4TH	5TH	6TH
Vatanen	33	13	2	3	-	2	Buffum	4	2	7	8	1	3	Kankkunen	1	1	4	8	8	6
Mikkola	12	29	5	2	1	3	Waldegard	2	-	1	3	-	-	McRae	1	-	3	3	5	15
Mouton	5	10	14	13	7	2	Eklund	1	3	9	9	9	6	Wilson	-	1	3	3	5	2

THE ROUTE

		SPECIAL STAGES	TOTAL DISTANCE	CREWS RUNNING
Etape 1 (1–7)	Chester (Sunday 0800) – Chester (Sunday 1815)	3 asphalt – 11 miles 4 mixed – 11 miles	296 miles	115
Etape 2 (8–14)	Chester (Monday 0500) – Hawick (Monday 1430)	6 gravel – 59 miles 1 mixed – 4 miles	314 miles	100
Etape 3 (15–20)	Hawick (Monday 1600) – Middlesbrough (Monday 2315)	6 gravel – 89 miles	218 miles	86
Etape 4 (21–31)	Middlesbrough (Tuesday 0230) – Chester (Tuesday 1620)	8 gravel – 103 miles 1 asphalt – 2 miles 2 mixed – 5 miles	409 miles	75
Etape 5 (32–41)	Chester (Wednesday 0800) – Aberafan (Wednesday 1910)	8 gravel – 81 miles 2 mixed – 7 miles	340 miles	60
Etape 6 (42–48)	Aberafan (Wednesday 2200) – Dolgellau (Thursday 0640)	7 gravel – 109 miles	264 miles	54
Etape 7 (49–56)	Dolgellau (Thursday 0900) – Chester (Thursday 1450)	8 gravel – 55 miles	167 miles	52
		56 stages – 536 miles	2008 miles	

Weather was mostly dry but slippery. 25 stages held in darkness.

RECENT WINNERS

1974 Timo Makinen/Henry Liddon Ford Escort RS1600
1975 Timo Makinen/Henry Liddon Ford Escort RS1800
1976 Roger Clark/Stuart Pegg Ford Escort RS1800
1977 Bjorn Waldegard/Hans Thorszelius Ford Escort RS1800
1978 Hannu Mikkola/Arne Hertz Ford Escort RS
1979 Hannu Mikkola/Arne Hertz Ford Escort RS
1980 Henri Toivonen/Paul White Talbot Sunbeam Lotus
1981 Hannu Mikkola/Arne Hertz Audi Quattro
1982 Hannu Mikkola/Arne Hertz Audi Quattro
1983 Stig Blomqvist/Bjorn Cederberg Audi Quattro

World Championship Charts

For 1984 FISA decreed that the old groups 2 and 4 were to be excluded from participation in rounds of the World Championships, thereby finalising the period of transition from the old to the new and permitting cars only from groups B, A and N.

Points scoring, however, remained as in previous years with only positions in the top ten qualifying. In the Drivers Championship points were allocated as follows – 1st 20; 2nd 15; 3rd 12; 4th 10; 5th 8; 6th 6; 7th 4; 8th 3; 9th 2; 10th 1. In the Manufacturers Championship points were allocated for position in the top ten with 10 points for 1st descending to 1 point for 10th, plus position in group down to eighth with 8 points for

1st in group down to 1 point for 8th. Should there be less than five starters in a group then the group points are ignored with only the overall points to count. Only the highest placed car from each manufacturer scores points, with a maximum of seven scores to count for both Driver and Manufacturer Championships.

World Championship for Rallies 1984

	MC Monte Carlo	P Portugal	EAK Safari	F Corsica	GR Acropolis	NZ New Zealand	RA Argentina	SF 1000 Lakes	I Sanremo	GB RAC	Total
1 Audi	18	18	14	(10)	18	18	18	(12)	(7)	16	120
2 Lancia	(10)	16	12	18	14	16	-	16	16	-	108
3 Peugeot	-	-	-	12	-	-	8	18	18	18	74
4 Toyota	-	10	18	-	-	10	-	10	-	14	62
5 Renault	12	10	-	14	-	-	15	4	-	-	55
6 Opel	-	-	16	2	-	-	11	2	7	10	48
7 Nissan	2	-	10	-	8	12	-	6	-	8	46
8 Volkswagen	9	12	-	-	-	-	-	-	13	-	34
9 Subaru	-	-	-	-	-	11	-	-	-	-	11
10 Alfa Romeo	-	-	-	9	-	-	-	-	-	-	9
10 Fiat	-	-	-	-	-	-	-	-	9	-	9
12 Ford	-	-	-	-	-	6	-	-	-	-	6
13 Citroen	-	4	-	-	-	-	-	-	-	-	4
14 Vauxhall	-	2	-	-	-	-	-	-	-	-	2
14 Mazda	-	-	-	-	2	-	-	-	-	-	2
14 Mitsubishi	-	-	-	-	-	2	-	-	-	-	2

World Championship for Drivers 1984

	MC Monte Carlo	S Sweden	P Portugal	EAK Safari	F Corsica	GR Acropolis	NZ New Zealand	RA Argentina	SF 1000 Lakes	I Sanremo	CI Ivory Coast	GB RAC	Total
1 Stig Blomqvist (S)	15	20	-	-	(8)	20	20	20	10	-	20	-	125
2 Hannu Mikkola (SF)	(12)	-	20	12	-	15	12	15	-	-	15	15	104
3 Markku Alen (SF)	3	-	15	10	20	12	15	-	15	-	-	-	90
4 Ari Vatanen (SF)	-	-	-	-	-	-	-	-	20	20	-	20	60
5 Attilio Bettega (I)	8	-	12	-	4	10	-	-	-	15	-	-	49
6 Massimo Biasion (I)	6	-	10	-	15	-	-	-	-	12	-	-	43
7 Per Eklund (S)	-	12	-	-	-	-	-	-	6	-	-	12	30
8 Bjorn Waldegard (S)	-	-	-	20	-	-	8	-	-	-	-	-	28
9 Shekhar Mehta (EAK)	-	-	-	8	-	4	-	-	-	-	12	3	27
9 Timo Salonen (SF)	1	-	-	4	-	6	10	-	-	-	-	6	27
11 Walter Rohrl (D)	20	-	6	-	-	-	-	-	-	-	-	-	26
12 Michele Mouton (F)	-	15	-	-	-	-	-	-	-	-	-	10	25
13 Jean Ragnotti (F)	-	-	8	-	12	-	-	-	-	-	-	-	20
14 Jean-Pierre Nicolas (F)	-	-	-	-	10	-	-	-	-	8	-	-	18
15 Rauno Aaltonen (SF)	-	-	-	15	-	-	-	-	-	-	-	-	15
16 Jorge Recalde (RA)	-	-	-	-	-	-	-	12	-	-	-	-	12
16 Henri Toivonen (SF)	-	-	-	-	-	-	-	-	-	12	-	-	12
16 Kalle Grundel (S)	2	-	4	-	-	-	-	-	-	6	-	-	12

19 Jean-Luc Therier (F), Mats Jonsson (S), Mario Stillo (RA), Fabrizio Tabaton (I), Alain Ambrosino (CI) (all 10 points).

24 Lars-Erik Torph (S), John Buffum (USA), Yasuhiro Iwase (EAK), Juha Kankkunen (SF), David Horsey (EAK), Russell Brookes (GB) (all 8 points).

30 Bjorn Johansson (S), Vic Preston Jnr (EAK), Jean-Claude Andruet (F), Reg Cook (NZ), Miguel Torras (RA), Patrick Tauziac (CI) (all 6 points).

36 Bernard Darniche (F), Kenneth Eriksson (S), Malcolm Stewart (NZ), Carlos Bassi (RA), Erkki Pitkanen (SF), Massimo Ercolani (RSM), Jimmy McRae (GB) (all 4 points).

43 Stig Andervang (S), Jorge Ortigao (P), Franz Wittmann (A), Yoshio Iwashita (J), Francois Chatriot (F), George Moschous (GR), 'Possum' Bourne (NZ), Gerhard Kalnay (A), Hugo Hernandez (RA), Bruno Saby (F) (all 3 points).

53 Gunnar Pettersson (S), Christian Dorche (F), Guy Frequelin (F), Achim Warmbold (D), Tony Teesdale (NZ), Monnenmacher Perez (RA), Jouko Poysti (SF), Michele Rayneri (I), Bertie Fisher (GB) (all 2 points).

62 Jerry Ahlin (S), Russell Gooding (GB), Basil Criticos (EAK), Yves Loubet (F), Blair Robson (NZ), Walter D'Agostini (RA), Kalevi Aho (SF), Werner Grissmann (A), Mikael Ericsson (S) (all 1 point).

Rally Cars
Prototypes

Ford RS200

After a break of five years, Ford announced their hope to re-enter world championship rallying. After aborting the RS1700T, they decided to go ahead with a purpose-built car. Special features of the RS200 are non-permanent four-wheel drive, mid-located turbocharged engine and a front-mounted transaxle which provides a 50–50 weight distribution, in a body which bears no direct resemblance to an existing production model.

The car was announced at the Turin Motor Show in deference to work carried out by Ghia, and hopes were expressed that the car will be homologated in time for the 1000 Lakes Rally, 1985. The car is initially to be used in competition in basic (i.e. not evolution) form, with an 1803cc engine (originally produced for the RS1700T). This brings it into the 3-litre class and permits substantial increases in engine capacity when the need for a more powerful engine arises.

Mitsubishi Starion 4WD Rally

After delays in finalising the basic design, Mitsubishi produced a rally version of their 4×4 production based prototype, with detailed design carried out in Britain by a team headed by Andrew Cowan and Allan Wilkinson. The car appeared in the poorly-supported prototype category of the 1984 Rallye 1000 Pistes which it won, but gradually plans to homologate the car were deferred. The car uses the Pajero/Shogun transmission system with 50/50 torque split and permanent four-wheel drive, and the layout closely followed the production car.

The turbocharged engine has the same block, single-cam two valve cylinder head as the old group 4 cars though the engine size has been increased to the capacity limit. Although sharing many characteristics with the Quattro, most of the engine is located between the axles which offers better handling balance.

Opel Kadett 400

Until mid-year Opel were well set on their programme of making a four-wheel drive rally car, but the German car workers strike deferred plans – and the designs – for the moment. While concepts were being considered came a request from South Africa for help; the current Manta 400 did not relate to a design offered locally for sale and they sought a different car which could be used on rallies. By coincidence Opel at Russelsheim had experimented with fitting the Manta 400 running gear into an old style front-wheel drive Kadett bodyshell. The merger worked surprisingly smoothly and this was the car which finally went to South Africa. In due course it is hoped to use this prototype for testing four-wheel drive designs in rally conditions, including the X-trac system designed for Schanche's rally-cross Escort.

a Delta S4

Announced at their December press conference was Lancia's hope for the immediate rallying future – the 038 Delta S4. Unlike the 037 Lancia the car has been identified with an existing model. The spaceframe chassis is traditional, the permanent four-wheel drive transmission offers few novelties and the unequal weight distribution (42–58) and the big wheels (18″ front, 16″ rear) shows continued circuit racing influence.

It is Lancia's new engine which attracted greatest attention. Unlike the 037 it is over-square, though not to so great an extent as the Stratos. Internally it is the first rally engine with ceramic application, and it is the first competition engine to combine turbocharging with the traditional Lancia compressor. At 227 bhp/litre it is also the most efficient engine in rallying to date.

Skoda

Czechoslovakia hoped to enter group B competition in 1984 with the Skoda 130LR but production delayed homologation a few months. Run through the season on Czech national rallies in a special prototype class, the 130LR promises to be highly competitive in the 1300cc group B class, being the only rear-drive car for rallying homologated in this category. The car will not only have a performance potential parallel to the Talbot Samba but also have the advantage of being run by an official team. Completely unrelated to the 130LR, using a 1600cc engine from the rival Lada factory in Russia is the MTX160. With the end of the career for the group 2 Skoda 130RS cars, the reigning Czech champion Vaclav Blahna wanted a car to use for his home events and Metalex built this hybrid which could challenge the 130LRs. Without hope of homologation, Blahna had to forsake this car and use a group B Lada VFTS on foreign events.

Nissan Langley

Apart from the Kadett 400 and the Ford RS1700T South Africa saw another prototype in action, a rear-drive version of the Nissan Langley. Built by its driver, Nissan's team member Hannes Grobler, the car was fitted with engine and transmission from a 240RS, which being Silvia-based was not commercially relevant to the team. This car showed surprising speed and was often able to challenge the all-conquering Quattros.

The British Prototypes

No country produced as many rallying prototypes in 1984 as Britain. The national Shell Oils/Autosport series admitted these cars openly, and until the final round a prototype had been leading the series outright. AUSTIN-ROVER took full advantage in running their 6R4 prototype on these events. This Metro-based car featured a special normally aspirated V6 version of the Rover V8 engine, mid-mounted and straddling the rear axle, with permanent four-wheel drive and 50/50 torque split, but was badly hampered by the use of a two-valve test engine which restricted power outputs to less than 250bhp.

HOLMES

Escort 4x4

Alan Edwards V6 Engine

R-E-D 4T

Audi 80 Quattro

The most successful prototype seen on British special stages was the rear-drive turbocharged R-E-D 4T, a Sierra project discarded by Ford themselves and taken over by MCD's restructured rally car operation in Cheshire. Only one example was built and was driven by the girl Louise Aitken-Walker. Although capable of higher outputs, the 2-litre BDA engine was detuned progressively during the year in aid of better traction and driveability. For 1985 R-E-D hope to continue the project, this time with four-wheel drive.

A project which started with promise but collapsed for financial reasons in mid-season was the turbocharged Audi 80 Quattro of Darryl Weidner. This had group B Quattro running gear fitted into an 80 body which despite its four doors was lighter than a Quattro. A similar car had also been built by Andy Bentza for use in European rallycross events. Built by David Sutton in London, Weidner's car first appeared on the York National Rally.

Other private projects were also seen in Britain in 1984. The most exciting of these was Alan Edwards' four-wheel drive Escort. Fitted with a Ford V6 Essex engine it showed amazing speed but the power often proved too much for the gearbox. The Safety Devices accessory company in Cambridge undertook the construction of a special rear-drive Vauxhall Astra. This car was fitted with a longitudinal 2.6 Chevette engine and a surplus rear transaxle from the Ford RS1700T. This car was driven by George Hill but on the one occasion it went well the engine failed.

Rally Cars
Prototype Car Specifications

	ENGINE SIZE	INDUCTION	VALVES/ CYLINDER	BHP	ENGINE LOCATION	DRIVE LOCATION	WEIGHT (KG)
Ford RS200	1803cc	Ford inj. Garrett Turbo	4	380	Mid Longitudinal	RWD/4WD	1000
Mitsubishi Starion 4WD Rally	2140cc	Mitsubishi ECI Turbo	2	350	Front Longitudinal	4WD	1050
Opel Kadett 400	2420cc	2 Weber 50DCOE	4	275	Front Longitudinal	RWD	1000
Lancia Delta S4	1759cc	Volumex Compressor & KKK Turbo	4	400	Mid Longitudinal	4WD	950
Skoda 130LR	1295cc	2 Weber 45DCOE	2	140	Rear Longitudinal	RWD	820
MG Metro 6R4	2495cc	2 Weber	2	240	Mid Longitudinal	4WD	900
Nissan Langley	2340cc	2 Solex 50PHH	4	265	Front Longitudinal	RWD	970

Vauxhall Astra

Rally Cars
Groups B and A

Audi

The SPORT QUATTRO is an attempt to get better performance on asphalt by using a shorter chassis and a four-valve engine which offers considerably more power. First seen at the Tour de Corse, it took several months before the engine worked well and almost a half year before the car was reliable enough even to finish a world rally.

Audi's development of the road-going version created a long delay before the evolution Sport Quattro was available for competition. The car follows Audi's qualities of strength through weight and performance through power at a time when other companies were seeking more subtle solutions. One novelty is the homologation of an alternative six-speed gearbox, to extend the range of overall axle ratios.

Lancia

The 037 RALLY was given a second evolution change in time for Monte Carlo. Main features included an engine bored out to 2111cc, closer to the class limit, different fuel injection slides and revised rear bodywork. Kits were prepared for owners of older cars to update their vehicles. The rear-wheel drive car was in reality only a stop-gap while the 038 Delta S4 was being prepared, although it gained the European title with Capone.

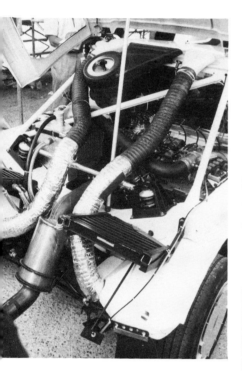

Peugeot

The 205 TURBO 16 was homologated simultaneously with an evolution version for competition. It was the first car to be able to split the transmission torque, and provision was made for three facilities: 50/50 for very slippery conditions, 33/67 for gravel and 25/75 for asphalt. This gave the car a major advantage over the Quattros. The other main feature of the car was its reliability. By the end of 1984 Peugeot recognised they had a power deficiency and wanted to improve this when they were allowed to homologate their second evolution in mid-1985.

Mazda

The first rotary engined group B car was the RX7, part of a long-term programme of integration into the world rally scene with both the RX7 and the 323, the latter being a group A car. The RX7 was simultaneously homologated in basic and evolution form, utilizing considerable plastic bodywork, an oil cooler in the rear wing, rear mounted dry sump tank, parallel rear axle links and an engine mounted 10cm rearwards in the chassis. The basic group B car was improved from the old group 2 and group A cars by using rack and pinion steering and the alternative 2.6 litre 13B engine. These cars are the most powerful works rally cars using normally aspirated engines.

The 323 saloon is still under constant development. Monte Carlo 1985 saw the debut of the 175bhp 1490cc (2.5 litre class) 323 TURBO; more powerful versions are planned for the future, including sixteen valves and four-wheel drive.

Toyota

With future plans to run mid-engined four-wheel drive cars, 1984 was a technically low year in group B for Toyota, but in group A the rear-drive COROLLA 16-VALVE made an increasingly important impact on rallying. Used in probably more countries than a group A model from any other company, the Corolla now produces 160bhp, and development work will centre around lightening the car in 1985. Despite difficulties in tuning the electronically controlled engine the car has gained successes in many countries, but most significantly in Britain.

Volvo

Although most of their competition activities have been in Touring Car racing and rallycross events, some 240 TURBOs appeared in Swedish rallies but without success. This was only the second car in group A to be produced in evolution form and features water injection, though in rallying this was not used. In this form the cars were also fitted with a bigger turbo, spoilers and an intercooler, and are potentially the most powerful cars in group A rallying.

Volkswagen

One of rallying's longest-running group A models received a facelift in 1984 when the GOLF GTI was homologated with a 75mm longer wheelbase and new bodywork. The old 1800cc GTI engine and most of the running gear were retained and plans begun for turning to 16-valves in 1985. The track of the new model is 30mm wider which demands longer driveshafts.

Rally Cars
Groups B and A Specifications

	Alfa Romeo GTV6	Audi Quattro A2	Audi Sport Quattro	Citroen Visa 1000 Pistes	Fiat Ritmo Abarth 130TC	Lancia Rally E2	Mazda RX7
GROUP	A	B	B	B	A	B	B
NO. CYLINDERS il=in line	V6	5 il	5 il	4 il	4 il	4 il	2 rotary
CC	2492	2142/2999	2142/2999	1434	1995	2111/2955	2616
BORE/STROKE (mm)	88/68.3	79.5/86.4	79.5/86.4	77/77	84/90	85/93	n/a
COMP. RATIO	11.5	6.6	7.5	10.8	9.4	9.0	9.0
MAX. POWER (bhp) @ REVS.	218 7500	360 7000	400 7500	145 7000	130 5900	325 8000	300 8200
MAX. TORQUE (Kg/m) @ REVS.	25 5000	46 4000	46.9 5500	15.3 5500	18.0 3600	30 5500	27 7500
INDUCTION TYPE	Bosch Injection	Bosch Motronic KKK Turbo	Bosch Motronic KKK Turbo	2 Weber 45DCOE	2 Weber 45DCOE	Bosch Inj. Abarth compressor	1 Weber 51IDA
NO. VALVES	12	10	20	8	8	16	2×2
NO. +POSITION CAMS	1 ohc × 2	1 ohc	2 ohc	1 ohc	2 ohc	2 ohc	Peripheral Ports
LUBRICATION	Wet	Dry	Dry	Wet	Wet	Dry	Dry
ENGINE LOCATION	Front-Long.	Front-Long.	Front-Long.	Front-Trans.	Front-Trans.	Mid-Long.	Front-Long.
DRIVE LOCATION	Rear	Perm 4WD	Perm 4WD	4WD	Front	Rear	Rear
CLUTCH NO. PLATES	2	1	1	1	1	1	2
NO. FORWARD GEARS	5	5	5 or 6	5	5	5	5
FRONT BRAKES D=DISC (Ø=mm) DR=DRUM	DV279	DV295	DV295	DV244.5	DV243	DV300	DV304
REAR BRAKES V=VENTED	DV254	DV295	DV295	D244.5	DR185	DV300	DV304
FRONT SUSPENSION	W+T	McPh	McPh	McPh	McPh	W+C	McPh
REAR SUSPENSION	de Dion	McPh	McPh	Semi TA+ McPh.	McPh	W+C	C+L
STEERING	R/P	R/P	R/P	R/P	R/P	R/P	R/P
LENGTH (mm)	4260	4404	4160	3725	4014	3890	4250
WIDTH (mm)	1605	1733	1790	1590	1663	1800	1770
HEIGHT (mm)	1330	1344	1344	1398	1374	1245	1260
WHEELBASE (mm)	2400	2524	2204	2436	2432	2445	2420
FRONT TRACK (mm)	1365	1465	1465	1390	1455	15.8	1420
REAR TRACK (mm)	1367	1502	1502	1380	1420	1490	1400
WEIGHT (kg)	1100	1200	1250	770	950	965	990 (asphalt)
DATE 1st HOMOLOGATION + NUMBER	(Transfer) A5839	1.5.83 B243	1.5.84 B264	1.3.84 B258 (evolution 1.4.84)	1.1.84 A5189	1.4.82 B210 (evolution 1.1.84)	1.5.84 B255
1st MAJOR RALLY	Monte Carlo 1983	Corsica 1983	Corsica 1984	Safari 1984	Monte Carlo 1984	Monte Carlo 1984 (evolution)	Acropolis 1984

Nissan 240RS	Opel Manta 400	Opel Ascona	Peugeot 205 Turbo 16	Renault 5 Turbo 'Tour de Corse'	Subaru Leone 4×4	Toyota Corolla 1600GT 3 door AE86	Toyota Celica Twincam Turbo	VW 19 Golf GTI
B	B	A	B	B	A	A	B	A
4 il	4 il	4 il	4 il	4 il	Flat 4	4 il	4 il	4 il
2340	2420	1979	1775/2484	1397/1956	1781	1599	2090/2926	1781
92/88	95/85	95/69.8	83/82	76/77	92/67	81.3/77	89/84	81.0/86.4
11.5	11.2	10	7	7	11.5	11.5	8	11.2
265 8000	275 7500	170 5500	350 7500	295 7000	145 6800	160 8000	350 7750	170 6800
26.5 6400	30 5500	17 4000	40 5000	34 5000	18.5 4800	13.8 6500	35 7500	20 7500
2 Solex 50PHH	2 Weber 50DCOE	2 Solex 45 ADDHE	Bosch K Jetronic Inj. KKK Turbo	Bosch Inj. Garrett Turbo	Twin Makuni	Nippodenso Inj.	Nippodenso Inj. KKK Turbo	Bosch K-Jetronic Inj.
16	16	8	16	8	8	16	8	8
2 ohc	2 ohc	1 cih.	2 ohc	1 push	1 push	2 ohc	2 ohc	1 ohc
Dry	Dry	Wet	Dry	Dry	Wet	Wet	Dry	Wet
Front-Long.	Front-Long.	Front-Long.	Mid-Trans.	Mid-Long.	Front	Front-Long.	Front-Long.	Front-Trans.
Rear	Rear	Rear	4WD	Rear	FWD or 4WD	Rear	Rear	Front
2	2	1	1	2	1	1	2	1
5	5	4	5	5	4h.+4l.	5	5	5
DV292	DV290	DV256	DV300	DV276	D229	DV260	DV267	DV280
DV292	DV278	D253	DV300	DV276	DR180	DV264	DV267	D280
McPh	W+C	Double W+C	Double W+C	W+C	McPh	McPh	McPh	McPh
L+C	L+C	L+C	Double W+C	W+C	W+T	L+C	L+C	TA+C
RB	R/P	R/P	R/P	R/P	R/P	R/P	R/P	R/P
4300	4463	4333	3825	3664	4265	4180	4284	3987
1800	1770	1654	1674	1746	1620	1625	1785	1680
1310	1320	1320	1353	1328	1410	1335	1320	1405
2400	2518	2518	2540	2430	2450	2400	2500	2475
1410	1384	1394	1430	1346	1400	1355	1395	1432
1395	1379	1389	1430	1474	1410	1350	1385	1429
970	980	1010	940	925	980	910	1020	880
1.1.83 B233	1.3.83 B237	(Transfer) A5067	1.4.84 B262	1.2.82 B205	1.4.83 A5128	1.1.84 A5180	1.7.83 B239	1.4.84 A5212
Monte Carlo 1983	Corsica 1983 (evolution)	Bandama 1978 (Gp2)	Corsica 1984	Corsica 1983 (evolution)	Safari 1983	National Breakdown 1984	Mille Pistes 1983	1000 Lakes 1984

Key: cih=cam in head: C=Coil: D=Dead: h=high ratio: l.=low ratio: L=Live: Long.=Longitudinal: McPh=McPherson: R/P=Rack&Pinion: RB=Recirculating Ball: T=Torsion Bar: TA=Trailing Arm: Trans.=Transverse: W=Wishbone

European Championship for Rallies – Results

ECR1   ZIMMERMANN

ECR2   FOTO KAJ

ECR3   WEYENS

ECR1 JANNER (A) Freistadt 5/7 January 1984 *Coeff 2*
1	Wittmann/Nestinger	Audi Quattro	gB	3h.21m.33s.
2	Wurz/WALDEGARD	Audi Quattro	B	3h.26m.28s.
3	EKLUND/Whittock	Audi 80 Quattro	A	3h.28m.17s.
4	Ericsson/Melleroth	Audi 80 Quattro	A	3h.31m.31s.
5	Wiedner/Zehetner	Audi 80 Quattro	A	3h.31m.58s.
6	Grissmann/Pattermann	Audi 80 Quattro	A	3h.39m.35s.
7	Mattig/Cantonati	Opel Manta 400	B	3h.51m.31s.
8	SURER/Wyder	Renault 5 Turbo	B	3h.54m.39s.
9	Bauer/de Cillia	Porsche 911SC	B	4h.01m.39s.
10	S. MEHTA/Y. Mehta	Opel Ascona 400	B	4h.04m.40s.

62 starters. 34 finishers. 4 A-PRIORITY DRIVERS. No group N finishers.

ECR2 ARCTIC (SF) Rovaniemi 27/29 January 1984 *Coeff 2*
1	A. Laine/Virtanen	Audi Quattro	gB	3h.27m.16s.
2	Ericsson/B. Thorszelius	Audi 80 Quattro	A	3h.29m.08s.
3	Arpiainen/Hantunen	Audi 80 Quattro	A	3h.29m.37s.
4	Sundstrom/Silander	Opel Ascona	A	3h.33m.27s.
5	Laakso/Lehtonen	VW Golf GTI	A	3h.43m.07s.
6	Kinnunen/Hokkanen	Ford Escort RS	B	3h.44m.16s.
7	Kauppinen/Leinonen	Ford Escort RS	B	3h.44m.39s.
8	Mustonen/Pakkanen	Opel Manta	A	3h.44m.50s.
9	Sohlbero/Jaasalo	Audi 80 Quattro	A	3h.45m.46s.
10	Uotila/Leino	Ford Escort RS	B	3h.48m.15s.
16	Alamaula/Heinonen	Audi 80 Quattro	N	3h.57m.42s.

52 starters. 27 finishers. NO A-PRIORITY DRIVERS.

ECR3 BOUCLES DE SPA (B) Spa 3/5 February 1984 *Coeff 2*
1	Capone/Cresto	Lancia Rally	gB	4h.44m.51s.
2	Pond/Arthur	Nissan 240RS	B	4h.46m.44s.
3	Snyers/Colebunders	Porsche 911	B	4h.54m.06s.
4	G. Colsoul/Lopes	Opel Manta 400	B	4h.56m.31s.
5	Lareppe/Jamar	Opel Ascona	A	5h.24m.00s.
6	Van der Wauver/Peeters	Audi 80 Quattro	N	5h.30m.04s.
7	Maaskant/Oosterbaan	Citroen Visa Chrono	B	5h.31m.16s.
8	Probst/Bozet	VW Golf GTI	A	5h.36m.20s.
9	Brasseur/Raway	Opel Ascona 400	B	5h.41m.20s.
10	Munster/Loncke	Opel Manta	A	5h.43m.07s.

91 starters. 25 finishers. 1 A-PRIORITY DRIVER (Eklund).

ECR4 SWEDISH (S) Karlstad 10/12 February 1984 *Coeff 4*
See the results of WCD round 2 on page 49

ECR5 WEYENS

ECR7 WAGNER

ECR9

ECR6 FOTO KAJ

ECR8 ARCHE

ECR10 MORELLI

ECR5 COSTA BRAVA (E)   Lloret de Mar 17/19 February 1984
Coeff 4

1	Cinotto/Radaelli	Audi Quattro	gB	6h.57m.40s.
2	Servia/J. Sabater	Opel Manta 400	B	7h.00m.30s.
3	Frigola/Bou	Renault 5 Turbo	B	7h.23m.21s.
4	Ferjancz/Tandari	Renault 5 Turbo	B	7h.23m.42s.
5	C. Santacreu/A. Santacreu	Opel Ascona	A	7h.33m.13s.
6	Candela/Villalba	VW Golf GTI	N	7h.47m.48s.
7	Probst/Bozet	VW Golf GTI	A	7h.48m.55s.
8	de Boey/Dierickx	Opel Ascona 400	B	7h.46m.56s.
9	Hugot/Ozoux	Opel Ascona	A	8h.02m.37s.
10	Giraud/Faoro	Audi 80 Quattro	N	8h.02m.50s.

59 starters. 25 finishers. NO A-PRIORITY DRIVERS.

ECR8 COSTA BLANCA RACE (E)   Alicante 17/19 March 1984
Coeff 3

1	Capone/Cresto	Lancia Rally	gB	4h.06m.32s.
2	ZANINI/Autet	Ferrari 308GTB 2v.	B	4h.09m.46s.
3	B. Fernandez/Sala	Porsche 911SC RS	B	4h.10m.57s.
4	McRAE/Arthur	Opel Manta 400	B	4h.14m.41s.
5	Sainz/Boto	Renault 5 Turbo	B	4h.24m.04s.
6	Onoro/Orozco	Opel Manta 400	B	4h.27m.58s.
7	C. Santacreu/A. Santacreu	Opel Ascona	A	4h.38m.30s.
8	Orti/Criado	Porsche 911SC	B	4h.39m.20s.
9	Nieto/Martinez	Renault 5 Turbo	B	4h.42m.27s.
10	Arque/Aluma	Opel Manta	A	4h.42m.38s.
13	Candela/Villalba	VW Golf GTI	N	4h.50m.32s.

105 starters. 48 finishers. 2 A-PRIORITY DRIVERS.

ECR6 HANKI (SF)   Helsinki 24/26 February 1984   *Coeff 2*

1	LAMPI/Kuukkala	Audi Quattro	gB	4h.30m.05s.
2	Harri Toivonen/Wrede	Audi 80 Quattro	A	4h.36m.27s.
3	Sundstrom/Silander	Opel Ascona	A	4h.36m.32s.
4	Stromberg/P. Carlsson	Saab 99 Turbo	A	4h.40m.39s.
5	Jonsson/Gustavsson	Opel Ascona 400	B	4h.43m.31s.
6	Makela/Palve	Talbot Sunbeam Lotus	B	4h.44m.40s.
7	Laakso/V. Salonen	VW Golf GTI	A	4h.45m.18s.
8	Uotila/Leino	Ford Escort RS2000	B	4h.45m.38s.
9	Lindholm/Ohman	Opel Ascona	A	4h.46m.21s.
10	K. Aho/Vyorykka	Citroen Visa Trophee	B	4h.47m.08s.
28	Lindstrom/Ollila	Audi 80 Quattro	N	5h.07m.11s.

72 starters. 38 finishers. 1 A-PRIORITY DRIVER.

ECR9 TARGA FLORIO (I)   Palermo-Cefalu 29/31 March 1984
Coeff 3

1	'TONY'/Sghedoni	Lancia Rally	gB	6h.08m.57s.
2	'Lucky'/Berro	Ferrari 308GTB 4v.	B	6h.09m.36s.
3	ZANINI/Autet	Ferrari 308GTB 2v.	B	6h.24m.32s.
4	Del Zoppo/B. Tognana	Talbot Samba	B	6h.36m.23s.
5	Bentivogli/Evangelisti	Alfa Romeo GTV6	A	6h.40m.32s.
6	Vazzana/Provenza	Porsche 911SC	B	6h.44m.22s.
7	Rossi/Amati	Opel Ascona 400	B	6h.46m.08s.
8	'Dielis'/Spataro	Porsche 911SC	B	6h.49m.59s.
9	Montalto/'Flai'	VW Golf GTI	A	6h.52m.31s.
10	Savioli/Mauro	Opel Kadett GT/E	A	6h.58m.08s.
12	Carrotta/Schermi	Fiat Abarth 130	N	7h.01m.40s.

86 starters. 31 finishers. 3 A-PRIORITY DRIVERS (also Vudafieri).

ECR7 SACHS WINTER (D)   Bad Harzburg 24/26 February 1984
Coeff 2

1	Demuth/Lux	Audi Quattro	gB	2h.43m.18s.
2	Hero/Muller	Porsche 930 Turbo	B	2h.48m.47s.
3	Kissel/Michel	VW Golf GTI	A	2h.57m.11s.
4	Mayer/Stock	VW Golf GTI	A	2h.57m.34s.
5	Beck/Bruder	Opel Kadett GT/E	A	2h.57m.43s.
6	Nies/Siems	Audi Quattro	B	2h.57m.50s.
7	R. Holzer/G. Holzer	Opel Manta 200	B	2h.58m.39s.
8	Petersen/Bockelmann	Opel Ascona 400	A	2h.59m.26s.
9	Brauer/Hage	VW Golf GTI	A	3h.01m.59s.
10	Kern/Ufer	VW Golf GTI	A	3h.02m.22s.

61 starters. 41 finishers. NO A-PRIORITY DRIVERS. No group N starters.

ECR10 GARRIGUES (F)   Nimes 30/31 March 1984   *Coeff 2*

1	Andruet/Rick	Lancia Rally	gB	3h.57m.51s.
2	FREQUELIN/'Tilber'	Opel Manta 400	B	3h.58m.19s.
3	Henri Toivonen/Piironen	Porsche 911SC RS	B	3h.58m.30s.
4	Chatriot/Perin	Renault 5 Turbo	B	3h.58m.38s.
5	Saby/Fauchille	Renault 5 Turbo	B	4h.03m.07s.
6	DARNICHE/Mahe	Audi Quattro	B	4h.06m.20s.
7	Touren/Neyroy	Renault 5 Turbo	B	4h.11m.04s.
8	Sarrazin/Ginoux	Renault 5 Turbo	B	4h.20m.12s.
9	Rouby/Martin	Renault 5 Turbo	B	4h.21m.12s.
10	B. Abric/D. Abric	Renault 5 Turbo	B	4h.24m.16s.
12	Frau/Denison	Opel Ascona	A	4h.32m.40s.
13	Clemens/Lefebvre	Alfa Romeo GTV6	N	4h.36m.11s.

102 starters. 44 finishers. 2 A-PRIORITY DRIVERS.

ECR11   WAGNER

ECR13   MORELLI

ECR16   FEKETE

ECR12   BOZIC

ECR15   PHOTO 4

ECR17   PHOTO 4

ECR11   SAARLAND   (D)   Saarbrucken 7/8 April 1984   *Coeff 2*

1	Demuth/Lux	Audi Quattro	gB	2h.56m.33s.
2	Weber/Wanger	Opel Manta 400	B	2h.58m.29s.
3	Hero/Muller	Porsche 930 Turbo	B	3h.03m.07s.
4	R. Holzer/G. Holzer	Opel Manta 200	B	3h.11m.47s.
5	Brusch/Schaller	Opel Manta 200	B	3h.13m.57s.
6	Mayer/Stock	VW Golf GTI	A	3h.14m.21s.
7	Werner/Feltz	Ford Escort RS	B	3h.16m.42s.
8	Blome/Baerdges	Talbot Samba	B	3h.18m.07s.
9	Brauer/Hage	VW Golf GTI	A	3h.20m.34s.
10	J. Brack/M. Brack	Porsche 930 Turbo	B	3h.21m.10s.
22	Schaeffer/Joero	Talbot Samba	N	3h.45m.02s.

107 starters. 58 finishers. NO A-PRIORITY DRIVERS.

ECR12   ARBO   (A)   Vienna 12/15 April 1984   *Coeff 1*

1	Wiedner/Zehetner	Audi Quattro	gB	8883pt
2	Haider/Hinterleitner	Opel Manta 400	B	8891
3	Hopfer/Strobl	Renault 5 Turbo	B	9564
4	Wallner/Groesslhuber	Ford Escort RS	B	9586
5	Husar/Fekonia	Porsche 911SC	B	9841
6	T. Kottulinsky/Zeltner	Audi 80 Quattro	B	10002
7	Hahling/Appe	Opel Kadett GT/E	A	10145
8	Spreitzhofer/Gersthofer	Opel Kadett GT/E	A	10197
9	Anderson/Peisel	Toyota Starlet	A	10260
10	Roth/Schutzl	Porsche 911	B	10499

21 starters. 10 finishers. NO A-PRIORITY DRIVERS. No group N starters.

ECR13   CRITERIUM ALPIN   (F)   Grasse 14/15 April 1984   *Coeff 3*

1	RAGNOTTI/Thimonier	Renault 5 Turbo	gB	4h.12m.27s.
2	Henri Toivonen/Piironen	Porsche 911SC RS	B	4h.13m.15s.
3	FREQUELIN/'Tilber'	Opel Manta 400	B	4h.19m.38s.
4	Auriol/Occelli	Renault 5 Turbo	B	4h.21m.01s.
5	De Meyer/Borie	Renault 5 Turbo	B	4h.23m.05s.
6	DARNICHE/Mahe	Audi Quattro	B	4h.25m.23s.
7	C. Spiliotis/I. Spiliotis	Porsche 911SC	B	4h.43m.44s.
8	Panciatici/Sappey	Alfa Romeo GTV6	N	4h.45m.58s.
9	Clemens/Lefevre	Alfa Romeo GTV6	N	4h.52m.59s.
10	Orengo/Brezzo	Alfa Romeo GTV6	N	4h.56m.13s.
11	Badou/Dard	Opel Ascona	A	4h.56m.39s.

106 starters. 56 finishers. 3 A-PRIORITY DRIVERS.

ECR14   CIRCUIT OF IRELAND   (GB/IRL)   Belfast 19/24 April 1984
Coeff 2
See the results of Rothmans/RAC Championship round 2 on page 135

ECR15   COSTA SMERALDA   (I)   Porto Cervo 26/29 April 1984
Coeff 4

1	Henri Toivonen/Piironen	Porsche 911SC RS	gB	6h.53m.47s.
2	Capone/Cresto	Lancia Rally	B	6h.54m.44s.
3	Cerrato/Cerri	Opel Manta 400	B	7h.07m.04s.
4	'Lucky'/Berro	Ferrari 308GTB 4v.	B	7h.18m.53s.
5	Servia/Sabater	Opel Manta 400	B	7h.23m.55s.
6	Del Zoppo/B. Tognana	Talbot Samba	B	7h.37m.43s.
7	Noberasco/Cianci	Fiat Abarth 130	A	7h.38m.58s.
8	Carlino/Silvetti	Lancia Rally	B	7h.39m.13s.
9	Vittadini/Novaro	Ford Escort RS	B	7h.49m.49s.
10	'Tchine'/Borie	Opel Manta	A	8h.01m.00s.
18	Chiti/Boretti	Fiat Abarth 130	N	9h.09m.06s.

72 starters. 20 finishers. 3 A-PRIORITY DRIVERS (Bettega, Vudafieri and 'Tony').

ECR16   ZLATNI PIASSATZI   (BG)   Albena 12/13 May 1984   *Coeff 4*

1	Capone/Cresto	Lancia Rally	gB	4h.08m.04s.
2	Henri Toivonen/Grindrod	Porsche 911SC RS	B	4h.08m.40s.
3	Droogmans/Joosten	Porsche 911SC RS	B	4h.25m.40s.
4	Kaby/Gormley	Nissan 240RS	B	4h.28m.34s.
5	Ferjancz/Tandari	Renault 5 Turbo	B	4h.40m.05s
6	Noberasco/Spollon	Fiat Abarth 130	A	4h.41m.56s.
7	Petkov/Montchev	Nissan 240RS	B	4h.46m.52s.
8	Brundza/Girdauskas	Lada VFTS	B	4h.47m.33s.
9	Vukovich/Zvingevicz	Lada VFTS	B	4h.51m.09s.
10	Tameka/Kiulgevee	Lada VFTS	B	4h.59m.13s.
20	Van der Wauwer/Manset	Audi 80 Quattro	N	5h.11m.24s.

77 starters. 43 finishers. NO A-PRIORITY DRIVERS.

ECR17   FOUR REGIONS   (I)   Salice Terme 18/20 May 1984   *Coeff 2*

1	VUDAFIERI/Pirollo	Lancia Rally	gB	7h.28m.40s.
2	Cerrato/Cerri	Opel Manta 400	B	7h.29m.53s.
3	Del Zoppo/B. Tognana	Talbot Samba	B	7h.58m.40s.
4	Rayneri/Bartolich	Fiat Abarth 130	A	8h.07m.42s.
5	Bentivogli/Evangelisti	Alfa Romeo GTV6	A	8h.13m.18s.
6	Cerutti/Perazzi	Opel Manta 400	B	8h.19m.09s.
7	Cravero/Mandrile	Opel Manta	A	8h.28m.28s.
8	Guggiari/Ambrosoli	Citroen Visa Trophee	B	8h.29m.13s.
9	Fabbri/Farfoglia	Fiat Abarth 130	N	8h.31m.55s.
10	Gerbino/Cavalleri	Fiat Abarth 130	N	8h.33m.09s.

66 starters. 28 finishers. 2 A-PRIORITY DRIVERS (also 'Tony').

ECR18   LINDBERG

ECR20

ECR22

ECR 19   SLICK

ECR21   WEYENS

ECR24 (seen on 1984 ECR16)   FEKETE

ECR18 SOUTH SWEDISH (S) Kristianstad 18/20 May 1984 *Coeff 2*

1	WALDEGARD/Billstam	Toyota Celica TCT	gB	2h.03m.10s.
2	Stromberg/P. Carlsson	Saab 99 Turbo	A	2h.04m.10s.
3	Torph/Svanstrom	Opel Ascona	A	2h.04m.22s.
4	L-E. Walfridsson/Baeckman	Renault 5 Turbo	B	2h.04m.23s.
5	B. Johansson/Olsson	Opel Ascona	A	2h.04m.37s.
6	E. Johansson/Ostensson	Saab 99 Turbo	A	2h.05m.08s.
7	Grundel/Uppsaell	VW Golf GTI	A	2h.05m.34s.
8	Jensen/Stamnes	Ford Escort RS	B	2h.06m.43s.
9	Ahlin/Karlsson	Opel Ascona	A	2h.06m.57s.
10	P. Strid/B. Strid	Opel Manta 200	B	2h.06m.59s.
64	A. Carlsson/Lindberg	VW Golf GTI	N	2h.45m.39s.

133 starters. 64 finishers. 1 A-PRIORITY DRIVER.

ECR19 VOLTA A PORTUGAL (P) Lisbon 24/27 May 1984 *Coeff 2*

1	Santos/M. Oliveira	Ford Escort RS	gB	5h.27m.58s.
2	Bica/Prata	Ford Escort RS	B	5h.32m.56s.
3	Souto/Cid	Ford Escort RS	B	5h.39m.15s.
4	Ortigao/Batista	Toyota Corolla 16v.	A	5h.40m.44s.
5	'Tchine'/Borie	Opel Manta	A	5h.49m.46s.
6	Fernandes/Monteiro	Fiat Abarth 130	A	6h.00m.52s.
7	Breyner/Villar	Audi 80 Quattro	N	6h.04m.20s.
8	Simoes/Duraes	Opel Manta	A	6h.07m.01s.
9	Segurado/Sena	Opel Ascona	A	6h.13m.35s.
10	Lemos/Tavares	Toyota Starlet	A	6h.16m.14s.

53 starters. 13 finishers. NO A-PRIORITY DRIVERS.

ECR20 GUNAYDIN (TR) Istanbul 26/27 May 1984 *Coeff 1*

1	Wurz/Geist	Audi Quattro	gB	3h.53m.31s.
2	Petkov/Montchev	Nissan 240RS	B	4h.06m.28s.
3	K. Aho/T. Aho	Opel Ascona	A	4h.18m.09s.
4	Constine/Barbu	Renault 5 Alpine	A	4h.27m.47s.
5	Urdea/Amarica	Dacia 1310	A	4h.27m.50s.
6	Yerlici/Guvendiren	Peugeot 104ZS	A	4h.29m.03s.
7	Lammila/Nyman	Opel Ascona	A	4h.30m.32s.
8	Vasile/Scobai	Dacia 1310	A	4h.34m.16s.
9	Karacen/Elver	Ford Escort	A	4h.35m.51s.
10	Taslica/Tumay	Fiat 131	A	4h.41m.59s.
15	Beauld/Barral	Alfa Romeo GTV6	N	5h.02m.32s.

68 starters. 15 finishers. 1 A-PRIORITY DRIVER (Tchubrikov).

ECR21 HASPENGOUW (B) Landen 1/3 June 1984 *Coeff 1*

1	Droogmans/Joosten	Porsche 911SC RS	gB	4h.05m.20s.
2	Andervang/Schoonenwolf	Ford Escort RS	B	4h.11m.21s.
3	McRAE/Arthur	Nissan 240RS	B	4h.11m.36s.
4	Vandermaesen/Aerts	Opel Ascona 400	B	4h.13m.49s.
5	Lietaer/Martens	Talbot Sunbeam Lotus	B	4h.17m.41s.
6	Lareppe/Lambert	Opel Ascona	A	4h.19m.16s.
7	Reginster/Delmelle	Opel Kadett GT/E	A	4h.21m.02s.
8	Goudezeune/Messine	Alfa Romeo GTV6	A	4h.22m.08s.
9	H. Colsoul/Ulens	Opel Ascona 400	B	4h.28m.15s.
10	Munster/Loncke	Opel Manta	A	4h.28m.49s.
18	Van der Wauver/Peeters	Audi 80 Quattro	N	4h.36m.19s.

90 starters. 40 finishers. 1 A-PRIORITY DRIVER.

ECR22 ELBA (I) Portoferraio 7/9 June 1984 *Coeff 2*

1	Cunico/Sghedoni	Lancia Rally	gB	6h.31m.41s.
2	'Lucky'/Berro	Ferrari 308GTB 4v.	B	6h.33m.28s.
3	Cerrato/Cerri	Opel Manta 400	B	6h.36m.36s.
4	VUDAFIERI/Pirollo	Lancia Rally	B	6h.46m.30s.
5	Del Zoppo/B. Tognana	Talbot Samba	B	6h.57m.33s.
6	Ormezzano/Amati	Ferrari 308GTB 2v.	B	6h.58m.29s.
7	Rayneri/Bartolich	Fiat Abarth 130	A	7h.07m.16s.
8	Bardi/Mazzei	Ford Escort RS	B	7h.11m.39s.
9	Ercolani/Carlotto	Opel Ascona 400	B	7h.14m.00s.
10	Grossi/Parri	Alfa Romeo GTV6	A	7h.19m.54s.
11	Fabbri/Amati	Fiat Abarth 130	N	7h.29m.15s.

54 starters. 24 finishers. 1 A-PRIORITY DRIVER.

ECR23 SCOTTISH (GB) Glasgow 9/12 June 1984 *Coeff 2*
See the results of Rothmans/RAC Championship round 4 on page 137

ECR24 DANUBE (R) Sibiu 22/24 June 1984 *Coeff 1*

1	Ferjancz/Tandari	Renault 5 Turbo	gB	4h.00m.58s.
2	Velikov/Iliev	Lada 1600	B	4h.11m.05s.
3	Koper/Waniowski	Renault 5 Alpine	A	4h.24m.09s.
4	Petrov/Streschnov	Lada 1600	B	4h.24m.21s.
5	Lavrinovich/Niel	Lada 1600	B	4h.25m.31s.
6	Hristov/Radev	Lada 1600	B	4h.25m.44s.
7	Filimonov/Devel	Moskvich	A	4h.25m.58s.
8	Vasile/Scobai	Dacia 1310	A	4h.28m.53s.
9	Chtykov/Titov	Moskvich	A	4h.29m.37s.
10	H. Veselinov/P. Veselinov	Lada 1600	B	4h.32m.47s.

74 starters. 30 finishers. 1 A-PRIORITY DRIVER (Tchubrikov).
No group N starters.

ECR25

ECR 27   FEKETE

ECR29   FEKETE

ECR26   PHOTO 4

ECR28   (center photo, car #6 Rothmans Porsche)

ECR30   BAKES

ECR25 HESSEN (D) Kirchheim 22/24 June 1984 *Coeff 2*

1	Weber/Wanger	Opel Manta 400	gB	3h.57m.14s.
2	Hero/Muller	Porsche 930 Turbo	B	3h.59m.27s.
3	FREQUELIN/'Tilber'	Opel Manta 400	B	4h.01m.00s.
4	Kristiansen/Kischkel	Opel Manta 400	B	4h.10m.16s.
5	Schewe/Ricken	Opel Ascona 400	B	4h.11m.45s.
6	R. Hofler/B. Hofler	Opel Ascona 400	B	4h.17m.23s.
7	Schwarz/Drobe	Ford Escort RS	B	4h.19m.33s.
8	R. Holzer/G. Holzer	Opel Manta 200	B	4h.20m.21s.
9	Richter/Wendel	Opel Ascona 400	B	4h.20m.27s.
10	Blome/Bardges	Talbot Samba	B	4h.23m.23s.
11	Brauer/Hage	VW Golf GTI	A	4h.23m.46s.
56	R. Deubel/C. Deubel	Audi 80 Quattro	N	5h.25m.59s.

101 starters. 59 finishers. 1 A-PRIORITY DRIVER.

ECR28 YPRES (B) Ypres 29 June/1 July 1984 *Coeff 4*

1	Henri Toivonen/Grindrod	Porsche 911SC RS	gB	5h.16m.24s.
2	Snyers/Colebunders	Porsche 911SC RS	B	5h.21m.33s.
3	Capone/Cresto	Lancia Rally	B	5h.22m.39s.
4	McRAE/Arthur	Opel Manta 400	B	5h.29m.36s.
5	G. Colsoul/Lopes	Opel Manta 400	B	5h.34m.42s.
6	Mathon/Hanoca	Renault 5 Turbo	B	5h.36m.10s.
7	P. Dumoulin/J. Dumoulin	Porsche 911SC	B	5h.46m.21s.
8	Lareppe/Lambert	Opel Ascona	A	5h.49m.35s.
9	Goudezeune/Messine	Alfa Romeo GTV6	A	5h.52m.10s.
10	Guliker/Van den Brink	Porsche 911SC	B	6h.01m.26s.
13	Panciatici/Sappey	Alfa Romeo GTV6	N	6h.09m.09s.

147 starters. 70 finishers. 1 A-PRIORITY DRIVER.

ECR26 LANA (I) Biella 28/30 June 1984 *Coeff 2*

1	VUDAFIERI/Pirollo	Lancia Rally	gB	6h.11m.50s.
2	'Lucky'/Berro	Ferrari 308GTB 4v.	B	6h.18m.51s.
3	Cunico/Sghedoni	Lancia Rally	B	6h.23m.03s.
4	Ercolani/Roggia	Opel Ascona 400	B	6h.36m.30s.
5	Serena/Amerio	Lancia Rally	B	6h.37m.38s.
6	Del Zoppo/B. Tognana	Talbot Samba	B	6h.41m.12s.
7	Giorgio/Gruppo	Porsche 911	B	6h.46m.59s.
8	Cravero/Mandrile	Opel Manta	A	6h.59m.29s.
9	Martini/Mondino	Opel Ascona 400	B	7h.00m.47s.
10	Grossi/Parri	Alfa Romeo GTV6	A	7h.08m.10s.
11	Chiti/Boretti	Fiat Abarth 130	N	7h.10m.36s.

75 starters. 26 finishers. 1 A-PRIORITY DRIVER.

ECR29 POLISH (PL) Wroclaw 6/7 July 1984 *Coeff 2*

1	I. Carlsson/Melander	Mazda RX7	gB	3h.43m.58s.
2	Vukovich/Zvingevicz	Lada VFTS	B	3h.58m.35s.
3	Koper/Geborys	Renault 5 Alpine	A	4h.02m.44s.
4	Moskovskih/Girdauskas	Lada VFTS	B	4h.04m.22s.
5	Petkov/Montchev	Nissan 240RS	B	4h.08m.29s.
6	Tumaleviclus/Videcka	Lada VFTS	B	4h.08m.51s.
7	Hristov/Radev	Lada 2105	B	4h.09m.50s.
8	Polak/Bajorska	Talbot Sunbeam TI	A	4h.11m.37s.
9	Przybylski/Sadowski	Polonez 1600	A	4h.14m.02s.
10	Petrov/Tonev	Lada 2105	B	4h.14m.03s.

54 starters. 25 finishers. NO A-PRIORITY DRIVERS. No group N finishers.

ECR27 BARUM (CS) Gottwaldov 29/30 June 1984 *Coeff 1*

1	Demuth/Lux	Audi 80 Quattro	gA	4h.05m.41s.
2	Moosleitner/Cantonati	Opel Manta 400	B	4h.14m.09s.
3	Pavlik/Schimek	Opel Manta 200	B	4h.15m.14s.
4	Lank/Tyce	Lada VFTS	B	4h.16m.40s.
5	Blahna/Schovanek	Lada VFTS	B	4h.18m.30s.
6	Krecek/Motl	Skoda 120LS	A	4h.21m.29s.
7	Kvaizar/Janecek	Skoda 120LS	A	4h.24m.03s.
8	Sedlar/Castulik	Skoda 120LS	A	4h.25m.57s.
9	Salvan/Cigala	Fiat Abarth 130	A	4h.27m.08s.
10	Pech/Soukup	Skoda 120LS	A	4h.29m.03s.

74 starters. 28 finishers. 1 A-PRIORITY DRIVER (Tchubrikov).
No group N starters.

ECR30 SKODA (CS) Prague 14/15 July 1984 *Coeff 1*

1	Cinotto/Radaelli	Audi Quattro	gB	3h.02m.10s.
2	I. Carlsson/Melander	Mazda RX7	B	3h.08m.55s.
3	Haugland/Bohlin	Skoda 120LS	A	3h.16m.45s.
4	Sellholm/K. Andersson	Toyota Starlet	A	3h.18m.24s.
5	Aitken/Eckardt	Ford Escort RS 1600i	A	3h.24m.33s.
6	Svendsen/Gulband	Ford Escort RS2000	B	3h.25m.02s.
7	Wachs/Dobberphul	Opel Manta 200	B	3h.25m.56s.
8	Widerstroem/P. Johansson	Toyota Starlet	A	3h.26m.28s.
9	Ellingsen/Johnsen	Opel Ascona	A	3h.27m.12s.
10	Simek/Broulik	Skoda 120LS	A	3h.27m.19s.
52	Schindler/Gams	Fiat Abarth 130	N	3h.54m.53s.

126 starters. 65 finishers. NO A-PRIORITY DRIVERS.

ECR31   CHYTIL

ECR33   WAGNER

ECR35   PHOTO 4

ECR32   ARCHIVE

ECR34   WEYENS

ECR36   WEYENS

ECR31 VIDA (BG) Vidin 28/29 July 1984 *Coeff 1*

1	Petkov/Montchev	Nissan 240RS	gB	2h.09m.21s.
2	Velicov/Iliev	Lada 2105	B	2h.10m.35s.
3	E. Halivelakis/Papageorgieu	Ford Escort RS2000	A	2h.15m.58s.
4	Guerguiev/Marcov	Lada 2105	B	2h.19m.00s.
5	P. Tchubrikov/Grekov	Renault 5 Turbo	B	2h.22m.06s.
6	Vraj/Nerusil	Skoda 120LS	A	2h.23m.34s.
7	Stephanov/Tsvetcov	Lada 2105	B	2h.24m.13s.
8	Sivik/Vita	Skoda 120LS	A	2h.25m.14s.
9	Tesar/Ondrousek	Skoda 120LS	A	2h.27m.33s.
10	Jupam/Bojadzievski	Zastava 101	A	2h.29m.18s.

53 starters. 27 finishers. NO A-PRIORITY DRIVERS. No group N starters

ECR34 HALKIDIKIS (GR) Porto Carras 20/22 August 1984 *Coeff 4*

1	Capone/Cresto	Lancia Rally	gB	5h.04m.28s.
2	S. MEHTA/Y. Mehta	Nissan 240RS	B	5h.09m.04s.
3	Moschous/Makrinos	Nissan 240RS	B	5h.10m.10s.
4	'Stratissino'/Fertakis	Nissan 240RS	B	5h.17m.40s.
5	Kirkland/Levitan	Nissan 240RS	B	5h.19m.34s.
6	Petkov/Montchev	Nissan 240RS	B	5h.39m.55s.
7	'Melas'/Halaris	Lancia Rally	B	5h.40m.41s.
8	Papatriantafillou/Stefanis	Toyota Corolla	A	5h.52m.14s.
9	Hatzitsopanis/Athanasiou	Ford Escort	A	5h.55m.08s.
10	Pesmazoglu/Kilivridis	Opel Ascona 400	B	5h.55m.27s.
14	Van der Wauver/Droeven	Audi 80 Quattro	N	6h.01m.51s.

64 starters. 32 finishers. 1 A-PRIORITY DRIVER.

ECR32 MADEIRA (P) Funchal 4/5 August 1984 *Coeff 4*

1	Henri Toivonen/Piironen	Porsche 911SC RS	gB	5h.53m.33s.
2	Snyers/Colebunders	Porsche 911SC RS	B	6h.03m.18s.
3	Mandelli/Borghi	Lancia Rally	B	6h.06m.18s.
4	Chantriaux/Bernard	Citroen Visa Chrono	B	6h.16m.39s.
5	Gooding/Jenkins	Vaux. Chevette 2300HSR	B	6h.21m.47s.
6	P. Oliveira/Caldeira	Opel Manta GT/E	A	6h.27m.43s.
7	Bica/Prata	Ford Escort RS1800	B	6h.35m.33s.
8	Ortigao/Batista	Toyota Corolla 16v.	A	6h.36m.19s.
9	Guerreiro/Suarez	Toyota Corolla 16v.	A	6h.37m.35s.
10	Roussely/Villeminot	Porsche 911SC	B	6h.38m.29s.
17	Brustel/Maner	Fiat Abarth 125	N	7h.09m.32s.

66 starters. 25 finishers. NO A-PRIORITY DRIVERS.

ECR35 PIANCAVALLO (I) Piancavallo 30 August/2 September 1984 *Coeff 1*

1	VUDAFIERI/Pirollo	Lancia Rally	gB	6h.21m.52s.
2	Cunico/Sghedoni	Lancia Rally	B	6h.31m.27s.
3	'Pau'/Zanella	Lancia Rally	B	6h.48m.02s.
4	Bentivogli/Evangelisti	Alfa Romeo GTV6	A	6h.53m.32s.
5	Rayneri/Bartolich	Fiat Abarth 130	A	6h.55m.11s.
6	Moosleitner/Cantonati	Opel Manta 400	B	7h.12m.26s.
7	Russolo/Bigoni	Fiat Abarth 130	A	7h.25m.30s.
8	Fabbri/Ferfoglia	Fiat Abarth 130	N	7h.26m.20s.
9	Comelli/Del Put	Fiat Abarth 130	N	7h.33m.47s.
10	Dallacoletta/Groppello	Opel Ascona	A	7h.39m.17s.

56 starters. 16 finishers. 1 A-PRIORITY DRIVER.

ECR33 HUNSRUCK (D) Trier 17/18 August 1984 *Coeff 3*

1	Demuth/Lux	Audi Quattro	gB	4h.54m.23s.
2	Weber/Wanger	Opel Manta 400	B	4h.56m.18s.
3	Hero/Muller	Porsche 930 Turbo	B	5h.06m.09s.
4	Buffum/N. Wilson	Audi Quattro	B	5h.10m.03s.
5	Pond/Arthur	Austin Rover Vitesse	A	5h.17m.08s.
6	Brusch/Schaller	Opel Manta 200	B	5h.20m.12s.
7	Tuumi/Schneppenheim	Opel Ascona	A	5h.21m.35s.
8	Van der Marel/Beltzer	Opel Manta 400	B	5h.22m.30s.
9	Lareppe/Lambert	Opel Ascona	A	5h.23m.11s.
10	Moenchmeyer/Jahns	Toyota Corolla 16v.	A	5h.24m.43s.
43	'Doum'/'Chou'	Talbot Samba	N	6h.08m.54s.

130 starters. 63 finishers. NO A-PRIORITY DRIVERS.

ECR36 BIANCHI (B) Beaumont-Charleroi 31 August/2 September 1984 *Coeff 1*

1	Droogmans/Joosten	Porsche 911SC RS	gB	4h.25m.19s.
2	Dumont/Richard	Renault 5 Turbo	B	4h.40m.32s.
3	Vandermaesen/Aerts	Opel Ascona 400	B	4h.40m.55s.
4	Lareppe/Lambert	Opel Ascona	A	4h.47m.51s.
5	Van der Marel/Beltzer	Opel Manta 400	B	4h.50m.33s.
6	Reginster/Delmelle	Opel Kadett GT/E	A	4h.53m.56s.
7	Probst/Bozet	VW Golf GTI	A	4h.56m.17s.
8	Hendrickx/Bauduin	Opel Manta 200	B	4h.56m.51s.
9	Munster/Decock	Opel Kadett GT/E	A	5h.03m.17s.
10	Soulet/Willem	Porsche 911	B	5h.05m.46s.
12	Van der Wauver/Droeven	Audi 80 Quattro	N	5h.06m.54s.

165 starters. 72 finishers. NO A-PRIORITY DRIVERS.

ECR37   SMITH

ECR40   ARCHE

ECR42   TAYLOR

ECR39   BOZIC   ECR41

ECR43   WEYENS

ECR37 HEBROS (BG) Plovdiv 1/2 September 1984 *Coeff 2*

1	Ferjancz/Tandari	Renault 5 Turbo	gB	3h.38m.04s.
2	I. TCHUBRIKOV/Dimitrov	Renault 5 Turbo	B	3h.40m.42s.
3	Dounev/Marinov	Renault 5 Turbo	B	3h.42m.46s.
4	Krupa/Mystkowski	Renault 11 Turbo	A	3h.51m.18s.
5	Petrov/Tonev	Lada 2105	B	3h.52m.27s.
6	Christov/Radev	Lada 2105	B	3h.55m.02s.
7	E. Halivelakis/Panahotoonis	Toyota Corolla	A	3h.59m.20s.
8	Karacan/Yuvali	Ford Escort RS2000	B	4h.01m.57s.
9	Mali/Klimek	Lada 2105	B	4h.03m.08s.
10	Kokkinis/Pavli-Kokkini	Renault 5 Alpine	A	4h.06m.28s.
13	Poyaud/Vinoy	Talbot Samba	N	4h.14m.06s.

69 starters. 24 finishers. 1 A-PRIORITY DRIVER.

ECR38 MANX (GBM) Douglas 13/15 September 1984 *Coeff 2*
See the results of Rothmans/RAC Championship round 6 on page 138

ECR39 YU (YU) Sarajevo 14/16 September 1984 *Coeff 2*

1	Wittmann/Pattermann	Audi Quattro	gB	3h.52m.13s.
2	Droogmans/Joosten	Porsche 911SC	B	3h.55m.42s.
3	Ferjancz/Tandari	Renault 5 Turbo	B	4h.01m.05s.
4	Fischer/Hinterleitner	Mitsubishi Lancer T.	B	4h.03m.26s.
5	Kuzmic/Sali	Renault 5 Turbo	B	4h.07m.58s.
6	Krupa/Mystkowski	Renault 11 Turbo	A	4h.19m.48s.
7	M. Halivelakis/C. Halivelakis	Ford Escort RS2000	A	4h.27m.43s.
8	Prokopiou/Stellios	Opel Ascona	A	4h.28m.36s.
9	Kruegel/Schenk	Wartburg 353	A	4h.34m.30s.
10	Valant/Patarcic	Zastava GT65	A	4h.39m.59s.

67 starters. 47 finishers. NO A-PRIORITY DRIVERS. No group N starters.

ECR40 ASTURIAS (E) Oviedo 20/23 September 1984. *Coeff 2*

1	Servia/Sabater	Opel Manta 400	gB	4h.19m.18s.
2	A. Tognana/De Antoni	Ferrari 308GTB 4v.	B	4h.22m.33s.
3	Fombona/Menendez	Renault 5 Turbo	B	4h.24m.29s.
4	Llewellin/Arthur	Ford Escort RS	B	4h.29m.32s.
5	Moratal/Rodriguez	Talbot Samba	B	4h.34m.01s.
6	Gooding/Jenkins	Vaux. Chevette 2300HSR	B	4h.42m.53s.
7	Cardin/Grancedo	Lancia Rally	B	4h.44m.47s.
8	C. Santacreu/A. Santacreu	Opel Ascona	A	4h.45m.06s.
9	Wood/Bond	Talbot Samba	A	4h.48m.06s.
10	Holke/Puigdengolas	Ford XR3i	A	4h.51m.35s.
11	Candela/Villalba	VW Golf GTI	N	4h.53m.20s.

67 starters. 37 finishers. NO A-PRIORITY DRIVERS.

ECR41 TOUR DE FRANCE (F) Paris-Nice 24/28 September 1984 *Coeff 4*

1	RAGNOTTI/Thimonier	Renault 5 Turbo	gB	6h.26m.44s.
2	Andruet/Peuvergne	Lancia Rally	B	6h.27m.05s.
3	FREQUELIN/'Tilber'	Opel Manta 400	B	6h.34m.27s.
4	DARNICHE/Mahe	Audi Quattro	B	6h.35m.29s.
5	Auriol/Occeli	Renault 5 Turbo	B	6h.48m.29s.
6	Balas/E. Laine	Alfa Romeo GTV6	A	7h.13m.15s.
7	Gardavot/Levivier	Porsche 911SC	B	7h.15m.38s.
8	Defour/Roux	Talbot Samba	B	7h.18m.22s.
9	Panciatici/Sappey	Alfa Romeo GTV6	N	7h.27m.21s.
10	Zele/Bichet	Renault 5 Turbo	B	7h.29m.19s.

96 starters. 55 finishers. 3 A-PRIORITY DRIVERS.

ECR42 CYPRUS (CY) Nicosia 26/30 September 1984 *Coeff 3*

1	Buffum/Gallagher	Audi Quattro	gB	11h.49m.31s.
2	Brookes/Broad	Opel Manta 400	B	11h.57m.19s.
3	Mavropoulos/Adams	Talbot Sunbeam Lotus	B	12h.37m.02s.
4	Terzian/Thephanous	Nissan 240RS	B	12h.52m.09s.
5	Bin Sulayem/Daniels	Opel Manta 400	B	13h.06m.30s.
6	Tabatoni/Cadier	Citroen Visa 1000 P.	B	13h.07m.41s.
7	Saleh/Samia	Opel Ascona 400	B	13h.19m.48s.
8	Gemenis/Kepezis	Toyota Corolla 16v.	A	13h.55m.02s.
9	Eliades/Vassiliades	Citroen Visa Chrono	B	13h.55m.58s.
10	'Icaros'/Laos	Talbot Samba	B	14h.01m.59s.

70 starters. 30 finishers. 2 A-PRIORITY DRIVERS (McRae and Tchubrikov). No group N starters.

ECR43 VIN (CH) Martigny 26/30 September 1984 *Coeff 2*

1	Demuth/Lux	Audi Quattro	gB	4h.49m.25s.
2	Ferreux/Audemars	Renault 5 Turbo	B	4h.50m.17s.
3	SURER/Wyder	Renault 5 Turbo	B	4h.52m.12s.
4	Balmer/Indermuhle	Opel Manta 400	B	4h.52m.24s.
5	Christian Jacquillard/ Christine Jacquillard	Lancia Rally	B	4h.56m.12s.
6	Snyers/Peeters	Porsche 911SC RS	B	5h.00m.48s.
7	Roux/Schaer	Nissan 240RS	B	5h.01m.43s.
8	Carron/Lattion	Porsche 930 Turbo	B	5h.02m.43s.
9	Corthay/Cotting	Porsche 930 Turbo	B	5h.03m.35s.
10	Andervang/Schoonenwolf	Ford Escort RS	B	5h.07m.48s.
14	Toedtli/Rea	Opel Ascona	A	5h.22m.04s.
21	Terrani/Polli	Alfa Romeo GTV6	N	5h.38m.17s.

72 starters. 32 finishers. 1 A-PRIORITY DRIVER.

ECR44   ARCHE

ECR46   ARCHE

ECR48   WEYENS

ECR45   MORELLI

ECR47   SLICK

ECR 49

ECR44 CORTE INGLES (E) Las Palmas 5/7 October 1984 *Coeff 1*

1	Kaby/Gormley	Nissan 240RS	gB	2h.56m.19s.
2	Alonso/Sarmiento	Opel Ascona 400	B	2h.57m.19s.
3	M. Etchebers/C. Etchebers	Porsche 911SC	B	3h.00m.49s.
4	Ponce/I. Fernandez	BMW 635 CSI	A	3h.03m.37s.
5	S. MEHTA/Y. Mehta	Nissan 240RS	B	3h.04m.28s.
6	Alvarez/Leon	Renault 5 Turbo	B	3h.07m.23s.
7	ZANINI/Autet	Talbot Samba	B	3h.11m.41s.
8	Acosta/Rivero	Toyota Corolla GT	A	3h.13m.35s.
9	Gonzalez/Hidalgo	Toyota Corolla GT	A	3h.17m.32s.
10	Schweizer/Gleich	Opel Manta 200	B	3h.20m.10s.
11	Guerra/Reyes	VW Golf GTI	N	3h.21m.02s.

80 starters. 46 finishers. 2 A-PRIORITY DRIVERS.

ECR45 ANTIBES (F) Antibes 12/13 October 1984 *Coeff 3*

1	Capone/Cresto	Lancia Rally	gB	5h.03m.27s.
2	Beguin/Lenne	BMW M1	B	5h.04m.00s.
3	FREQUELIN/'Tilber'	Opel Manta 400	B	5h.04m.04s.
4	RAGNOTTI/Thimonier	Renault 5 Turbo	B	5h.06m.14s.
5	Vincent/Huret	Ferrari 308GTB	B	5h.08m.23s.
6	Gardavot/Levivier	Porsche 911SC	B	5h.29m.29s.
7	Rouby/Martin	Renault 5 Turbo	B	5h.31m.17s.
8	Loubet/Vieu	Alfa Romeo GTV6	A	5h.33m.36s.
9	Baroni/Barthelet	Ford Escort RS1600i	A	5h.42m.53s.
10	A. Oreille/S. Oreille	Renault 11 Turbo	N	5h.46m.20s.

118 starters. 45 finishers. 2 A-PRIORITY DRIVERS.

ECR46 CATALUNA (E) Barcelona 26/28 October 1984 *Coeff 3*

1	Servia/J. Sabater	Opel Manta 400	gB	4h.57m.49s.
2	Sainz/Orozco	Opel Manta 400	B	5h.00m.05s.
3	Ortiz/Barreras	Renault 5 Turbo	B	5h.02m.46s.
4	Pons/Grane	Lancia Rally	B	5h.07m.24s.
5	Mandelli/Borghi	Lancia Rally	B	5h.12m.47s.
6	Ferjancz/Tandari	Renault 5 Turbo	B	5h.16m.10s.
7	Frigola/Bou	Renault 5 Turbo	B	5h.16m.41s.
8	Moratal/Rodriguez	Talbot Samba	B	5h.22m.07s.
9	Arque/Romani	Opel Manta	A	5h.28m.21s.
10	C. Santacreu/A. Santacreu	Opel Ascona	A	5h.31m.00s.
12	Candela/Villalba	VW Golf GTI	N	5h.40m.33s.

83 starters. 42 finishers. 1 A-PRIORITY DRIVER (Zanini).

ECR47 ALGARVE (P) Alvor 1/3 November 1984 *Coeff 2*

1	Santos/M. Oliveira	Ford Escort RS	gB	6h.29m.21s.
2	Bica/Alegria	Ford Escort RS	B	6h.32m.35s.
3	Amaral/Neto	Citroen Visa Trophee	B	6h.37m.25s.
4	Fontainhas/Seromenho	Ford Escort RS	B	6h.52m.36s.
5	Schweizer/Schneider	Opel Manta 400	B	6h.56m.55s.
6	Mendes/Cunha	Nissan 240RS	B	6h.57m.19s.
7	R. Fernandes/Monteiro	Fiat Abarth 130	A	7h.05m.33s.
8	Moreno/Pereira	Opel Corsa	A	7h.21m.16s.
9	Coutinho/Junior	Toyota Corolla GT	A	7h.27m.29s.
10	Lemos/Tavares	Toyota Starlet	A	7h.32m.15s.
13	Hauser/Martin	Peugeot 205GTI	N	7h.55m.41s.

52 starters. 24 finishers. NO A-PRIORITY DRIVERS.
*results provisional subject to appeal.

ECR48 CONDROZ (B) Huy 2/4 November 1984 *Coeff 1*

1	Droogmans/Joosten	Porsche 911SC RS	gB	3h.47m.22s.
2	G. Colsoul/Lopes	Opel Manta 400	B	3h.49m.17s.
3	Dumont/Richard	Renault 5 Turbo	B	3h.51m.48s.
4	Vandermaessen/Aerts	Opel Ascona 400	B	3h.59m.16s.
5	Dechesnes/Michaux	Opel Ascona 400	B	4h.04m.22s.
6	Viane/Ostyn	Opel Kadett GT/E	A	4h.04m.53s.
7	Hendrickx/Baudoin	Opel Manta	A	4h.06m.09s.
8	Budo/Malais	Citroen Visa Trophee	B	4h.10m.06s.
9	Snoeck/Van der Sluys	Opel Manta 200	B	4h.11m.32s.
10	Probst/Bozet	VW Golf GTI	A	4h.11m.43s.
11	Van der Wauver/Droeven	Audi 80 Quattro	N	4h.11m.43s.

114 starters. 40 finishers. 1 A-PRIORITY DRIVER (Surer).

ECR49 SAN MARINO (RSM/I) San Marino 9/11 November 1984 *Coeff 3*

1	VUDAFIERI/Pirollo	Lancia Rally	gB	7h.10m.24s.
2	Demuth/Short	Audi Quattro	B	7h.13m.02s.
3	BETTEGA/Perissinot	Lancia Rally	B	7h.11m.15s.
4	Rossi/Cassini	Opel Manta 400	B	7h.50m.45s.
5	Bentivogli/Evangelisti	Alfa Romeo GTV6	A	7h.55m.25s.
6	P. Alessandrini/ A. Alessandrini	Porsche 911SC	B	8h.04m.59s.
7	Chiti/Boretti	Fiat Abarth 130	N	8h.09m.03s.
8	Cravero/Ercole	Opel Manta	A	8h.10m.08s.
9	Comelli/del Pup	Fiat Abarth 130	N	8h.17m.52s.
10	Fabbri/Cassina	Fiat Abarth 130	N	8h.22m.04s.

55 starters. 23 finishers. 2 A-PRIORITY DRIVERS.

European Championship for Rallies – Leading Positions

Rally	Janner	Arctic	Spa	Swedish	Costa Brava	Hanki	Sachs Winter	RACE	Targa Florio	Garrigues	Saarland	Arbo	Alpin	Circuit of Ireland	Costa Smeralda	Zlatni Piassatzi	Four Regions	South Swedish	Volta a Portugal	Gunaydin	Haspengouw	Elba	Scottish	Danube	Hessen	Lana
Country	A	SF	B	S	E	SF	D	E	I	F	D	A	F	GB	I	BG	I	S	P	TR	B	I	GB	R	D	I
Round No.	1	2	3	4	5	6	7	8	9	10	11	12	13	14	15	16	17	18	19	20	21	22	23	24	25	26
Coefficient	2	2	2	4	4	2	2	3	3	2	2	1	3	2	4	4	2	2	2	1	1	2	2	1	2	2
FISA Group A Challenge	-	-	-	-	-	1	-	-	-	-	-	-	-	-	2	3	-	4	-	-	-	-	-	-	-	-
Carlo Capone (I)				40					60						60	80										
Henri Toivonen (SF)										24			45		80	60										
Harald Demuth (D)							40				40															
Salvador Servia (E)					60										32											
Guy Frequelin (F)										30			36												24	
Adartico Vudafieri (I)																40					20					40
Attila Ferjancz (H)					40											32								20		
Jean Ragnotti (F)													60													
Patrick Snyers (B)		24																								
Jimmy McRae (GB)								30														12	30			
'Lucky' (I)									45						40							30				30
Robert Droogmans (B)																48					20					
Jean-Claude Andruet (F)										40																
	1	2	3	4	5	6	7	8	9	10	11	12	13	14	15	16	17	18	19	20	21	22	23	24	25	26

Scoring Basic Points: 20 for 1st, 15 for 2nd, 12 for 3rd, 10 for 4th, 8 for 5th, 6 for 6th, 4 for 7th, 3 for 8th, 2 for 9th and 1 for 10th.
These points are then multiplied by the coefficient concerned.
Best eight scores only to count.

For the third year running and the fourth time in six years an Italian driver (27 year old Turin native CARLO CAPONE) has won the European championship. A comparative unknown, he drove a factory prepared Lancia sponsored by West cigarettes. A back injury forced his rival HENRI TOIVONEN to withdraw in mid-season when leading the series. Capone started rallying with an Autobianchi in 1977 coming second in 1978 in the one-make series for these cars. From 1979 till 1982 he drove Ritmos, taking the Italian group A title in 1982.

Behind Capone and Toivonen came the former German champion 34 year old HARALD DEMUTH and the little known 40 year old Spaniard SALVADOR SERVIA. Apart from his annual entry at Monte Carlo Servia is normally only seen on Spanish events though in 1984 he also gained ECR points in Sardinia. The battle for fifth place between GUY FREQUELIN, JEAN RAGNOTTI and ADARTICO VUDAFIERI (the first two already guaranteed 1985 A-status) was only decided on the final round.

The ladies' award went for the third year running to the Italian ANTON-ELLA MANDELLI and the ECR co-drivers' title was won by the Italian-based American SERGIO CRESTO. The FISA group A challenge strongly favoured Scandinavian drivers who could gain high overall placings on their events due to their national championship excluding group B cars. Only the champion OLA STROMBERG (25 points) took two high placings; HARRI TOIVONEN (15) had one good overall position to finish ahead of LARS-ERIK TORPH (10) and BJORN JOHANSSON (8). In 1985 the points will be awarded to positions in the group.

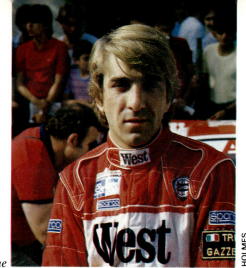

Henri Toivonen *Carlo Capone*

HOLMES

Rally	Barum	Ypres	Polish	Skoda	Vida	Madeira	Hunsruck	Halkidikis	Piancavallo	Bianchi	Hebros	Manx	YU	Asturias	Tour de France	Cyprus	Vin	Corte Ingles	Antibes	Cataluna	Algarve	Condroz	San Marino	Var	Total
Country	CS	B	PL	CS	BG	P	D	GR	I	B	BG	GBM	YU	E	F	CY	CH	E	F	E	P	B	RSM	F	
Round No.	27	28	29	30	31	32	33	34	35	36	37	38	39	40	41	42	43	44	45	46	47	48	49	50	
Coefficient	1	4	2	1	1	4	3	4	1	1	2	2	2	2	4	3	2	1	3	3	2	1	3	1	
FISA group A Challenge	-	5	-	-	-	-	6	7	-	-	-	8	-	-	-	9	-	-	10	11	12	-	-	-	
Carlo Capone (I)		48						80											60						428
Henri Toivonen (SF)		80			80																				369
Harald Demuth (D)	20						60										40							45	245
Salvador Servia (E)														40						60					192
Guy Frequelin (F)																48			36					15	189
Adartico Vudafieri (I)									20														60		180
Attila Ferjancz (H)											40		24							18					174
Jean Ragnotti (F)																80			30						170
Patrick Snyers (B)		60				60											12								156
Jimmy McRae (GB)		40										40													152
'Lucky' (I)																									145
Robert Droogmans (B)										20			30									20			138
Jean-Claude Andruet (F)																60								20	120
	27	28	29	30	31	32	33	34	35	36	37	38	39	40	41	42	43	44	45	46	47	48	49	50	

Salvador Servia *Harald Demuth* *Ola Stromberg*

British Championship

Rothmans/RAC Open Rally Championship

National Breakdown

After previous seasons in which it attracted regular support from a large contingent of manufacturers and star drivers, the 1984 British series was lower-key, with only an Audi Quattro for World Champion driver Hannu Mikkola and a group A Toyota Corolla for Per Eklund, both cars run by UK-based semi-official teams. The Citroen importers also supplied a Visa Chrono to British driver John Weatherley, promising that a four-wheel drive 1000 Pistes would appear later in the year.

Despite its new sponsor and title, the opening round of the Championship was very similar to the Mintex Rally of years past, featuring the same stages (mainly the north Yorkshire forest), the same format (32 hours rallying with only one brief rest halt), the same weather (fog and ice) – and the same organisation problems.

The overall result was never in any doubt, Mikkola (using the car with which Stig Blomqvist had won the 1983 Lombard-RAC Rally) being about one second per stage kilometre faster than any of his rivals and winning by over five minutes. British drivers Jimmy McRae and Russell Brookes, both driving factory Opel Manta 400s this year, fought hard over second place with the Scot coming out on top; fourth was Eklund in the new 16-valve Corolla. The Swede had been briefly led in group A by Mikael Sundstrom (Talbot Sunbeam TI), but the Finn went off and then broke three gearboxes. Malcolm Wilson made a first appearance in his private Quattro (the car used by Blomqvist to win the 1983 Open Championship), but he broke a driveshaft while holding fourth place.

The rally was marred by the death of Iceland's leading rally driver, Hafsteinn Hauksson (Ford Escort RS), who went off at a notorious bend in Dalby Forest and rolled sideways into a tree.

Jimmy McRae (left) and Mike Nicholson celebrate victory in the 1984 Rothmans/RAC Open Rally Championship.

TAYLOR

Round 1 28th NATIONAL BREAKDOWN York 17/18 Feb

1	MIKKOLA/Hertz	Audi Quattro	gB	3h.29m.51s.
2	McRAE/Nicholson	Opel Manta 400	B	3h.35m.29s.
3	Brookes/Broad	Opel Manta 400	B	3h.35m.51s.
4	EKLUND/Whittock	Toyota Corolla 16-valve	A	3h.51m.30s.
5	Tilke/Freeman	Ford Escort RS	1	3h.52m.44s.
6	Weatherley/R. Morgan	Citroen Visa Chrono	B	3h.55m.53s.
7	Brise/Bond	Talbot Sunbeam TI	A	4h.01m.37s.
8	Nicholson/Millington	Ford Escort RS	B	4h.02m.46s.
9	Jackson/Reed	Ford Escort RS	4	4h.05m.00s.
10	Mann/Goodman	Toyota Corolla	A	4h.08m.17s.
28	Wiggins/Shepherd	Vauxhall Astra GT/E	N	4h.23m.10s.

66 starters. 33 finishers. 3 A-PRIORITY DRIVERS.

Rally Leaders
Mikkola stages 1–50.
Stages: 3 asphalt, 3 mixed, 40 gravel; numbers 14+15 cancelled before start, 33+40 cancelled.

Leading Retirements

				STAGES CPLTD
Haugland/Eckhardt	Skoda 120LS	gA	gearbox mountings	17
Sundstrom/Orrick	Talbot Sunbeam TI	A	gearbox	30
Hauksson/Halldorsson	Ford Escort RS	B	accident	32
Lord/Gormley	VW Golf GTI	A	differential	36
Wilson/Harryman	Audi Quattro	B	driveshaft	37

Circuit of Ireland

As usual, this all-asphalt event proved to be the toughest rally in Britain – and probably one of the hardest in Europe. The challenge attracted an entry low in numbers but rich in quality, although the clash with the Safari Rally meant that some familiar cars were driven by new faces. In addition to Open Championship regulars McRae and Brookes, the event sponsors entered Henri Toivonen in a Porsche 911SC RS; German Harald Demuth replaced Mikkola in the Audi UK Quattro; Juha Kankkunen sat in for Eklund in the group A Toyota and Colin Malkin appeared in a 300bhp factory Rover Vitesse, also group A.

The rally started dramatically, Brookes retiring with propshaft failure on the first stage, Toivonen losing six minutes with an accident on the third stage and Malkin succumbing to axle failure after stage 5. The early leader was Northern Irishman Bertie Fisher, but he had halfshaft failure and McRae then led from Demuth. Toivonen was much the fastest driver, however, and had taken the lead by the time crews reached the new southern base of Waterford. Both McRae and Demuth suffered engine failures, leaving Toivonen with a six-minute advantage until his gearbox broke. The rally

BELOW

Billy Coleman and Ronan Morgan won the Circuit of Ireland in their Opel Manta 400.

BELOW

A Nissan 240RS was used on the series by Davy Evans who finished twice in the top ten. Competing here with Roy Kernaghan on the Circuit of Ireland.

was then fought between Irish Opel drivers Billy Coleman and Austin McHale, with Coleman leading until he was passed by McHale, whose engine exploded three stages from the finish. It was Coleman's third Circuit victory and the winning margin was one of the largest in the event's history.

Kankkunen punctured on the first stage, but pulled back to lead group A until his engine failed, leaving honours to Alan Johnston in Eklund's 1983 championship-winning car. Tim Brise (Sunbeam) also led group A briefly, but gearbox problems and an accident put him out of the event. Remarkable results were produced by Ernest Kidney, whose second place was one of the highest ever achieved by a genuine private driver on a British Championship rally; and by third-placed Davy Evans, the former World Hot Rod Champion, who was taking part in his first-ever rally!

Round 2 45th ROTHMANS CIRCUIT OF IRELAND Belfast 19/24 Apr *ECR14*

1	Coleman/R. Morgan	Opel Manta 400	gB	8h.59m.39s.
2	Kidney/McCanny	Talbot Sunbeam Lotus	B	9h.19m.43s.
3	Evans/Kernaghan	Nissan 240RS	B	9h.31m.18s.
4	Price/Davies	Renault 5 Turbo	B	9h.33m.30s.
5	Johnston/Willis	Toyota Corolla GT	A	9h.36m.07s.
6	McKinstry/Philpott	Ford Escort RS	A	9h.43m.21s.
7	Mann/West	Toyota Corolla GT	A	9h.46m.02s.
8	Brise/Bond	Talbot Sunbeam TI	A	9h.53m.59s.
9	Craig/Kniveton	Ford Escort RS	B	9h.56m.21s.
10	Roderick/Holmes	Vauxhall Chevette 2300HSR	B	9h.57m.24s.
22	Wiggins/Shepherd	Vauxhall Astra GT/E	N	10h.31m.59s.

75 starters. 36 finishers. 1 A-PRIORITY DRIVER.

Rally Leaders
Toivonen stages 1+2, McRae 3–9, Fisher 10–19, Toivonen 20–34, Coleman 35–41, McHale 42–51, Coleman 52–55.
Stages: 54 asphalt; number 14 cancelled.

Leading Retirements				STAGES CPLTD
Brookes/Broad	Opel Manta 400	gB	propshaft	0
Lord/Gormley	VW Golf GTI	A	oil loss	4
Malkin/Arthur	Rover Vitesse	A	transmission	5
McRAE/Nicholson	Opel Manta 400	B	engine	15
Kankkunen/Gallagher	Toyota Corolla GT	A	engine	16
Fisher/Frazer	Opel Manta 400	B	halfshaft	19
Demuth/Short	Audi Quattro	B	engine	23
Toivonen/Grindrod	Porsche 911SC RS	B	gearbox	43
McHale/Farrell	Opel Manta 400	B	engine	51

Welsh

After the dramas and surprises of the Circuit of Ireland, the Welsh Rally offered a return to normality, with Mikkola resuming his place in the Audi UK Quattro and winning the rally much as he pleased. As usual, the interest centred on the battle for second place between McRae and Brookes, although this event saw another Manta 400, the private car of Phil Collins, challenging the regular teams.

Because of unusually dry weather, the risk of fire in the forests of South Wales was too great, forcing the last-minute cancellation of many gravel stages and the addition of extra mileage over the asphalt roads of the Epynt military ranges.

This suited Brookes and Collins (both experts on Epynt) and they held first and second until Collins crashed. John Weatherley (who had been sacked by the UK Citroen team after rolling their new 1000 Pistes in testing) entered a private Mazda RX7 in group A and also led the established teams over these asphalt sections, although this car was withdrawn before the gravel stages.

Once the route reached the forests of central Wales, which made up all the second-half stages, four-wheel drive took over and Brookes could do nothing. McRae had several accidents and was beaten by Wilson's private Quattro as well as by Brookes. Finnish privateer Antero Laine appeared with his private Quattro, but only reached sixth place before retiring with engine failure.

BELOW
Tim Brise had some good results in the Talbot Sunbeam TI and finished the championship 3rd overall in the Group A. In action here on the Welsh with Steve Bond.

TAYLOR

Scottish

The hard, rocky forests of Scotland offered their usual challenge, made tougher this year by hot, dry conditions which produced clouds of choking dust for all except the first car on the road. That car was, once again, the Quattro of Mikkola, who cruised to his third victory in the championship by a margin of over six minutes. He was fastest on over two-thirds of the stages and never set a time outside the top four.

Second place was quite another matter, being hotly contested between three British drivers – McRae, Brookes and Wilson. The Quattro privateer was the quickest, even beating Mikkola on some early stages, but his front suspension broke after hitting a rock; Brookes then held second before crashing and losing 12 minutes, allowing McRae to finish runner-up on his home event for the fourth year in succession.

Although the tough nature of the stages and the sheer length of the rally proved unappealing to club competitors – only 63 homologated cars (plus some Army Landrovers) started – the organisers attracted some interesting overseas drivers; Swede Mats Jonsson set 18 times in the top five before breaking a halfshaft on stage 23 and the Finn Harri Uotila pleased spectators by continuing after a huge accident on the fifth stage, only to have his group A Ascona engine fail later in the event. There were some excellent performances by British private drivers: Vince Wetton finished seventh in his old Ascona 400, while Colin Valentine finished 11th overall to win the 1300cc group A class in his Talbot Samba

The British Citroen Visa 1000 Pistes (quickly rebuilt after the accident mentioned above) made its debut in the hands of Mark Lovell and was well driven into ninth place and a comfortable class win. After the initial fright from Weatherley, Eklund again dominated group A, winning by three minutes from Alan Johnston; expected rival Mikael Sundstrom suffered many punctures on his Sunbeam and could finish only 25th.

Round 3 20th CASTROL WELSH Llandrindod Wells 5/6 May

1	MIKKOLA/Hertz	Audi Quattro	gB	2h.49m.43s.
2	Brookes/Broad	Opel Manta 400	B	2h.52m.23s.
3	Wilson/Harris	Audi Quattro	B	2h.53m.32s.
4	McRAE/Nicholson	Opel Manta 400	B	2h.59m.52s.
5	EKLUND/Whittock	Toyota Corolla GT	A	3h.07m.18s.
6	Fisher/Frazer	Opel Manta 400	B	3h.07m.24s.
7	Tilke/Freeman	Ford Escort RS	B	3h.07m.26s.
8	Gooding/Jenkins	Vauxhall Chevette 2300HSR	B	3h.08m.00s.
9	Lovell/Davies	Citroen Visa 1000 Pistes	B	3h.08m.42s.
10	Johnston/Willis	Toyota Corolla GT	A	3h.10m.03s.
27	Wiggins/Shepherd	Vauxhall Astra GT/E	N	3h.26m.08s.

91 starters. 47 finishers. 3 A-PRIORITY DRIVERS.

Rally Leaders
Brookes stages 1–15, Mikkola 15–28.
Stages: 6 asphalt, 16 gravel; 28 stages planned (4 asphalt, 24 gravel) but new route issued before start.

Leading Retirements				STAGES CPLTD
Collins/Derry	Opel Manta 400	gB	accident	4
Uotila/Rydman	Opel Ascona	A	gearbox	15
Laine/Hokkanen	Audi Quattro	B	engine	22

ABOVE
Hannu Mikkola and Arne Hertz, who won three of the six rounds in this year's series are seen here on the Scottish in their Audi Quattro.

TAYLOR

Rallye, beating John Haugland's factory Skoda (which did not appear in the series again) by over ten minutes. Lovell's second outing in the factory Citroen Visa 1000 Pistes ended with early transmission failure, although he managed to equal Wilson's second-fastest time on one stage.

Group A was yet again dominated by Eklund, who won the category by two minutes from Brise, after Johnston retired with engine failure. Brian Wiggins won group N to clinch that class on the Open Championship with two rounds to run.

Round 4 25th ARNOLD CLARK SCOTTISH Glasgow 9/12 Jun
ECR 23

1 MIKKOLA/Short	Audi Quattro	gB	5h.07m.30s.
2 McRAE/Nicholson	Opel Manta 400	B	5h.13m.45s.
3 Brookes/Broad	Opel Manta 400	B	5h.25m.46s.
4 EKLUND/Whittock	Toyota Corolla GT	A	5h.34m.46s.
5 Brise/Bond	Talbot Sunbeam TI	A	5h.36m.54s.
6 Heggie/Mungall	Ford Escort RS	B	5h.38m.11s.
7 Wetton/Allen	Opel Ascona 400	B	5h.42m.45s.
8 Tilke/Roberts	Ford Escort RS	B	5h.44m.29s.
9 Lord/Daniels	VW Golf GTI	A	5h.46m.57s.
10 Girvan/McGilvray	Vauxhall Chevette 2300HSR	B	5h.53m.39s.
17 Wiggins/Shepherd	Opel Kadett GT/E	N	6h.07m.36s.

63 starters (in groups B, A and N). 37 finishers. 3 A-PRIORITY DRIVERS.

Rally Leaders
Mikkola stages 1–50.
Stages: 3 asphalt, 47 gravel.

ABOVE
Brian Wiggins won the Group N Championship with a Vauxhall Astra GT/E, seen here on the Scottish with Tony Shepherd where they finished 17th overall.

Leading Retirements

				STAGES CPLTD
Fisher/Frazer	Opel Manta 400	gB	accident damage	9
Lovell/Davis	Citroen Visa 1000 Pistes	B	differential	10
Jonsson/Gustavsson	Opel Ascona 400	B	rear axle	23
Wilson/Harris	Audi Quattro	B	accident damage	29

Ulster

With the gravel events completed, the Ulster Rally began the final phase of the championship, to be contested entirely on asphalt stages with pacenotes permitted. With Mikkola away in Argentina, Demuth again took his place in the Quattro, but the Audi UK effort was completely overshadowed by the appearance of Walter Rohrl in one of the new Sport Quattros from the German Audi factory team. Although the powerful short-wheelbase car was clearly very hard to drive Rohrl led the 26-hour event from start to finish, covering the opening stages over one second per kilometre faster than anyone else and winning by over four minutes.

McRae and Brookes had their customary battle, the English driver with a brand new car proving clearly superior on this occasion: he beat the Scot despite stopping on one stage with electrical troubles and going off later. Demuth had turbo problems, then was forced out after an electrical fire, so fourth place was contested between the Irish Manta 400 drivers Coleman and Fisher. Austin McHale (also Manta 400) was faster than either, but only until a major accident on the third stage. Private drivers filled the bottom half of the top ten and there was a notable performance from Andrew Wood, who finished 11th in a 1235cc group A Samba.

Eklund again led group A, but was stopped by a camshaft problem. Tim Brise (Sunbeam) and Alan Johnston (Corolla) both crashed, leaving the category to be won by David Mann's private Corolla. Group N saw the first UK appearance of the Fiat Abarth 130, which in Norman Thompson's hands proved far too powerful for the Astra GT/E and Talbot Samba opposition.

BELOW
The Audi Sport Quattro on its first outing in Britain was driven to victory on the Ulster Rally by Walter Rohrl and Christian Geistdorfer.

Round 5 9th RENTATRUCK ULSTER Belfast 27/28 Jul

1 ROHRL/Geistdorfer	Audi Sport Quattro	gB	3h.20m.37s.
2 Brookes/Broad	Opel Manta 400	B	3h.24m.52s.
3 McRAE/Nicholson	Opel Manta 400	B	3h.25m.08s.
4 Fisher/Frazer	Opel Manta 400	B	3h.38m.37s.
5 Coleman/R. Morgan	Opel Manta 400	B	3h.40m.50s.
6 Bolton/Ervine	Vauxhall Chevette 2300HSR	B	3h.40m.59s.
7 Tilke/Wray	Ford Escort RS	B	3h.44m.48s.
8 McKinstry/Philpott	Nissan 240RS	B	3h.45m.46s.
9 Dunnion/Fitzsimmons	Talbot Sunbeam Lotus	B	3h.50m.08s.
10 Mann/West	Toyota Corolla	A	3h.53m.48s.
18 L. Gibson/R. Gibson	Triumph TR8	4	4h.07m.27s.
23 Mills/Hill	Ford Escort	2	4h.11m.58s.
32 N. Thompson/ T. Thompson	Fiat Abarth 130	N	4h.16m.56s.

70 starters. 46 finishers. 3 A-PRIORITY DRIVERS.

Rally Leaders
Rohrl stages 1–27.
Stages: 27 asphalt.

Leading Retirements

				STAGES CPLTD
Brise/Bond	Talbot Sunbeam TI	gA	accident	0
Demuth/Short	Audi Quattro	B	engine fire	0
Wilson/Arthur	Audi Quattro	B	transmission	2
McHale/Farrell	Opel Manta 400	B	accident	2
EKLUND/Whittock	Toyota Corolla GT	A	camshaft	13

Manx

The most popular event in the championship also attracted the most varied entry, with 104 drivers from eight countries starting a rally which also qualified for the European Championship, the West Euro Cup, the FISA Group A Challenge and the national series of Belgium, Luxembourg and Ireland. Covering three days of all-asphalt daylight stages, it is the best organised event in the Open Championship.

This was the final year of sponsorship by Rothmans, who intended to repeat their 'in-house' victory of last year when Henri Toivonen won after a huge battle with Ari Vatanen. They entered Toivonen in the Porsche which had dominated the Circuit of Ireland, but the Finn injured his back at 1000

ABOVE

TAYLOR

Winning the Manx Rally in style Jimmy McRae and Mike Nicholson in their Opel Manta 400.

Lakes and had to be replaced by the promising Juha Kankkunen, who retired with engine failure after only four stages. Mikkola, who needed to win in the Sport Quattro to have any chance of the title, retired at the same place with the gearbox jammed.

As in 1983, the rally therefore turned into a battle between two Manta 400 drivers, this time McRae and Brookes. Brookes was the early leader until a puncture encouraged McRae to attack; the English driver made up some time, but crashed out of the rally on the second day. McRae made no mistakes and won his second Manx Trophy, thereby taking his third Open Championship title in four years.

Group A was considerably enlivened by the appearance of Tony Pond (a past winner of the event and an expert on the

Manx roads) in a factory Rover Vitesse, the 300bhp car proving faster than most of the group B cars and finishing third overall. Pond had several axle changes during the rally, and the team resorted to a device which squirted soapy water onto the rear tyres to reduce their grip and preserve the transmission! Eklund, however, finished second in group, won his class and clinched the overall Manufacturer's title for Toyota.

Round 6 22nd ROTHMANS MANX INT'L 13/15 Sep *ECR 38*

1	McRAE/Nicholson	Opel Manta 400	gB	5h.42m.34s.
2	Fisher/Frazer	Opel Manta 400	B	5h.55m.05s.
3	Pond/Arthur	Rover Vitesse	A	5h.57m.47s.
4	Corkhill/Byron	Ford Escort RS	B	6h.05m.01s.
5	Bengry/Watkins	Opel Ascona 400	B	6h.12m.07s.
6	Evans/Kernaghan	Nissan 240RS	B	6h.13m.42s.
7	EKLUND/Whittock	Toyota Corolla GT	A	6h.17m.49s.
8	Sundstrom/Silander	Opel Ascona	A	6h.21m.40s.
9	Lovell/Davis	VW Golf GTI	A	6h.25m.24s.
10	Price/Davies	Renault 5 Turbo	B	6h.28m.32s.
26	Wiggins/Shepherd	Vauxhall Astra GT/E	N	6h.56m.59s.

104 starters. 45 finishers. 3 A-PRIORITY DRIVERS.

Rally Leaders
Brookes stages 1–4, McRae 5–49.
Stages: 48 asphalt; number 16 cancelled.

Leading Retirements

				STAGES CPLTD
Weber/Berglund	Opel Manta 400	gB	engine	2
MIKKOLA/Hertz	Audi Sport Quattro	B	gearbox	4
Kankkunen/Piironen	Porsche 911SC RS	B	engine	4
Lord/McMahon	VW Golf GTI	A	accident	18
Bolton/Ervine	Vauxhall Chevette 2300HSR	B	accident	24
Brookes/Broad	Opel Manta 400	B	accident	29

		National Breakdown	Circuit of Ireland	Castrol Welsh	Arnold Clark Scottish	Rentatruck Ulster	Rothmans Manx	Total (best five)
1	**Jimmy McRae**	12	–	8	12	10	15	57
2	**Hannu Mikkola (SF)**	15	–	15	15	–	–	45
3	**Russell Brookes**	10	–	12	10	12	–	44
4	**Per Eklund (S)**	8	–	6	8	–	4	26
5	**Bertie Fisher**	–	–	5	–	8	12	25
6	**Billy Coleman (IRL)**	–	15	–	–	6	–	21
7	**Ian Tilke**	6	–	4	3	4	–	17
8	**Walter Rohrl (D)**	–	–	–	–	15	–	15
9	**Davy Evans**	–	10	–	–	–	5	15
10	**Tim Brise**	4	3	–	6	–	–	13

Group A winner: Per Eklund
Manufacturer: Toyota

ABOVE

TAYLOR

The Manufacturers title went for the second year running to Toyota. The Corolla 1600GT being driven here on the Manx Rally by Per Eklund and Dave Whittock.

Shell Oils/Autosport

Round 1 10 Mar SKIP BROWN GWYNEDD Llandudno   69s 43f
1 Weidner/Short   Audi Quattro   1h.17m.40s.
2 Collins/Freeman   Opel Manta 400   1h.18m.29s.
3 Llewellin/James   Opel Ascona 400 1h.18m.32s.

Round 2 31 Mar YORK NATIONAL Teesside   100s 64f
1 Weidner/Short   Audi 80 Quattro 1h.14m.15s.
2 Edwards/Watkins   Ford Escort RS   1h.15m.25s.
3 Aitken/E. Morgan   R-E-D 4T   1h.15m.47s.

Round 3 14 Apr JOHN CLARK BMW GRANITE CITY Aberdeen
                                      86s 58f
1 Wood/Brown   Rover Vitesse   1h.12m.45s.
2 Lymburn/Hutchinson Ford Escort RS   1h.13m.18s.
3 Heggie/Mungall   Ford Escort RS   1h.13m.47s.*
4 Aitken/E. Morgan   R-E-D 4T   1h.13m.50s.

Round 4 12 May ROTHMANS MANX STAGES Douglas, IOM
                                     126s 72f
1 Collins/Freeman   Opel Manta 400   1h.31m.22s.
2 Pattison/Taylor   Ford Escort G3   1h.32m.38s.
3 Dobie/Spokes   Opel Manta 400   1h.33m.12s.

Round 5 4 Aug PETER RUSSEK MANUALS Swansea   79s 49f
1 Llewellin/Evans   Ford Escort RS
                                       1h.28m.59s.
2 Aitken-Walker/   R-E-D 4T   1h.29m.23s.
  E. Morgan
3 Fowden/H. Thomas Rover Vitesse   1h.32m.31s.

Round 6 26 Aug RADIO LINK MEWLA STAGES Llanwrtyd Wells
                                     74s 50f
1 Collins/Freeman   Opel Manta 400   1h.18m.47s.
2 Pattison/Watts   Ford Escort G3   1h.20m.50s.
3 Pond/Arthur   MG Metro 6R4   1h.20m.58s.*
5 Chilman/B. Thomas Ford Escort RS   1h.22m.08s.

Round 7 1 Sep NEWCASTLE MOAT HOUSE LINDISFARNE
Newcastle-upon-Tyne   57s 44f
1 Collins/Freeman   Opel Manta 400   1h.04m.46s.
2 Chilman/B. Thomas Ford Escort RS   1h.05m.27s.
3 Aitken-Walker/E. Morgan R-E-D 4T   1h.05m.55s.

Round 8 29 Sep ANDREWS HEAT FOR HIRE CUMBRIA
Carlisle   49s 31f
1 Wilson/Harris   Audi Quattro   1h.23m.29s.*
2 Llewellin/Evans   Nissan 240RS   1h.28m.02s.
3 Chilman/B. Thomas Ford Escort RS   1h.29m.30s.
4 Marshall/Black   Vauxhall Chevette 1h.30m.15s.
                        2300HSR

Round 9 20 Oct AUDI SPORT NATIONAL Aberystwyth   83s 59f
1 Wilson/Harris   Audi Quattro   1h.17m.08s.*
2 Mouton/Gullick   Audi Quattro   1h.18m.56s.*
3 Eklund/Whittock   Toyota Celica TCT 1h.21m.19s.*
4 Collins/Freeman   Opel Manta 400   1h.21m.19s.
5 Llewellin/Evans   Nissan 240RS   1h.21m.57s.
7 Chilman/B. Thomas Ford Escort RS   1h.22m.42s.

* not registered for championship

Shell Oils/Autosport
RAC National Rally Champion: Dai Llewellin 147 pts
                           2nd Phil Collins 143
                           3rd Louise Aitken-Walker 136
                           4th Roger Chilman 122
                           5th John Midgley 95

Group A Champion: John Midgley 169

Esso/BTRDA Rally Champion: Clinton Smith
Esso/BTRDA Production Champion: Mike Price
Esso/Scottish Rally Champion: Ken Wood
Nicolet Welsh Stage Champion: Les Hurdley
Ford Escort Turbo Rally Champion: Rob Stoneman
Astra Challenge Champion: Stuart Nicholls
Lada Challenge Champion: Clive Wheeler
Rally Sport Champion: Kevin Maxted
Motoring News/BTRDA Rally Champion: Gwyndaf Evans
Castrol/Motoring News Tarmac Stage Champion: John Price

Llewellin   TAYLOR

Smith   LODGE

Wood   LODGE

Hurdley   LODGE

Stoneman   LODGE

Nicholls   LODGE

Wheeler   LODGE

Maxted   LODGE

John Price   LODGE

International Championship Rally Results

African Continent Championship

Round 1 13/15 Jan GRANDS LACS (ZAI, RW and BU)   20s 7f
1 Colette/Colette	Renault 5 Alpine	291 pts*
2 Anwar/Yusuf	Nissan 160J	314*
3 Duncan/Bennett	Nissan Pickup 1400	325*
5 Mancat/Moulad	Toyota Corolla	406
6 Paillocher/Potron	Peugeot 104ZS	474
7 Tomoni/Batavia	Mitsubishi Colt Turbo	638

Round 2 24/26 Feb SAFARI DU ZAIRE (ZAI)   s 5f
1 N'Gimbi/N'Gimbi	Range Rover	425 pts*
2 Van Ecke/Finet	Talbot Samba	465
3 Brose/Phitidis	Toyota Celica	495

Round 3 19/23 Apr MARLBORO SAFARI (EAK)
See the results of WCR round 3, WCD round 4 on page 61

Round 4 24/27 May ZIMBABWE CHALLENGE (ZW)   32s 15f
1 Horsey/Williamson	Peugeot 504 Pickup	1h.29m.
2 Bentley/Rowe	Ford Escort 1700TC	1h.33m.
3 Watt/Higson-Smith	Ford Escort RS2000	2h.04m.

Round 5 7/12 Jul CASTROL (ZA/SD)   70s 27f
1 van der Merwe/Boshoff	Audi Quattro	6h.11m.20s.*
2 Grobler/Swanepoel	Nissan Langley	6h.45m.03s.*
3 Evertse/Kriek	VW Golf	6h.51m.30s.*

Round 6 22/28 Oct COTE d'IVOIRE
See the results of WCD round 11 on page 103

Note: The final round RWANDA (RW) (December).

*Not qualifying for championship

Saeed Al Hajri, Middle East Champion

Middle East Championship

Round 1 26/27 Jan QATAR (Q)   30s 11f
1 Al Hajri/Spiller	Porsche 911SC RS	4h.23m.51s.
2 Sulayem/Daniels	Opel Manta 400	4h.29m.16s.
3 Saleh/Samia	Toyota Celica	4h.43m.03s.*

Round 2 23/24 Feb KUWAIT (KWT)   28s 5f
1 Saleh/Samia	Toyota Celica	7h.02m.25s.*
2 Al Zaffeiri/Ashkenani	Nissan 240RS	7h.20m.36s.
3 Al Beirami/Zaid	Nissan Violet	7h.33m.52s.*
4 Walles/McCormack	Porsche 911SC RS	8h.38m.47s.

Round 3 29/30 May BAHRAIN (KWT)   42s 20f
1 Brookes/Broad	Talbot Sunbeam Lotus	2h.09m.37s.
2 Al Hajri/Spiller	Porsche 911	2h.11m.03s.
3 Saleh/Samia	Toyota Celica	2h.30m.17s.*

Round 4 27/28 Jul JORDAN (HKJ)   29s 12f
1 Sulayem/Ali Talib	Toyota Celica TCT	4h.50m.12s.
2 Saleh/Samia	Toyota Celica TCT	5h.05m.33s.
3 Al Hajri/Spiller	Porsche 911SC RS	6h.10m.31s.

Round 5 1/2 Nov OMAN (OM)   21s 9f
1 Al Hajri/Spiller	Porsche 911SC RS	1h.24m.02s.
2 Saleh/Samia	Toyota Celica TCT	1h.24m.53s.
3 Georgiou/Porter	Nissan 240RS	1h.43m.25s.

Round 6 6/7 Dec DUBAI (EAU)   41s 21f
1 Al Hajri/Spiller	Porsche 911SC RS	1h.58m.56s.
2 Sulayem/Shadoor	Toyota Celica TCT	2h.00m.35s.
3 Swaidan/Skennerton	Range Rover	2h.20m.05s.

Middle East Championship Champion: Saeed Al Hajri.

Note: Final positions and points not yet available in Championship.

* Not qualifying for championship

TAYLOR

Alpe Adria Cup

Round 1 12/15 Apr ARBO (A)
See the results of European Championship round 12 on page 126

Round 2 12/13 May SATURNUS (YU) Portoroz   97s 51f
1 Kuzmic/Sali	Renault 5 Turbo	2h.25m.38s.
2 Pasetti/Siega	Fiat Abarth 131	2h.26m.38s.
3 Colombi/Mattanza	Opel Ascona 400	2h.32m.05s.

Round 3 27/29 Jul TRE LAGHI (I) Brescia   167s 107f
1 Montini/Rovelli	Porsche 911	1h.15m.33s.
2 Triboldi/Malchiodi	Lancia Rally	1h.19m.36s.
3 Facetti/Arioli	Ferrari 308GTB	1h.20m.05s.

Round 4 1/3 Sep BRATSTVO I JEDINSTVO (YU) Kopaonik
    37s 25f
1 Kuzmic/Sali	Renault 5 Turbo	1h.31m.01s.
2 Colombi/Mattanza	Opel Ascona 400	1h.36m.22s.
3 Lulik/Vidmar	Opel Kadett GT/E	1h.41m.56s.

Round 5 29/30 Sep KARNTEN (A) Klagenfurt   46s 33f
1 Haider/Hinterleitner	Opel Manta 400	2h.06m.26s.
2 Fischer/Weinzierl	Mitsubishi Lancer Turbo	2h.14m.12s.
3 Wallner/Groesslhuber	Ford Escort RS	2h.16m.10s.

Round 6 12 Oct VALLI CAMONICA (I) Brescia   s   f
1 Bossini/Passoti	Alfa Romeo GTV6	1h.18m.05s.
2 Marion/Vinzioli	Renault 5 Turbo	1h.18m.26s.
3 Kuzmic/Sali	Renault 5 Turbo	1h.18m.48s.

Alpe Adria Cup Champion: Fabrizio Colombi (I) 272 pts
                        2nd Branislav Kuzmic (YU) 228
                        3rd Silvan Lulik (YU) 190
                        4th Andrej Erklavec (YU) 146
                        5th Manfred Riegler (A) 132

STP-Irish Tarmac

Round 1 10/11 Feb AGIP GALWAY Galway   68s 27f
1 Fagan/McNamee	V. Chevette 2300HS	4h.47m.25s.
2 Coleman/R. Morgan	Opel Manta 400	4h.52m.09s.
3 McMillan/Bole	Ford Escort RS	4h.53m.15s.

Round 2 19/24 Apr ROTHMANS CIRCUIT OF IRELAND
See the results of Rothmans-RAC Open Championship round 2 on page 135

Round 3 22/24 Jun SHELL OILS DONEGAL Letterkenny   151s 85f
1 Coleman/R. Morgan	Opel Manta 400	3h.09m.10s.
2 McHale/Farrell	Opel Manta 400	3h.09m.41s.
3 Fisher/Fraser	Opel Manta 400	3h.12m.28s.

Round 4 27/28 Jul ULSTER Belfast
See the results of Rothmans-RAC Open Championship round 5 on page 137

Round 5 13/15 Sep ROTHMANS MANX
See the results of Rothmans-RAC Open Championship round 6 on page 138

Round 6 6/7 Oct UNIROYAL CORK 20 Cork   54s 31f
1 Coleman/R. Morgan	Opel Manta 400	3h.07m.46s.
2 McHale/Farrell	Opel Manta 400	3h.10m.42s.
3 Fagan/McNamee	V. Chevette 2300HSR	3h.16m.21s.

Round 7 8/9 Dec GLENEAGLE RALLY OF THE LAKES
Killarney   79s 33f
1 Coleman/R. Morgan	Opel Manta 400	3h.24m.05s.
2 McHale/Farrell	Opel Manta 400	3h.33m.00s.
3 Cullen/S. Gormley	Ford Escort RS1800	3h.35m.44s.

STP-Tarmac Champion: Billy Coleman 80 pts
                    2nd Austin McHale 36
                    3rd Davy Evans 34
                    4th Brendan Fagan 33
                    5th Pat Dunnion 22

Fabrizio Colombi, Alpe Adria Champion   BOZIC

Mitropa Cup

Round 1 30 Mar/1 Apr LAVANTALLER (A) Wolfsburg   45s 26f
1 Wiedner/Zehetner	Audi Quattro	3h.35m.33s.
2 Haider/Stunde	Opel Ascona 400	3h.44m.06s.
3 Fischer/Mikes	Mitsubishi Lancer Turbo	3h.45m.31s.

Round 2 7 May ULM (D) Ulm   s   f
1 Bohne/Fricker	Mercedes-Benz 500SL	
2 Gaiser/Gaiser	Opel Manta 400	
3 Braumueller/Molitor	Ford Escort RS2000	

Round 3 26/27 May CARSO (I) Trieste   80s 48f
1 Egizii/Nieri	Lancia Rally	2h.42m.19s.
2 'Pau'/Roggia	Lancia Rally	2h.42m.39s.
3 Fabbri/Cecchini	Fiat Abarth 130	2h.50m.27s.

Round 4 15/17 Jun PYHRN EISENWURZEN (A) Kirchdorf   44s 20f
1 Wiedner/Zehetner	Audi Quattro	1h.52m.37s.
2 Haider/Hinterleitner	Opel Manta 400	1h.55m.50s.
3 Fischer/Mikes	Mitsubishi Lancer Turbo	2h.01m.58s.

Round 5 29/30 Jun BARUM (CS)
See results of European Championship round 27 on page 128

Round 6 14/15 Jul SKODA (CS)
See results of European Championship round 30 on page 129

Round 7 30 Aug/2 Sep PIANCAVALO (I)
See results of European Championship round 35 on page 129

Round 8 19/21 Oct 3 STADTE (D) Landshut   134s 63f
1 Rohrl/Geistdorfer	Audi Sport Quattro	2h.17m.08s. .
2 Demuth/Lux	Audi Quattro	2h.21m.53s.
3 Petersen/Bokelmann	Opel Manta 400	2h.32m.00s.

Mitropa Cup Champion: Mathias Moosleitner (D) 148 pts
                    2nd Miroslav Lank (CS) 104
                    3rd Ladislav Krecek (CS) 103
                    4th Svatopluk Kvaizar (CS) 84
                    5th Hermann Tomczyk (D) 75

Stig Andervang, West Euro Cup Champion RALLY PRINT

Nordic Rally Championship

Round 1 10/12 Feb SWEDISH
See the results of WCR round 2 on page 49

Round 2 24/26 Feb HANKI
See the results of European Championship round 6 on page 125

Round 3 18/20 May SOUTH SWEDISH
See the results of European Championship round 18 on page 127

Round 4 26/28 Sep 1000 LAKES
See the results of WCR round 8, WCD round 9 on page 91

Nordic Rally Champion: Stig Blomqvist 30 pts
2nd Ola Stromberg 25
3rd Lasse Lampi 20
4th Bjorn Waldegard 20
5th Ari Vatanen 20

Peace & Friendship Cup

Round 1 10/12 Feb BALTICA (SU) Tallinn		61s 50f
1 Soots/Putmaker	Lada 2105	2h.28m.45s.
2 Yunpuu/Timusk	Lada 2105	2h.29m.33s.
3 Filimonov/Devel	Lada 2105	2h.29m.35s.

Round 2 30 Mar/1 Apr SALGO (H) Salgotarjannt		44s 23f
1 Tammeka/Kulgevee	Lada VFTS	4h.02m.41s.
2 Hristov/Radev	Lada VFTS	4h.04m.29s.
3 Hideg/Ban	Lada VFTS	4h.06m.27s.

Round 3 13/14 Apr SACHSENRING (DDR) Zwikau		75s 44f
1 Bolshih/Bolshih	Lada VFTS	7582.9
2 Bublewicz/Zyszkowski	Polonez 2000	7617.3
3 Moskovskich/Girdauskas	Lada VFTS	8005.6

Round 4 12/13 May ZLATNI PIASSATZI (BG)
See the results of European Championship round 16 on page 126

Round 5 22/24 Jun DACIA (R)
See the results of European Championship round 24 on page 127

Round 6 6/7 Jul RAJD POLSKI (PL)
See the results of European Championship round 29 on page 128

Round 7 14/15 Sep TATRY (CS) Poprad		66s 37f
1 Joki/Ronnlov	Toyota Celica	2h.46m.04s.*
2 Bublewicz/Zyszkowski	Polonez 2000 Turbo	2h.47m.05s.
3 Tumalyavicius/Videika	Lada VFTS	2h.53m.05s.
5 Velikov/Iliev	Lada 2105	2h.54m.40s.

Peace & Friendship Cup Champion: Andrzej Koper (PL) 207 pts
2nd Slavtmo Hristov (BG) 206
3rd Zdcnck Pipota (CS) 173
4th Georgi Petrov (BG) 164
5th Jozef Wazny (PL) 164

*Does not qualify for championship

Soots and Putmaker winning the Baltica Rally MARSICEK

West Euro Cup

Round 1 16/18 Mar TRIFELS (D) Kniserslautern		61s 41f
1 Demuth/Lux	Audi Quattro	6997 points
2 Weber/Wanger	Opel Manta 400	7046
3 Hero/Muller	Porsche 911 Turbo	7264

Round 2 13/14 Apr TULPEN (NL) Barneveld		91s 51f
1 Andervang/Schoonenwolf	Ford Escort RS	9381s.
2 Gulliker/Dickhout	Porsche 911	9469s.
3 Hoes/Badenberg	Opel Manta 200	9599s.

Round 3 27/28 Apr ROTHMANS HELLENDOORN (NL)

Hellendoorn		170s 105f
1 Andervang/Schoonenwolf	Ford Escort RS	7016s.
2 Kristiansen/Pedersen	Opel Manta 400	7986s.
3 Vandermaesen/Aerts	Opel Ascona 400	7134s.

Round 4 11/13 May ROTHMANS BAC (NL) Breda		60s 37f
1 van der Marel/Beltzer	Opel Manta 400	5757s.
2 Maaskant/Oosterbaan	Citroen Visa	5901s.
3 Hoes/Badenberg	Opel Manta 200	5908s.

Round 5 1/3 Jun HASPENGOUW (B)
See the results of European championship round 21 on page 127

Round 6 17/18 Aug HUNSRUCK (D)
See the results of European Championship round 33 on page 129

Round 7 31 Aug/2 Sep BIANCHI (B)
See the results of European Championship round 36 on page 129

Round 8 13/15 Sep ROTHMANS-MANX (GBM)
See the results of Rothmans-RAC Open Championship round 6 on page 138

Round 9 26/30 Sep VIN (CH)
See the results of European Championship round 43 on page 130

Round 10 10 Nov KOLN AHRWEILER (D) Althenr		242s 154f
1 Pettersson/Joenson	Audi 80 Quattro	2h.04m.26s.
2 Smith/Baud	Ford Escort RS	2h.07m.45s.
3 Surer/Wyder	Renault 5 Turbo	2h.08m.24s.

West Euro Cup Champion 1984: Stig Andervang 242 pts
2nd Kurt Jesse 216.5
3rd Valere Vandermaesen 213
4th Peter Klodzinski 180
5th Jan van der Marel 169

Other International Rally Results

DUBAI (EAU) 6/7 Dec 1983		35s 20f
Omar/Ali	Toyota Celica GT	3h.02m.33s.

PENNZOIL DAYLIGHT (MAL) 26 Feb		77s 63f
Lyou/Skalak	Nissan 130Y	67.44 penalties

HIMALAYAN (IND) 28 Oct/3 Nov New Delhi-Mussorie		59s 37f
Shah/Drews	Nissan 240RS	1h.57m.

National Championship Rally Results

The results listed represent the first team scoring points in the national championship, not necessarily the outright winning team.

A Austria

Round 1 5/7 Jan JANNER
See the results of European Championship round 1 on page 124

Round 2 24/26 Feb DHL-WIENERWALD Neulengbach   57s 39f
Wittmann/Nestinger   Audi Quattro   1h.55m.03s.

Round 3 9/11 Mar SCHNEEROSEN Heidenreichstein   33s 21f
Wittmann/Nestinger   Audi Quattro   2h.15m.25s.

Round 4 30 Mar/1 Apr LAVANTTALER
See the results of Mitropa Cup round 1 on page 141

Round 5 12/15 Apr ARBO
See the results of European Championship round 12 on page 126

Round 6 3/5 May SALZBURG Hofgastein   36s 19f
Wittmann/Nestinger   Audi Quattro   1h.48m.03s.

Round 7 15/17 Jun PYHRN EISENWURZEN
See the results of Mitropa Cup round 4 on page 141

Round 8 5 Aug OSTSTEIRISCHE Hartberg   28s 20f
Wittmann/Nestinger   Audi Quattro   4142 pts

Round 9 26 Aug ADMONT Admont   32s 21f
Wittmann/Pattermann   Audi Quattro   4714 pts

Round 10 29/30 Sep KARNTEN
See the results of Alpe Adria Cup round 5 on page 141

Round 11 3 Nov SEMPERIT Waidhofen   85s 45f
Fischer/Weinzierl   Mit. Lancer Turbo   2h.02m.34s.

Austrian National Rally Champion: Franz Wittmann 143 pts
2nd Wilfried Wiedner 110
3rd Georg Fischer 105
4th Sepp Haider 77
5th Franz Wurz 75

AUS Australia

Round 1 24/25 Mar CANON ZODIAC Bairnsdale, VIC   31s 17f
D. Officer/Hobson   Mitsubishi Galant   4h.34m.14s.

Round 2 7/8 Apr MID-STATE TELEVISION Bathurst, NSW
55s 30f
Carr/Gocentas   Fiat Abarth 131   4h.02m.38s.

Round 3 5/6 May JAMES HARDIE NATIONAL Mt Coot-tha, QL
72s 38f
Carr/Gocentas   Fiat Abarth 131   4h.14m.12s.

Round 4 2/3 Jun SUNDAY TIMES R&I BANK SAFARI,
Busselton, WA   64s 35f
Nicoli/MacNeall   Datsun Stanza   3h.57m.02s.

Round 5 11/14 Aug DUNLOP/2GO Gosford, NSW   46s 23f
Hill/Bonser   Ford Escort RS   7h.27m.31s.

Round 6 17 Nov ALPINE Bright, VIC   93s 44f
D. Officer/K. Officer   Mitsubishi Galant   5h.36m.12s.

Australian National Rally Champion: David Officer 98 pts
2nd Ed Mulligan 90
3rd Greg Carr 68
4th Murray Coote 58
5th Jim Middleton 50

Production Class winner: Ed Mulligan 90

David Officer, Australian Champion   STENZEL

B   Belgium

Round 1 3/5 Feb BOUCLES DE SPA
See the results of European Championship round 3 on page 124

Round 2 9/11 Mar CIRCUIT DES ARDENNES Dinant   79s 36f
Snyers/Colebunders   Porsche 911SC RS   4h.27m.35s.

Round 3 15 Apr TAC Tielt   68s 39f
Snyers/Colebunders   Porsche 911SC RS   3h.39m.15s.

Round 4 4/6 May WALLONIE Namur   59s 30f
Snyers/Colebunders   Porsche 911SC RS   4h.05m.30s.

Round 5 1/3 Jun HASPENGOUW
See the results of European Championship round 21 on page 127

Round 6 29 Jun/1 Jul YPRES
See the results of European Championship round 28 on page 128

Round 7 31 Aug/2 Sep BIANCHI
See the results of European Championship round 36 on page 129

Round 8 21/23 Sep OMLOOP VAN VLAANDEREN Roeselare
                                                        50s 23f
Snyers/Colebunders   Porsche 911SC RS   4h.42m.48s.

Round 9 2/4 Nov CONDROZ
See the results of European Championship round 48 on page 131

Belgian Bastos Int'l Open Rally Champion:
          Patrick Snyers 163.6 pts
          2nd Robert Droogmans 140.4
          3rd Guy Colsoul 105.7
          4th Jose Lareppe 89.8
          5th Jean-Claude Probst 74.7

BG   Bulgaria

Round 1 28/29 Apr SLIVEN Sliven   92s 51f
Slavov/Yanakiev   Skoda 130

Round 2 2/3 Jun OSUM Lovech   273s 50f
Velikov/Iliev   Lada 21011

Round 3 16/17 Jun STARI STOLITZI Shumen   173s 73f
Velikov/Iliev   Lada 21011

Note: The final round DEVNIA (November).

BR   Brasil

Round 1 7/8 Jul ULTRACRED DA GRACIOSA Parana   28s 19f
Fleck/Schury   Fiat Oggi   1h.58m.59s.

Round 2 21 Jul ITAU DE NOVA FRIBURGO Rio de Janeiro
                                                       25s 19f
Rodriguez/Lanhoso   VW Voyage   2h.36m.48s.

Round 3 1 Sep OURO BRANCO Minas Gerais   25s 9f
Bordin/Cunha   Chevrolet Chevette 1.6 2h.52m.40s.

Round 4 21/22 Sep PLAZA CALDAS DA IMPERATRIZ Santa
Catarina   22s 11f
Bordin/Cunha   Chevrolet Chevette 1.6 1h.49m.37s.

Round 5 12/13 Oct SAO PAULO FIRESTONE/REMINGTON Sao
Paulo   26s 4f
Antunes/Barbour   VW Voyage

Round 6 24/25 Nov TOURING/FIRESTONE Rio Grande do Sul
                                                       25s 16f
Bordin/Cunha   Chevrolet Chevette 1.6 1h.40m.34s.

Brasilian National Rally Champion: Saby Bordin 102 pts
                                        2nd Cesar Villela 51
                                        3rd Claudio Antunes 45

Saby Bordin, Brasilian Champion

ROMEU

CDN Canada

Round 1 4 Feb PERCE-NEIGE Maniwaki, QUE. 25s 11f
Bergeron/Rousseau Toyota Corolla 4h.17m.12s.

Round 2 30 Jun BAIE DES CHALEURS New Richmond, QUE.
  27s 17f
Franke/Cyr Volvo 242 Turbo 1h.18m.07s.

Round 3 14 Jul NOVA SCOTIA HIGHLANDS Truro, N.S. 18s 13f
Bendle/Crundwell Datsun 510 2h.26m.47s.

Round 4 21 Jul MOLSON LOBSTER Shediac, N.B. 23s 14f
Castledine/Sakanashi Datsun 510 1h.02m.47s.

Round 5 8 Sep VOYAGEURS North Bay, ONT. 20s 12f
Bendle/Crundwell Toyota Corolla 2h.38m.20s.

Round 6 7 Oct DEFI STE-AGATHE Ste-Agathe des Monts, QUE.
  30s 16f
Normandin/Belanger Toyota Corolla 1h.44m.52s.

Round 7 24 Nov TALL PINES Peterborough, ONT. 32s 12f
Bendle/Crundwell Toyota Corolla 2h.21m.22s.

Canadian National Rally Champion: Tim Bendle 64 pts
2nd Bernard Franke 55
3rd Tim Mullin 45
4th François Arbique 36
5th André Normandin 30

Production Class A winner: Michel Poirier-Defoy 40

Production Class B winner: Francois Arbique 30

CH Switzerland

Round 1 18 Mar CRITERIUM JURASSIEN Delemont 72s 45f
Balmer/Indermuhle Opel Manta 400 2h.06m.53s.

Round 2 13 May NEUENBURG Neuenburg 85s 53f
Bering/Schertenleib Audi Quattro 1h.28m.05s.

Round 3 17 Jun SALLANCHES (F) Sallanches 89s 67f
Jaquillard/Jaquillard Lancia Rally 2h.32m.42s.

Round 4 1 Jul ALPES VAUDOISES Aigle 83s 55f
Ferreux/Audemars Renault 5 Turbo 1h.30m.47s.

Round 5 8 Jul ESSLINGEN (D) (West German round 7 on page 000)
Balmer/Indermuhle Opel Manta 400 5382 pts

Round 6 16 Sep ST-CERGUE St-Cergue 74s 46f
Ferreux/Audemars Renault 5 Turbo 1h.40m.56s.

Round 7 26/30 Sep VIN
See the results of European Championship round 43 on page 130

Round 8 21 Oct COURT Geneva 58s 39f
Ferreux/Audemars Renault 5 Turbo 1h.26m.55s.

Swiss National Rally Champion: Eric Ferreux 49 pts
2nd Jean-Pierre Balmer 47
3rd Christian Jacquillard 42
4th Laurent Nicolet 39

CI Ivory Coast

Round 1 4/5 Feb 3A (Coeff 2) Abidjan 17s 10f
Maurel/Guevel Toyota Celica 1h.37m.

Round 2 31 Mar/1 Apr DE BOUAKE (Coeff 1) Bouake 25s 12f
Assef/Tastet Mitsubishi Lancer 33m.
  Turbo

Round 3 21/23 Apr BOUCLE DU CACAO (Coeff 3) Abidjan 17s 4f
Assef/Barault Mitsubishi Lancer 3h.19m.
  Turbo

Round 4 9/11 Jun MARLBORO-PENTECOTE (Coeff 2) Abidjan
  31s 13f
Ambrosino/Le Saux Mitsubishi Lancer 2h.09m.46s.
  Turbo

Round 5 29 Oct/5 Nov COTE d'IVOIRE (Coeff 4)
See the results of WCD round 11 on page 103

Note: The final round d'AGBOVILLE (December).

CO Colombia

Round 1 7 Apr T&A CLUB DE COLOMBIA Bogata 15s 6f
Gomez/Garcia Renault 4 1884 penalty

Round 2 26 May T&A CLUB DE COLOMBIA Bogota 14s 9f
Yacaman/Amaya Fiat 147 759 penalty

Round 3 21 Jul ESCUDERIA LOS TOPOS Pasto 61s 56f
Yacaman/Amaya Fiat 147 91 penalty

Round 4 25 Aug AC DE OCCIDENTE Pereira 15s 13f
Yacaman/Amaya Fiat 147 109 penalty

Round 5 14 Oct CLUB DE ANTIOQUIA Pto. Triunfo 41s 29f
Cifuentes/Romero Fiat 147 116 penalty

Round 6 3 Nov CLUB LOS TORTUGAS Bogota 18s 9f
Chamas/Meissner Renault 12 1045 penalty

Colombian National Rally Champion: Gustavo Yacaman 87 pts
2nd Alfredo Rojas 75
3rd Jairo Cifuentes 63
4th Jaime Quintero Jnr. 35
5th Cesar Gomez 33

Gustavo Yacaman, Colombian Champion

PLANO

CS   Czechoslovakia

Round 1 9/11 Mar SUMAVA Klatovy — 90s 55f
Lank/Tyce — Lada 2105 MTX — 8859 penalty

Round 2 22 Apr SKOL-UNION Teplice — 97s 52f
Lank/Tyce — Lada 2105 MTX — 8784 penalty

Round 3 3 Jun PRIBRAM Pribram — 97s 47f
Maly/Klimek — Lada 2105 — 7968 penalty

Round 4 29/30 Jun BARUM
See the results of European Championship round 27 on page 128

Round 5 14/15 Jul SKODA
See the results of European Championship round 30 on page 128

Round 6 17/18 Aug TRIBEC Topolcany — 93s 57f
Blahna/Schovanek — Lada 2105 — 8982 penalty

Czechoslovakian National Rally Champion: Miroslav Lank 55 pts
2nd Vaclav Pech 32
3rd Jiri Urban 28
4th Rudolf Hahnel 25
5th Igor Drotar 23

CY   Cyprus

Round 1 11/12 Feb EAST CYPRUS SAFARI Larnaca — 27s 12f
Panayiotides/Yiapanas — VW Golf GTI — 3h.03m.18s.

Round 2 14/15 Apr INT'L TOUR OF CYPRUS Nicosia — 26s 14f
Kyprianou/Evripidou — Talbot Sunbeam — 5h.55m.05s.

Round 3 12/13 May TIGER Limassol — 27s 12f
Kaloyirou/
Christodoulides — Toyota Levin — 3h.12m.21s.

Round 4 28/31 May ACROPOLIS (WCR 5, WCD 6 on page 73)
Eliades/Vassiliades — Citroen Visa Chrono — 15h.07m.48s.

Round 5 26/30 Sep CYPRUS
See the results of European Championship round 42 on page 130

Round 6 24 Nov TULIP Nicosia — 33s 15f
Terzian/Theophanous — Nissan 240RS — 2h.42m.19s.

Note: The final round VENUS (December).

D   West Germany

Round 1 24/26 Feb SACHS WINTER
See the results of European Championship round 7 on page 125

Round 2 16/18 Mar TRIFELS
See the results of European Championship round 1 on page 142

Round 3 7/8 Apr SAARLAND
See the results of European Championship round 11 on page 126

Round 4 3 Jun VORDERPFALZ Ludwigshafen — 195s 142f
Weber/Wanger — Opel Manta 400 — 4536 pts

Round 5 22/24 Jun HESSEN
See the results of European Championship round 25 on page 128

Round 6 8 Jul ESSLINGEN Stuttgart — 115s 81f
Demuth/Lux — Audi Quattro — 5036 pts

Round 7 17/18 Aug HUNSRUCK
See the results of European Championship round 33 on page 129

Round 8 6/9 Sep DEUTSCHLAND Mainz — 57s 22f
Mikkola/Geistdorfer — Audi Sport Quattro — 5h.35m.44s.

Round 9 7 Oct BALTIC Damp 2000 — 69s 50f
Demuth/Lux — Audi Quattro — 7074 pts

Round 10 19/21 Oct 3-STADTE
See the results of Mitropa Cup round 8 on page|141

West German National Rally Champion: Harald Demuth 254 pts
2nd Manfred Hero 161
3rd Erwin Weber 144
4th Norbert Brauer 137
5th Karl-Friedrich Beck 127

E   Spain

Round 1 17/19 Feb COSTA BRAVA
See the results of European Championship round 5 on page 000

Round 2 17/19 Mar COSTA BLANCA RACE
See the results of European Championship round 8 on page 125

Round 3 7/8 Apr GUILLERIAS Viladrau — 100s 30f
Zanini/Autet — Ferrari 308GTB — 2h.21m.53s.

Round 4 29 Apr SIERRA MORENA Cordoba — 63s 38f
Zanini/Autet — Ferrari 308GTB — 2h.52m.32s.

Round 5 20 May BAVIERA Madrid — 71s 43f
Zanini/Autet — Ferrari 308GTB — 1h.37m.50s.

Round 6 10 Jun LLANES Llanes — 68s 36f
Ortiz/Barreras — Renault 5 Turbo — 2h.47m.49s.

Round 7 19 Aug SAN AGUSTIN Asturias — 50s 20f
Zanini/Autet — Ferrari 308GTB — 1h.45m.25s.

Round 8 20/23 Sep ASTURIAS
See the results of European Championship round 40 on page 130

Round 9 5/7 Oct CORTE INGLES
See the results of European Championship round 44 on page 131

Round 10 26/28 Oct CATALUNA
See the results of European Championship round 46 on page 131

Round 11 11 Nov VASCO-NAVARRO San Sebastian — 57s 38f
Zanini/Autet — Ferrari 308GTB — 2h.13m.23s.

Round 12 25 Nov GERONA Gerona — 63s 32f
Servia/Sabater — Opel Manta 400 — 2h.14m.03s.

Spanish Rally Champion: Antonio Zanini 1399 pts
2nd Salvador Servia 1263
3rd Carlos Santacreu 996
4th Octavio Candela 885
5th Borja Moratal 824

EAK   Kenya

Round 1 19/23 Apr MARLBORO SAFARI
See the results of WCR round 3, WCD round 4 on page 61

Round 2 26/27 May FIRESTONE Nairobi — 35s 16f
Criticos/Rose — Audi 80 Quattro — 9h.14m.

Round 3 23/24 Jun KENYA 2000 Nakuru — 29s 10f
S. Mehta/Combes — Nissan 240RS — 15h.01m.

Round 4 18/19 Aug BAMBURI BEACH HOTEL Mombasa — 28s 13f
Criticos/Rose — Ford Escort RS — 9h.18m.

Round 5 15/16 Sep COCA COLA Nairobi 49s 36f
S. Mehta/Combes   Nissan 240RS   14h.35m.

Round 6 6/7 Oct BP VISCO 2000 Nairobi 39s 16f
Patel/Kandola   Datsun Violet   9h.02m.

Round 7 27/28 Oct RAYMONDS Eldoret 27s 14f
Taieth/King   Opel Ascona 400   8h.19m.

Note: The final rounds GURU NANAK (November), JAMHURI
(December), COAST 600 (January 85) and RIFT 300 (February 85).

F   France

Round 1 3 Mar LYON CHARBONNIERES Lyon 160s 44f
Darniche/Mahe   Audi Quattro   2h.36m.38s.

Round 2 30/31 Mar GARRIGUES
See the results of European Championship round 10 on page 125

Round 3 14/15 Apr CRITERIUM ALPIN
See the results of European Championship round 13 on page 126

Round 4 4/5 May TOUR DE CORSE
See the results of WCR round 4, WCD round 5 on page 67

Round 5 19 May PROVENCE Gap 102s 62f
Frequelin/'Tilber'   Opel Manta 400   2h.41m.00s.

Round 6 30 Jun MILLE PISTES Canjeurs 142s 52f
Chatriot/Perin   Renault 5 Turbo   3h.03m.21s.

Round 7 8 Sep MONT BLANC Annecy 131s 57f
Ragnotti/Thimonier   Renault 5 Turbo   4h.01m.35s.

Round 8 24/28 Sep TOUR DE FRANCE
See the results of European Championship round 41 on page 130

Round 9 12/13 Oct ANTIBES
See the results of European Championship round 45 on page 131

Round 10 24/25 Nov VAR
See the results of European Championship round 50 on page 160

French National Rally Champion: Jean Ragnotti 104 pts
                                    2nd Guy Frequelin 85
                                    3rd Jacques Panciatici 75
                                    4th Bernard Darniche 65
                                    5th Alain Oreille 58

GR   Greece

Round 1 3 Mar PELOPONNISOS Peloponnisos 68s 44f
Moschous/Konstantakatos   Nissan 240RS   2h.01m.52s.

Round 2 17/18 Mar KENTAVROS Volos 58s 40f
Moschous/Konstantakatos   Nissan 240RS   56m. 18s.

Round 3 31 Mar/1 Apr ATTIKO Attiki-Biotia 148s 102f
'Iaveris'/Meletopoulos   Fiat Abarth 131   52m.16s.

Round 4 14/15 Apr CARINO Peloponnisos 42s 24f
Moschous/Konstantakatos   Nissan 240RS   2h.12m.25s.

Round 5 29 Apr MACEDONIA Macedonia-Halkidiki 26s 12f
'Iaveris'/Koudourakis   Fiat Abarth 131   1h.24m.34s.

Round 6 5/6 May OLYMPIAKO Peloponnisos 50s 34f
'Iaveris'/'El-Em'   Fiat Abarth 131   57m.46s.

Round 7 28/31 May ACROPOLIS
See the results of WCR round 5, WCD round 6 on page 73

Round 8 16/17 Jun FTHIOTIDOS Lamia 46s 31f
'Iaveris'/'El-Em'   Fiat Abarth 131   46m.00s.

Round 9 31 Jun/1 Jul ACHEOS Patras 50s 29f
'Stratissino'/Fertakis   Nissan 240RS   1h.07m.24s.

Round 10 14/15 Jul BIOTIA Livadia 40s 16f
'Iaveris'/'El-Em'   Fiat Abarth 131   2h.19m.55s.

Round 11 20/22 Aug HALKIDIKIS
See the results of European Championship round 34 on page 129

Round 12 15/16 Sep I.F.T. Macedonia-Halkidikis 48s 21f
Moschous/Makrinos   Nissan 240RS   2h.14m.38s.

Round 13 30 Sep PALADIO Attiki-Biotia 121s 90f
'Stratissino'/Fertakis   Nissan 240RS   47m.10s.

Round 14 10/13 Oct BLACK ROSE Attiki-Biotia 63s 35f
'Iaveris'/'El-Em'   Fiat Abarth 131   2h.17m.43s.

Round 15 17/18 Nov SCORPIO Attiki 137s 91f
'Leonidas'/Pavli-Kokkini   Renault 5 Turbo   47m.27s.

Greek National Rally Champion: George Moschous 389 pts
                                    2nd 'Stratissino' 305
                                    3rd 'Iaveris' 280

H   Hungary

Round 1 30/31 Mar SALGO-MOGURT (Coeff 2) Salgotarjan
                                    107s 44f
Hideg/Ban   Lada VFTS   4h.06m.27s.

Round 2 18/19 May PORAN (Coeff 1) Miskolc 70s 45f
Szabo/Ormenyi   Lada 1300   1h.51m.09s.

Round 3 21/22 Jul OSC-BUDAPEST (Coeff 1) Budapest 70s 40f
Hideg/Ban   Lada VFTS   1h.56m.04s.

Round 4 15/16 Sep FOTAXI (Coeff 0.5) Budapest 72s 41f
Wirtmann/Schneer   Lada 1300   2034

Round 5 6/7 Oct MECSEK (Coeff 2) Pecs 65s 40f
Ranga/Kurz   Lada 1300   1h.55m.21s.

Round 6 9/10 Nov TRAUBI-NEPSPORT (Coeff 1) Veszprem 51s 33f
Hideg/Ban   Lada VFTS   1h.29m.40s.

Hungarian National Rally Champion: Janos Hideg 99 pts
                                    2nd Laszlo Ranga 87
                                    3rd Gyula Dudas 42
                                    4th Andras Karsai 41
                                    5th Tamas Szabo 35

Janos Hideg, Hungarian Champion   FEKETE

David Jepson, Jordanian Champion ARCHIVE

Bertie Law, Irish National Shellsport Champion PATTERSON

HK   Hong Kong

Round 1 29/30 Oct 1983 Victoria   60s 47f
Lieu/Choi   Toyota Celica   2h.21m.04s.

Round 2 14/15 Jan 1984 Victoria   60s 54f
Leung/Wong   Daihatsu   1h.32m.06s.

Round 3 21/22 Jan 1984 Victoria   60s 53f
Leiu/Choi   Toyota Celica   1h.07m.02s.

Round 4 28/29 Apr 1984 Victoria   52s 42f
Leung/Wong   Daihatsu   1h.09m.37s.

1983/84 Rothmans Hong Kong Open Rally Champion:
                    K.M. Leung 54 pts
                    2nd Mike Lieu 30
                    3rd Henry Heung 22

HKJ   Jordan

Round 1 3 Feb PETRA BANK NATIONAL   39s 24f
Jepson/Jepson   Toyota Starlet   39m.50s.

Round 2 11 May BEITUNA NATIONAL   40s 20f
G. Haddad/N. Haddad   Toyota Celica   50m.45s.

Round 3 26/27 Jul JORDAN (Middle East Challenge Round 4 on page 000)
Jepson/Millward   Toyota Corolla   6h.23m.51s.

Round 4 8 Nov DAIHATSU   28s 16f
G. Haddad/Almond   Toyota Celica   47m.35s.

Jordanian National Rally Champion: David Jepson 152 pts
                                        2nd Antony Walter 119
                                        3rd George Khayyat 92
                                        4th George Haddad 92
                                        5th Haile Aguilar 74

Italy

Round 1 24/25 Mar MOLISE Campobasso   39s 21f
M. Boretti/M. Boretti   Lancia Rally   2h.49m.48s.

Round 2 14/15 Apr LANTERNA Genoa   86s 43f
Tabaton/Tedeschini   Lancia Rally   2h.41m.24s.

Round 3 5/6 May GRAN SASSO Teramo   24s 15f
Cinotto/Radaelli   Audi Quattro   2h.50m.50s.

Round 4 26/27 May CARSO
See the results of Mitropa Cup round 3 on page 141

Round 5 7/8 Jun LIMONE PIEMONTE Limone Piemonte   153s 67f
Tabaton/Tedeschini   Lancia Rally   2h.14m.53s.

Round 6 21/22 Sep LIBURNA Livorno   86s 46f
Tabaton/Tedeschini   Lancia Rally   2h.14m.53s.

Round 7 13/14 Oct CITTA DI SASSI Sassari   39s 20f
Tabaton/Tedeschini   Lancia Rally   2h.07m.05s.

Round 8 26/28 Oct CITTA' DIMESSINA Messina   87s 32f
A. Runfola/P. Runfola   Lancia Rally   2h.56m.55s.

Round 9 17/18 Nov AOSTA St. Vincent   138s f
Tabaton/Tedeschini   Lancia Rally   3h.14m.28s.

Note: The final round RODODENDRI (December). The Italian
International Champion is Adartico Vudafieri.

IRL   Ireland

Round 1 17/18 Mar ZANUSSI WEST CORK Clonakilty   180s 85f
Heeley/Meade   Ford Escort RS   3h.10m.35s.

Round 2 12 May BOREEN Wicklow   49s 31f
Law/Millar   V. Chevette 2300HSR   1h.27m.12s.

Round 3 2/3 Jun CIRCUIT OF MUNSTER Newcastle West 110s 73f
McHale/Kennedy   V. Chevette 2300HSR   2h.53m.26s.

Round 4 1 Jul CARLOW STAGE Carlow   73s 37f
Connolly/Meaney   Ford Escort RS   10m.52s.

Round 5 15 Jul GLENSIDE HOMES Ballycotton   70s 34f
Coleman/McCarthy   Opel Manta 400   1h.24m.04s.

Round 6 21/22 Jul SLIGO STAGES Sligo   134s 98f
Fisher/Fraser   Opel Manta 400   1h.16m.03s.

Round 7 12 Aug STONETHROWERS Clonmel   60s 35f
Law/Millar   V. Chevette 2300HSR   1h.28m.39s.

Round 8 1 Sep GALWAY SUMMER Headford   55s 32f
Connolly/Meaney   Ford Escort RS   1h.37m.40s.

Irish Shellsport National Stage Champion: Bertie Law 85 pts
                                    2nd Llangley Humphreys 57
                                    3rd Joe McHale 50

Group A Champion: Sam McKinstry

IS   Iceland

Round 1 28/29 Apr JOJO Keslavi   23s 12f
Bragasson/Fridriksson   Ford Escort 2000

Round 2 15/16 Jun DALA Keslavi   18s 9f
Ulfarsson/Hilmarsson   Toyota Corolla 1600

Round 3 20/21 Jul HUSAVIK Husavik   20s 8f
Ulfarsson/Hilmarsson   Toyota Corolla 1600

Round 4 20/23 Sep LJOMA INT'L Reykjavik   20s 6f
O. Ragnarsson/
J. Ragnarsson   Toyota Corolla 1600

Round 5 5 Oct HJOLABARDAHALLAR Reykjavik   18s 10f
Sigurgardarsson/
Fridriksson   Ford Escort 2000

Icelandic National Rally Champion: Omar Ragnarsson 62 pts
                                    2nd Halldor Ulfarsson 55
                                    3rd Birgir Bragasson 38
                                    4th Bjarmi Sigurgardarsson 35

J   Japan

Round 1 28/29 Jan CREST SNOW ADVENTURE Saporo   60s 42f
Katoo/Umino   Subaru 1.8 4WD   1115.4

Round 2 11/12 Feb DCCS WINTER Gunma-Nagano   60s 52f
Kamioka/Sakuma   Toyota Corolla 1.6   31m.31s.

Round 3 17/18 Mar ACK SPRING Ooita-Fukuoka   60s 36f
Hazu/Taguchi   Mit. Lancer 1800 Turbo 1339

Round 4 7/8 Apr KANSAI 84 Mie-Nara   60s 44f
Goto/Ito   Toyota Corolla 1.6   564

Round 5 19/20 May 84 TOUR DO SHIKOKU Ehime-Kochi   60s 46f
Yamauchi/Kamaguch   Mit. Lancer 1800 Turbo 765

Round 6 30 Jun/1 Jul THIBAULT IN HOKKAIDO Hokkaido
                                                        60s 41f
Kosaka/Uesaka   Toyota Corolla 1.6   774

Round 7 18/19 Aug 84 KURIKOMAYAMA ALPEN Iwate   60s 41f
Ooba/Odagiri   Mit. Lancer 1800 Turbo 2214

Round 8 15/16 Sep MONTORAY '84 Gunma-Nagano-Tochigi
                                                        60s 34f
Oosima/Ihara   Toyota Corolla 1.6   2025

Round 9 6/7 Oct MCSC HIRAND MASTERS 84 Nagano-Gifu
                                                        60s 28f
Kosaka/Uesaka   Toyota Corolla 1.6   336

Round 10 3/4 Nov R8 & 84 Ishikawa   60s 32f
Sonada/Kusaka   Toyota Corolla 1.6   1425

Japanese National Rally Champion:
                      Class C: Sinya Yamauchi
                      Class B: Tuneo Yoshizawa
                      Class A: Yasuo Kusakabe

MAL   Duckhams Malaysia

Round 1 24/25 Mar PETALING JAYA Selangor   36s 20f
Khong/Sia   Toyota Corolla LB   178.26

Round 2 26/27 May PETALING JAYA Selangor   33s 25f
Lee/Leow   Nissan Sunny 1.8   113.44

Round 3 28/29 Jul SEREMBAN N. Sembilan   49s 39f
Khong/Sia   Toyota Corolla GT   107.57

Round 4 31 Aug/3 Sep LUCKY STRIKE Kuala Lumpur   44s 29f
Khong/Sia   Toyota Corolla GT   6h.33m.12s.

Note: The final round is to be held in December. Yin Swan Khong cannot now be beaten in the Championship.

Yin Swan Khong, Malaysian Champion

ARCHIVE

MEX   Mexico

Round 1 28 Jan MONTANAS (Coeff B) Mexico City   39s 29f
Arnstein/de Silva   Ford Pickup   117 pts

Round 2 3 Mar XAC (Coeff B) Toluca   29s 11f
Solorzano/Vazquez   VW 1600   89 pts

Round 3 17 Mar ARCO 500 (Coeff C) Guadalajara   21s 17f
Gonzalez/Serrano   Ford Mustang   107 pts

Round 4 6/7 Apr MEDIANOCHE (Coeff B) Cuernavaca   43s 27f
Gonzalez/Serrano   Ford Mustang   160 pts

Round 5 5 May FERIA DE MAYO (Coeff B) Morelia   45s 40f
Gonzalez/Serrano   Ford Mustang   172 pts

Round 6 25/27 May AMERICA 2000 (Coeff A) Mexico City   39s 7f
Balmes/Romero   Chevrolet Citation Turbo 913 pts

Round 7 29/30 Jun CANADAS (Coeff B) Mexico City   30s 14f
Balmes/Romero   Chevrolet Citation Turbo 145 pts

Round 8 20/22 Jul 24 HORAS (Coeff A) Mexico City   36s 18f
Basurto/Marin   Renault 5 Alpine   198 pts

Round 9 25 Aug OCCIDENTE (Coeff B) Guadalajara   36s 19f
Gonzalez/Serrano   Ford Mustang   82 pts

Round 10 8 Sep PATRIO (Coeff C) Morelia   21s 11f
Gonzalez/Rodriguez   Ford Mustang   85 pts

Round 11 20 Oct RAC 1000 (Coeff A) Mexico City   29s 7f
Gonzalez/Serrano   Ford Mustang   1643 pts

Round 12 27/28 Oct RUTA DEL SOL (Coeff B) Guadalajara-Puerto Vallarta   26s 12f
Balmes/Romero   Chevrolet Citation Turbo 223 pts

Round 13 10 Nov TART (Coeff C) Toluca   185s 8f
Balmes/Romero   Chevrolet Citation Turbo 21 pts

Round 14 23/24 Nov ACAPULCO (Coeff A) Mexico City-Acapulco   42s 16f
Salas/De Silva   Ford Topaz   193 pts

Mexican National Rally Champion: Sergio Gonzalez 238 pts
2nd Jaime Balmes 158
3rd Luis Unikel 78
4th Guillermo Salas 72
5th Marco Basurto 54

N   Norway

Round 1 14 Jan SNOSVENGEN (S) Kil   52s 40f
Andersen/Jortun   VW Golf GTI 1800   33m.53s.

Round 2 21 Jan NORDMARKSNATTA (S) Arjang   47s 37f
Andersen/Jortun   VW Golf GTI 1800   30m.15s.

Round 3 28 Jan HURDAL (N) Eidsvoll   37s 26f
Stenshorne/Stenshorne   Ford Escort RS2000   1h.09m.53s.

Round 4 4 Feb SNOFRESER'N (N) Elverum   96s 81f
Andersen/Jortun   VW Golf GTI 1800   36m.30s.

Round 5 18 Feb EVJEMOEN (N) Evje   50s 36f
Jensen/Stamnes   Ford Escort RS   25m.52s.

Round 6 25 Feb FINNSKOG WINTER (N) Kongsvinger   96s 62f
Johansen/Hunsdal   VW Golf 1600   59m.34s.

Round 7 18/20 May SOUTH SWEDISH
See the results of European Championship round 18 on page 127

Round 8 8 Sept EDA (S) Eda   66s 49f
Frog/Fundemd   Opel Ascona   21m.51s.

Round 9 3 Nov VANERSBORG (S) Vanersborg   46s 37f
Matheson/Stamnes   Ford Escort RS2000   22m.15s.

Norwegian National Rally Champion:
Class 3 (group B):   Valter Jensen 55 pts
Class 2 (National):   Vidars Johansen 105
Class 1 (group A):   Rolf Jacob Andersen 115

NL   Netherlands

Round 1 3/5 Feb BOUCLES DE SPA (B)
See the results of European Championship round 3 on page 124

Round 2 9/11 Mar CIRCUIT DES ARDENNES (Belgium round 2 on page 144)
van der Marel/Van Traa   Opel Manta 400   4h.51m.15s.

Round 3 23/24 Mar AMSTERDAM-BP Amsterdam   35s 26f
Andervang/Schoonenwolf   Ford Escort RS   6820s.

Round 4 13/14 Apr TULPEN
See the results of West Euro Cup round 2 on page 142

Round 5 27/28 Apr ROTHMANS HELLENDOORN
See the results of West Euro Cup round 3 on page 142

Round 6 11/13 May ROTHMANS BAC
See the results of West Euro Cup round 4 on page 142

Round 7 26/27 May ELE Eindhoven   64s 38f
van der Marel/Beltzer   Opel Manta 400   8432s.

Round 8 1/3 Jun HASPENGOUW (B)
See the results of European Championship round 21 on page 127

Round 9 22/24 Jun HESSEN (D)
See the results of European Championship round 25 on page 128

Round 10 17/18 Aug HUNSRUCK (D)
See the results of European Championship round 33 on page 129

Round 11 25 Aug LIMBURGIA Maasbracht   90s 69f
van der Marel/Beltzer   Opel Manta 400   4142s.

Round 12 31 Aug/2 Sept BIANCHI (B)
See the results of European Championship round 36 on page 129

Round 13 15/16 Sep VISE-AUBEL (B) Aubel   128s 88f
van der Marel/Beltzer   Opel Manta 400   5320s.

Round 14 5/7 Oct GRENSLAND (B) Hasselt   120s 80f
Walfridsson/Kvarnhof   Renault 5 Turbo   8037s.

Round 15 13/14 Oct KOHLE UND STAHL (D)   96s 70f
van der Marel/Beltzer   Opel Manta 400   1h.46m.12s.

Round 16 10/11 Nov KOLN AHRWEILER (D) (West Euro Cup round 6 page 000)
Andervang/Schoonenwolf   Ford Escort RS   2h.15m.16s.

Netherlands Open International Rally Champion:
Jan van der Marel 443 pts
2nd Paul Maaskant 428
3rd Stig Andervang 422
4th Johnny Hoes 407
5th Henk Vossen 404

Netherlands National Rally Champion: Ron der Groot

NZ   New Zealand

Round 1 1 Apr WRIGHT CARS/4ZG South Island   54s 38f
Tulloch/Paterson   Ford Escort RS   2h.06m.46s.

Round 2 6 May TOKOROA North Island 72s 44f
Adams/Scott   Toyota Corolla   2h.49m.14s.

Round 3 12 May CANTERBURY South Island 68s 41f
Tulloch/Paterson   Ford Escort RS   2h.20m.23s.

Round 4 21 Jul HAWKES BAY North Island 83s 56f
Allport/Freeth   Ford Escort RS   3h.23m.08s.

Round 5 11 Aug NORTH OTAGO South Island 62s 38f
Stokes/Kerr   Ford Escort RS   2h.10m.51s.

Round 6 11/12 Aug HAMILTON North Island 44s 30f
Teesdale/Horne   Nissan 240RS   1h.35m.06s.

Round 7 8/9 Sep HELLA LIGHTS North Island 73s 43f
Stewart/Parkhill   Ford Escort RS   2h.12m.21s.

Round 8 29/30 Sep SOUTH CANTERBURY (PREMIER) South
Island   54s 32f
Cook/Lange   Nissan 240RS   3h.24m.35s.

New Zealand National Rally Champion: Tony Teesdale 86 pts
                                         2nd Reg Cook 80
                                         3rd Malcolm Stewart 78
                                         4th Paul Adams 70
                                         5th Inky Tulloch 63

National Group A Champion: Bruce McKenzie 105 pts

PL   Poland

Round 1 28/29 Apr ELMOT Swidnica 76s 55f
Bublewicz/Zyszkowski   Polonez 2000 Turbo   7388 pts

Round 2 8/9 Jun CRACOW Cracow 79s 43f
Bublewicz/Zyszkowski   Polonez 2000 Turbo   6262.8 pts

Round 3 29/30 Sep VISTULA Wisla 74s 46f
Koper/Geborys   Renault 5 Alpine   2686.1 pts

Round 4 27/28 Oct STOMIL Olsztyn 55s 36f
Koper/Geborys   Renault 5 Alpine   5938 pts

Polish National Rally Champion: Andrzej Koper 146 pts
                                    2nd Marian Bublewicz 141
                                    3rd Viktor Polak 130
                                    4th Pavel Przybylski 123
                                    5th Andrzej Baginski 99

PY   Paraguay

Round 1 1 Apr TRANS ITAPUA Encarnacion 39s 27f
J. Viveros/G. Viveros   Datsun 160J   125pts

Round 2 10 Jun PAZ DEL CHACO Emboscada 39s 19f
Sanabria/Gosling   Datsun 160J   2h.31m.55s.

Note: The final round ITAPUA MISIONES (RA) (December).

P   Portugal

Round 1 21/22 Jan SOPETE Povoa de Varzim 35s 20f
Moutinho/Fortes   Renault 5 Turbo   1h.48m.45s.

Round 2 4/5 Feb CAMELIAS Sintra 35s 22f
Moutinho/Fortes   Renault 5 Turbo   1h.31m.57s.

Round 3 7/10 Mar PORT WINE RALLY OF PORTUGAL
See the results of WCR round 2, WCD round 3 on page 55

Round 4 30/31 Mar FIGUERA DA FOZ Figuera da Foz-Arganil
                                             41s 18f
Moutinho/Fortes   Renault 5 Turbo   1h.44m.04s.

Round 5 13/15 Apr SERRA DO MARAO S. Marta de Penaguiao-
Vila Real   22s 14f
Santos/Oliveira   Ford Escort RS   1h.42m.54s.

Round 5 5/6 May ROTA DO SOL San Pedro de Moel 30s 21f
Moutinho/Fortes   Renault 5 Turbo   1h.19m.59s.

Round 6 24/27 May VOLTA A PORTUGAL
See the results of European Championship round 19 on page 127

Round 7 6/7 Jul S. MIGUEL Ponta Delgada 51s 19f
Moutinho/Fortes   Renault 5 Turbo   3h.33m.52s.

Round 8 4/5 Aug MADEIRA
See the results of European Championship round 32 on page 129

Round 9 22/23 Sep ALTO TAMEGA Vidago 16s 8f
Moutinho/Fortes   Renault 5 Turbo   1h.54m.01s.

Round 10 6/7 Oct CASTELO BRANCO Castelo Branco 24s 13f
Santos/Oliveira   Ford Escort RS1800   1h.55m.50s.

Round 11 1/3 Nov ALGARVE
See the results of European Championship round 47 on page 131

Provisional Portuguese National Rally Champion: Joaquim Santos

Note: Championship subject to appeal on Algarve results.

RA   Argentina

Round 1 2/4 Mar VILLA DOLORES Cordoba-Villa Dolores 60s 25f
Recalde/Del Buono   Renault 18GTX   4h.39m.10s.

Round 2 2/7 Apr VUELTA DE LA MANZANA General Roca
                                             83s 26f
Veronesi/Silva   Renault 18GTX   13h.42m.37s.

Round 3 19/22 Apr PROVINCIA DE BUENOS AIRES Henderson
                                             51s 4f
Veronesi/Silva   Renault 18GTX   6h.12m.07s.

Round 4 22/24 May LA RIOJA La Rioja 63s 29f
Soto/Christie   Renault 18GTX   4h.48m.15s.

Round 5 17/20 Jun DIA DE LA BANDERA Berrotaran-Capilla del
Monte   78s 23f
Recalde/Del Buono   Renault 18GTX   6h.50m.50s.

Round 6 27 Jul/1 Aug ARGENTINA
See the results of WCR round 7, WCD round 8 on page 85

Round 7 25/26 Aug VUELTA DEL NOROESTE Tucuman 66s 33f
Soto/Christie   Renault 18GTX   4h.53m.42s.

Round 8 14/16 Sep SAN LUIS San Luis 76s 38f
Recalde/Del Buono   Renault 18GTX   5h.37m.51s.

Round 9 5/7 Oct PAGOS DEL TUYU General Madariaga 75s 22f
Moroni/Campana   Renault 18GTX   4h.38m.11s.

Round 10 10/11 Nov 24 HORAS DE TANTI Cordoba 109s 27f
Soto/Christie   Renault 18GTX   5h.50m.21s.

Round 11 30 Nov/2 Dec GRAN PREMIO San Carlos de Bariloche
                                             70s 34f
Recalde/Del Buono   Renault 18GTX   8h.04m.42s.

Argentinian National Rally Champion:
                         Class 3: Ernesto Soto 119 pts
                         Class 2: Gabriel Raies 150
                         Class 1: Jose Ceccheto 115

S   Sweden

Round 1 7/8 Jan BERGSLAGS Nora   186s 97f
Pettersson/Pettersson   Audi 80 Coupe   2h.24m.30s.

Round 2 20/21 Jan OSTGOTA Norrkoping   147s 74f
Torph/Svanstrom   Opel Ascona   2h.35m.39s.

Round 3 10/13 Feb SWEDISH
See the results of WCD round 2 on page 49

Round 4 3/4 Mar NOLIA Umea   158s 82f
Ericsson/B. Thorszelius   Audi 80 Quattro   1h.45m.04s.

Round 5 18/20 May SOUTH SWEDISH
See the results of European Championship round 18 on page 127

Round 6 11/12 Aug GRANSFEJDEN Emmaboda   148s 92f
Andersson/Lundin   Opel Kadett GT/E   1h.20m.08s.

Round 7 22/23 Sep TREKLUBBAR Jonkoping   164s 111f
Grundel/Uppsall   VW Golf GTI   1h.17m.39s.

Round 8 27/28 Oct VERDEXA Lunds   141s 88f
Torph/Svanstrom   Opel Ascona   1h.21m.35s.

Swedish National Rally Champion:
                             Group A: Bjorn Johansson 46 pts
                             Group 2: Ingvar Carlsson 52
                             Standard: Leif Asterhag 51

SF   Finland

Round 1 14/15 Jan MANTTA 200-AJO Mantta   144s 50f
A. Laine/Kinnunen   Audi Quattro   1h.02m.03s.

Round 2 27/29 Jan ARCTIC
See the results of European Championship round 2 on page 124

Round 3 4/5 Feb SVEITSIN TALVI Hyvinkaa   165s 60f
A. Laine/Kinnunen   Audi Quattro   1h.06m.54s.

Round 4 24/26 Feb HANKI
See the results of European Championship round 6 on page 125

Round 5 16/17 Jun SALORA Salo   153s 98f
A. Laine/Kinnunen   Ford Escort RS   46m.43s.

Round 6 4/5 Aug IMATRA Imatra   100s 68f
Makela/Palve   Talbot Sunbeam Lotus 47m.57s.

Round 7 26/28 Aug 1000 LAKES
See the results of WCR round 8, WCD round 9 on page 91

Round 8 29/30 Sep TAMPERE Tampere   113s 68f
A. Laine/Hiltunen   Audi Quattro   1h.29m.32s.

Round 9 20/21 Oct TEBOIL Turlu   119s 86f
Lampi/Paarala   Audi Quattro   44m.15s.

Round 10 1/2 Dec POHJOLA Oulu   71s 27f
Arpianen/Hantunen   Audi 80 Quattro   2h.06m.31s.

Finnish National Rally Champion:
                             Group B: Antero Laine 80 pts
                             Group A: Mika Arpianen 78
                             Group 2: Koysti Hamalainen 91

SU   Soviet Union

Final Round 26/28 Oct GULBENE Latvia   41s 21f
Tumalyavicius/Videika   Lada   7770

Soviet Union National Rally Champion: Eugenius Tumalyavicius
                             2nd Igor Bolshih
                             3rd Joel Tammeka
                             4th Hardy Mets
                             5th Kotlyar

TR   Turkey

Round 1 28 Apr HITIT Ankara   31s 14f
Bacioglu/Ceker   Opel Manta 200   58m.17s.

Round 2 26/27 May GUNAYDIN
See the results of European Championship round 20 on page 127

Round 3 28/30 Jul BOGAZICI Istanbul   62s 12f
Kocibey/Unlu   Ford Escort   2h.09m.12s.

Round 4 27/28 Oct CUMHURIYET Ankara   32s 14f
Bacioglu/Ceker   Opel Manta   1h.34m.05s.

Round 5 17/18 Nov ALI SIPAHI Istanbul   41s 22f
Bacioglu/Ceker   Opel Manta   1h.02m.44s.

Turkish National Rally Champion: Ali Bacioglu 360 pts
                             2nd Renc Kocibey 290
                             3rd Emre Yerlici 230
                             4th Serdar Bostanci 150
                             5th Oguz Gursel 138

Eugenius Tumalyavicius, Soviet Union Champion

KUUSE

U   Uruguay

Round 1 29 Apr PANDO   14s 8f
Petruchelli/Arvelo   Renault 12TS   class 'B'
Trelles/Ivetich   Fiat 125   class 'C'

Round 2 3 Jun FLORIDA   s f
Petruchelli/Arvelo   Renault 12TS   class 'B'
Trelles/Ivetich   Fiat 125   class 'C'

Note: The final rounds MINAS (October) and MALDONADO
(November).

USA   United States of America

Round 1 14/15 Apr NOR'WESTER Tumwater, WA.   54s 40f
Buffum/Ward   Audi Quattro   2h.32.11m.

Round 2 21/22 Apr OLYMPUS Tumwater, WA.   55s 27f
R. Millen/Kraushaar   Mazda RX7 4WD   3h.38.68m.

Round 3 5/6 May MICHIGAN Midland, MI.   59s 33f
Buffum/Gallagher   Audi Quattro   1h.45.48m.

Round 4 9/10 Jun SUSQUEHANNOCK TRAIL Wellsboro, PA.
                                                    73s 33f
Buffum/Wilson   Audi Quattro   2h.16.28m.

Round 5 25/26 Aug BUDWEISER FOREST Chilicothe, OH.   79s 47f
Buffum/Wilson   Audi Quattro   1h.30.67m.

Round 6 8/9 Sep MANISTEE TRAILS Manistee, MI.   57s 43f
R. Millen/Kraushaar   Mazda RX7 4WD   1h.35.01m.

Round 7 26/28 Oct BUDWEISER PRESS ON REGARDLESS
Houghton, MI.   64s 33f
R. Millen/Kraushaar   Mazda RX7 4WD   4h.02.47m.

Round 8 17/18 Nov OREGON TRAIL Tualatin, OR.   46s 34f
Buffum/Grimshaw   Audi Quattro   2h.53.07m.

Round 9 8/9 Dec CARSON CITY Carson City, NV.   62s 29f
Mikkola/Shepherd   Audi Sport Quattro   3h.33m.18s.

SCCA-Pro Rally Overall Champion: John Buffum 130 pts
                                     2nd Rod Millen 120
                                     3rd Bruno Kreibich 55
                                     4th Doug Shepherd 48
                                     5th Steve Millen 42

GT Production Class Champion: Richard Kelsey
Production Class Champion: Doug Shepherd

John Buffum, SCCA-Pro Rally Champion

HOLMES

YU Yugoslavia

Round 1 14/15 May SATURNUS
See the results of Alpe Adria Rally Cup round 2 on page 141

Round 2 23/24 Jun INA DELTA Zagreb   45s 23f
Kuzmic/Sali   Renault 5 Turbo   3h.45m.04s.

Round 3 1/3 Sep BRATSTVO I JEDINSTVO
See the results of Alpe Adria Rally Cup round 4 on page 141

Round 4 14/16 Sep YU
See the results of European Championship round 39 on page 130

Round 5 6/7 Oct KOMPAS Ljubljana   32s 23f
Kuzmic/Sali   Renault 5 Turbo   1h.14m.04s.

Yugoslavian National Rally Champion: Branislav Kuzmic 140 pts
    2nd Drago Zonta 76
    3rd Andrej Erklavec 71.5
    4th Jakob Valant 59.5
    5th Stojan Pirjevec 45

ZA South Africa

Round 1 11 Feb TOUR DE VALVOLINE Durban, NATAL 77s 31f
Van der Merwe/Boshoff   Audi Quattro   3h.06m.00s.

Round 2 16/17 Mar BOSCH DIESEL ELECTRIC Nelstruit-Sabie, E.TVL   42s 24f
Van der Merwe/Boshoff   Audi Quattro   1h.57m.24s.

Round 3 13/14 Apr NISSAN INT'L Groenpunt, CAPE   53s 25f
Van der Merwe/Boshoff   Audi Quattro   3h.12m.50s.

Round 4 11/12 May ALGOA Port Elizabeth, CAPE   39s 20f
Van der Merwe/Boshoff   Audi Quattro   1h.30m.59s.

Round 5 7/12 Jul CASTROL INT'L
See the results of African Continent Championship round 5 on page 140

Round 6 11 Aug STANNIC Aliwal North, TVL   44s 19f
Grobler/Swanepoei   Nissan Langley   2h.07m.02s.

Bob Bentley, Zimbabwe Champion

Round 7 31 Aug/1 Sep JURGENS INT'L Barberton-Pretoria, TVL
    60s 22f
Van der Merwe/Boshoff   Audi Quattro   5h.30m.42s.

Round 8 19/20 Oct STANNIC INT'L Johannesburg, TVL   75s 37f
Demuth/Pegg   Audi Quattro   3h.32m.04s.

South African National Rally Champion:
    Sarel Van der Merwe 238 pts
    2nd Hans Grobler 180
    3rd Geoff Mortimer 135
    4th Johann Evertse 122
    5th Lappies Labuschagne 96

ZW Zimbabwe

Round 1 17 Mar MR THIRSTY CHAMPIONSHIP CHASE Harare
    16s 12f
Watt/Higson-Smith   Ford Escort RS2000   17m.00s.

Round 2 24/27 May ZIMBABWE CHALLENGE
See the results of African Continent Championship round 4 on page 140

Round 3 21 Jul GOULASH Harare   16s 13f
Watt/Higson-Smith   Ford Escort RS2000   11m.59s.

Round 4 18 Aug CALTEX MASHONALAND Harare   16s 5f
Van Heerden/Mitchell   Datsun P710   4h.04m.24s.

Round 5 16 Sep FRANK LE COUNT Wedza   15s 12f
Bentley/Rowe   Ford Escort 1700TC   1h.55m.47s.

Round 6 6 Oct PENHALONGA Mutare   11s 6f
Van Heerden/Mitchell   Datsun 160J   1h.12m.18s.

Round 7 24 Nov SELBAS Harare   12s 10f
Van Heerden/Mitchell   Datsun 160J   2h.25m.18s.

Zimbabwe National Rally Champion: Bob Bentley
Champion up to 1500cc: Colin Barnett

ARCHIVE

The Year in Retrospect

1984 was a year of change. One could dismiss it as the "Year of Peugeot", but Peugeot simply identified what we had been looking forward to for a long time – the chance to develop a rally car as an instrument for sport rather than an adaptation of a road car. As Ford and Lancia showed later in the year Peugeot represented a beginning rather than an end. Audi became the first team to win both world titles for four years, but they did this literally weeks before the Peugeot era started. The programme they offered Stig Blomqvist gave the Swede an unrivalled chance to get the drivers' title, but we must wait to see if

Audi will ever gain another title without radical changes in their competition policies.

The number of top drivers has continued to shrink. The list of A-drivers for 1985 has now come down to twenty, compared with thirty at the end of 1982. It was a shock when Peugeot announced, at the end of the season, they would employ Timo Salonen, a driver who had lost his A-seeding, in 1985. This was the best car in the business, yet the team could not find another suitable A-driver! Although events in the European championship remained low-key compared with the world series qualifiers, the end placings of the series – due to the back-door entry to the A-lists, became more important than ever. The 1984 ECR became a tragedy; the new champion hardly projected his identity at all and the driver who could have benefitted from success had to withdraw in mid-season.

If you scan the lists of ECR and national results in this book, it will become apparent that the high-technology is still mainly centred on the world series. A few good titles have gone to drivers of Audi Quattros, Lancia Rallys and Renault 5 Turbos, but most of them have been gained by cars which are "old-fashioned" – in other words, within the reach of ordinary teams and people. Soon this tendency to limit the big-spending to the top end of the sport will

ABOVE   HOLMES

The shape of things to come. In 1985 Ari Vatanen will lead a two-car team of Peugeot 205 Turbo 16s in the world championship.

LEFT

Stig Blomqvist won the Drivers title and Audi the Manufacturers. Both will again tackle the championships in 1985, but with new generation cars like the Peugeot, Lancia and Ford will they have a chance to retain the titles?

HOLMES

give encouragement to the smaller factories who might otherwise be frightened at what is going on. The mechanical achievements of rally cars in the mid-eighties are unbelievable. Rallying has opened up whole new areas of activities for so many people. The great worry now is whether organisers can cope.

155

Obituary

Hafsteinn Hauksson died instantly during the National Breakdown Rally in England on 18th February, when he crashed into a tree in Dalby Forest. He has so far been the only rally driver from Iceland to make his mark abroad, and had quickly become a popular competitor in Britain. He started rallying in 1978 with a Renault van but soon changed to Fords. After becoming Iceland's national champion in 1982 he looked further afield and in 1983 finished tenth on the Scottish Rally. Twenty-eight years old Hafsteinn lived in Reykjavik with his wife and daughter and worked as a freelance manager. It was a double tragedy. It had been the first major accident in Britain for many years, and Hauksson had achieved his successes after overcoming a special fear of Icelanders, the danger of trees – which do not exist in his home country.

Addenda

ECR45 AOSTA (I) St Vincent 10/11 December 1983 *Coeff 1*

1	Cunico/Bartolich	Lancia Rally	gB	3h.59m.48s.
2	Tabaton/Tedeschini	Lancia Rally	B	4h.01m.00s.
3	Biasion/Siviero	Lancia Rally	B	4h.03m.11s.
4	Cerrato/Cerri	Opel Manta 400	B	4h.04m.23s.
5	Del Zoppo/ B. Tognana	Talbot Samba	B	4h.25m.19s.
6	Fornicola/Clari	Porsche 911SC	B	4h.33m.00s.
7	Vuillermin/ Albanese	Opel Ascona 400	B	4h.34m.54s.
8	Gattoni/Conti	Porsche 911SC	B	4h.40m.46s.
9	'Tchine'/Jenot	Opel Manta	A	4h.42m.28s.
10	Signori/Gargiulo	Fiat Abarth 125	N	4h.45m.01s.
11	Biasuzzi/Vittori	Opel Kadett GT/E	2	4h.46m.05s.
23	Battiato/Lanzetti	Fiat Abarth 131	4	5h.05m.29s.

72 starters. 39 finishers. NO A-PRIORITY DRIVERS.

ECR45   PHOTO 4

Outstanding International Championship Results from 1983

African Continent Championship

The final round SENEGAL was not held so:

1983 African Continent Champion:
- Alain Ambrosino 30 pts*
- 2nd Hannu Mikkola 30*
- Equal 3rd Guy Collette, Christian Brose
- Ari Vatanen and Sarel van der Merwe 20

* Decided by number of wins

Peace & Friendship Cup

1983 Peace & Friendship Cup Champion:
- Svatopluk Kvaizar (CS) 230 pts
- 2nd Vello Soots (SU) 207
- 3rd Marian Bublewicz (PL) 196
- 4th Todor Medialkov (BG) 153
- 5th Joel Tammeka (SU) 140

Irish Tarmac Championship

Round 5 3/4 Dec 1983 GLENEAGLE RALLY OF THE LAKES
Killarney   95s 44f
Coleman/Murphy   Opel Ascona 400   3h.38m.36s.

1983 Irish Tarmac Champion: Austin McHale 37 pts
- 2nd Russell Brookes 35
- 3rd Bertie Fisher 25

West Euro Cup

1983 West Euro Cup Champion: Helge Abendroth (D) 161.5 pts
- 2nd Robert Droogmans (B) 159
- 3rd Renger Gulliker (NL) 153.5
- 4th Per Eklund (S) 143
- 5th Peter Klodzinski (D) 129

Outstanding National Championship Results from 1983

CDN   Canada

Round 10 26 Nov 1983 TALL PINES Peterborough, ONT   32s 19f
Anderson/Jackson   Toyota Celica   2h.38m.56s.

1983 Canadian National Rally Champion: Randy Black 119 pts
2nd Chris Castledine 110
3rd Bjorn Anderson 85
4th John Buffum 60
5th Tim Bendle 32

Production A Champion: Michel Poirier-Defoy 37

CI   Ivory Coast

Round 5 26/27 Nov 1983 ROHOE d'AGBOVILLE Agboville   27s 14f
Assef/Barault   Toyota Celica   1h.13m.

1983 Ivorian National Rally Champion: Samir Assef 240 pts
2nd Eugene Salim 136
3rd Jean Ferber 99
4th Alain Ambrosino 90
5th Michel Molinie 77

CY   Cyprus

Round 7 26/27 Nov 1983 TULIP Nicosia   34s 14f
Panayiotides/Yiapanas   VW Golf GTI   2h.07m.08s.

Round 8 17 Dec 1983 PILOT Nicosia   23s 18f
Panayiotides/Yiapanas   VW Golf GTI   No penalties

1983 Cyprus National Rally Champion: Vahan Terzian 95 pts
2nd Costas Panayiotides 67
3rd Dinos Mashias 61
4th Costas Theocharides 54
5th 'Fouis' 43

D   West Germany

1983 West German National Rally Champion:
Erwin Weber 223 pts
2nd Kalle Grundel 217
3rd Manfred Hero 175
4th Gustel Brusch 161
5th Walter Smolej 151

E   Spain

Round 17 4 Dec 1983 SHALYMAR Madrid   93s 50f
Fernandez/Sala   Porsche 911SC   1h.20m.06s.

1983 Spanish National Rally Champion: Eugenio Ortiz 928 pts
2nd Beny Fernandez 828
3rd Carlos Pineiro 690
4th Marc Etchebers 653
5th Carlos Santacreu 584

EAK   Kenya

Round 8 10/11 Dec 1983 JAMHURI Nairobi   33s 14f
Horsey/Williamson   Datsun 1300 pickup   1h.12m.

Round 9 28/29 Jan 1984 FIRESTONE COAST 600 Mombasa   28s 11f
Kirkland/Levitan   Nissan 240RS   1h.14m.

Round 10 11/12 Feb RIFT 300 Nakuru   19s 10f
Preston/Lyall   Lancia Rally   4h.36m.

1983/4 Kenyan National Rally Champion: Jayant Shah 130 pts
2nd David Horsey 115
3rd Vic Preston 88
4th John Hellier 63
5th Yasuhiro Iwase 48

GR   Greece

Round 14 13/14 Nov 1983 SCORPIO Attiki-Biotia   120s 90f
Moschous/Fertakis   Nissan 240RS   42m.29s.

1983 Greek National Rally Champion:
George Moschous 340 pts
2nd 'Leonidas' 320
3rd Andreas Papatriantafillou 247
4th Emmanuel Panagiotopoulos 176
5th Evangelos Gallo 129

I   Italy

Round 10 10/11 Dec 1983 AOSTA (I)
See the results of European Championship round 45 on page 157

1983 Italian National Rally Champion: Massimo Biasion 381 pts
2nd Gianfranco Cunico 376
3rd Dario Cerrato 335
4th Carlo Capone 230
5th Bruno Bentivogli 190

IRL   Ireland

1983 Irish National Rally Champion: Bertie Law

MAL   Malaysia

Round 4 17/19 Dec HYPERGRADE Kuala Lumpur   14s 14f
Khong/Sia   Toyota Corolla   2h.15m.12s.

1983 Malaysian National Rally Champion: Mudzaffar Tunku 47 pts
2nd Yin Swan Khong 46
3rd Kwai Leong Lee 34
4th Ariff Ridzwan 28
5th William Mei 28

PY   Paraguay

Round 4 26/27 Nov 1983 PRESIDENTE DE LA REPUBLICA
Paraguari   43s 22f
Saurini/Biedermann   Isuzu Gemini   3h.52m.08s.

1983 Paraguayan National Rally Champion:
Edgar Molas 55 pts
2nd Santiago Silguero 44
3rd Oscar Saurini 28
4th Hector Risso 26
5th Rodrigo Izaguirre 16.5

RA   Argentina

Round 9 8/10 Dec 1983 GRAN PREMIO DE TURISMO YPF San
Juan   65s 29f
Recalde/Christie   Renault 18GTX   8h.01m.20s.

1983 Argentinian National Rally Champion
Class 3: Jorge Recalde 107 pts
Class 2: Carlos Celis 91
Class 1: Sergio Colosi 109

U   Uruguay

Round 5 15 Nov MALDONADO Piriapolis   s   f
Martinez/Cipolina   Mazda 324   class B
Stagnari/Zunino   Datsun 160J   class C

1983 Uruguayan National Rally Champion
Class B: A. Martinez
Class C: H. Stagnari

USA   United States of America

Round 11 3/4 Dec 1983 SNO*DRIFT Grayling, MI.   40s 22f
R. Millen/Parris   Mazda RX7   1h.55.49m.

Round 12 10/11 Dec 1983 CARSON CITY Carson City, NV.   64s 21f
Buffum/Shepherd   Audi Quattro   3h.48.14m.

1983 SCCA-Pro Overall Rally Champion: John Buffum 120 pts
2nd Rod Millen 100
3rd Jon Woodner 86
4th Steve Nowicki 49
5th Mark Hardymon 43

Production Champion: Steve Nowicki 102

ZW   Zimbabwe

Round 7 3 Dec 1983 SELBAS Harare   17s 12f
C. Landman/J. Landman   Ford Escort   3h.52m.07s.

1983 Zimbabwe National Rally Champion: Bob Bentley
Champion up to 1500cc: L. Finaughty

Edgar Molas, Paraguayan Champion 1983

GONZALEZ

Errata/Stop Press

Errata

Audi Sport World of Rallying 6

p2   *Gerard* Lallement
p28   Blomqvist Born 29 *July* 1946
p29   Blomqvist 1976 SF Saab 99EMS
p33   Ragnotti *MH* = Martin Holmes
p73   Chomat Reg No: 554DVF75 (F)
p91   Blomqvist *IN-YA34 (D)*
p110   NZ *New Zealand*
p128   3. Bjorn Waldegard/*Claes Billstam*
p140   Audi Quattro: cc *2135/2939*
       bore/stroke *79.3/96.4*
       Citroen Visa Chrono: Rear Brakes *D244.5*
p149   Antibes (F) *Antibes*
p168   NL = Renger *Gulliker*
p169   RA town of headquarters =
       Round 3 *Cordoba*
       Round 4 *Rio Negra*
p170   USA = Round 1 Salem, *MO*
p171   Round 9 Nowick*i*
p173   ECR47 Tedesch*ini*
p175   National Champions *Ali* Bacioglu

Stop Press

ECR50   MORELLI

ECR50 VAR (F) Ste.-Maxime 24/25 November 1984 *Coeff 1*
1	Andruet/Peuvergne	Lancia Rally	gB	4h.21m.51s.
2	FREQUELIN/'Tilber'	Opel Manta 400	B	4h.24m.04s.
3	Chatriot/Perin	Renault 5 Turbo	B	4h.26m.36s.
4	D. Gauthier/M. Gauthier	Lancia Rally	B	4h.30m.24s.
5	Manzagol/Argeti	Renault 5 Turbo	B	4h.31m.06s.
6	Balas/E. Laine	Alfa Romeo GTV6	A	4h.49m.40s.
7	Rouby/Martin	Renault 5 Turbo	B	4h.50m.23s.
8	Colombet/Jamarin	Ford Escort RS	B	4h.56m.57s.
9	A. Oreille/S. Oreille	Renault 11 Turbo	N	4h.57m.30s.
10	Azzena/Rimbaud	Opel Manta	B	4h.57m.36s.

189 starters. 90 finishers. 1 A-PRIORITY DRIVER.

A-priority drivers for 1985

A-priority drivers for 1985		Expiry	Rally creating priority
Rauno Aaltonen	SF	1985	2nd Safari 1984
Markku Alen	SF	1987	1st Tour de Corse 1984
Attilio Bettega	I	1985	2nd Sanremo 1984
Massimo Biasion	I	1986	European Champion 1983
Stig Blomqvist	S	1987	1st Sweden, Acropolis, New Zealand, Argentina and Cote d'Ivoire 1984
Carlo Capone	I	1987	European Champion 1984
Harald Demuth	D	1985	3rd European Championship 1984
Per Eklund	S	1985	3rd Sweden, RAC 1984
Guy Frequelin	F	1985	5th European Championship 1984
Shekhar Mehta	EAK	1985	1st Safari 1982 and 3rd Cote d'Ivoire 1984
Hannu Mikkola	SF	1987	1st Portugal 1984
Michele Mouton	F	1985	1st Portugal, Acropolis and Brasil 1982, 2nd Sweden 1984
Jean Ragnotti	F	1985	1st Tour de Corse 1982, 3rd Tour de Corse 1984
Jorge Recalde	RA	1985	3rd Argentina 1984
Walter Rohrl	D	1987	1st Monte Carlo 1984
Salvador Servia	E	1985	4th European Championship 1984
Henri Toivonen	SF	1985	3rd 1000 Lakes and 2nd European Championship 1984
'Tony' Fassina	I	1985	European Champion 1982
Ari Vatanen	SF	1987	1st 1000 Lakes, Sanremo, RAC 1984
Bjorn Waldegard	S	1987	1st Safari 1984

Drivers who have regained A-status for 1985 are:

GUY FREQUELIN born 2 April 1945 at Langres, first rally car Renault 8 Gordini in 1967
HENRI TOIVONEN born 25 August 1956 at Jyvaskyla, first rally car Simca Rallye 2 in 1975

Drivers who have A-status for the first time in 1985 are:

CARLO CAPONE born 12 April 1957 at Chivasso, first rally car Autobianchi A112 in 1977
HARALD DEMUTH born 2 July 1950 at Bad Tolz, first rally car BMW 2002 Automatic in 1972
SALVADOR SERVIA born 29 June 1944 in Pals, Gerona, first rally car SEAT 600 in 1968

National Champions

Since going to press the African Continent Championship has been won by David Horsey, the Cyprus Championship by Vahan Terzian, and the Ivory Coast Championship by Alain Ambrosino.

International Championship Calendar for 1985

Date	Event	Country	WCR	ECR
Jan 1–6	Janner	A		2
18–20	Arctic	SF		2
Feb 8–10	Boucles de Spa	B		2
15–17	**Swedish**	S	M+D	4
21–24	Costa Brava	E		3
22–24	Sachs Winter	D		2
22–24	Hanki	SF		2*
Mar 5–10	**Portugal**	P	M+D	–
15–17	Ciocco	I		1
22–24	RACE	E		3*
28–31	Garrigues	F		3
Apr 4–8	**Safari**	EAK	M+D	–
5–9	Circuit of Ireland	GB/IRL		2
12–14	Criterium Alpin	F		3
17–20	Costa Smeralda	I		4*
19–21	Arbo	A		1
May 4–6	**Corsica**	F	M+D	–
11–13	Zlatni Piassatzi	BG		4*
16–19	South Swedish	S		2*
17–19	Haspengouw	B		1
19	Saturnus	YU		1
23–25	Elba	I		3
23–27	Volta Portugal	P		2
24–27	Gunaydin	TR		1
25–31	**Acropolis**	GR	M+D	–
Jun 6–9	Hessen	D		2*
8–11	Scottish	GB		2
14–15	Danube	R		1
14–16	El Corte Ingles	E		2
15–16	4 Regions	I		2
21–23	Barum	CS		2
28–30	Ypres	B		2*
27–3	**New Zealand**	NZ	M+D	–
Jul 4–6	Sicily	I		3
5–7	Poland	PL		2
11–14	San Marino	RSM/I		2
11–14	Hunsruck	D		3
18–20	Skoda	CS		2
25–28	Lana	I		2
27–3	**Argentina**	RA	M+D	–
Aug 3–4	Madeira	P		4
20–22	Vida	BG		2
21–25	**1000 Lakes**	SF	M+D	–
26–29	Halkidikis	GR		4*
29–1	Piancavallo	I		2
Sep 1–2	Hebros	BG		2
5–8	Saarland-Deutschland	D		2
6–8	Bianchi	B		2
11–14	Manx	GB		3*
20–22	Cyprus	CY		4*
20–22	Asturias	E		2
20–22	YU	YU		2
21–28	Tour de France	F		4*
25–29	Valais	CH		2
30–5	**Sanremo**	I	M+D	–
Oct 17–20	Antibes	F		2
25–28	Cataluna	E		4
29–3	**Ivory Coast**	CI	D	–
30–3	Algarve	P		2*
Nov 9–11	Condroz	B		1
23–28	**RAC**	GB	M+D	–
29–1 Dec	Var	F		1

*Qualifying rounds for FISA Amateur group A challenge.

Shell Oils RAC Open Rally Championship 1985

Feb 22–24	National Breakdown
Apr 5–9	Circuit of Ireland
May 3–6	Welsh
Jun 8–11	Scottish
July 26–27	Ulster
Sep 11–14	Manx

Shell Oils/Autosport RAC National Rally Championship 1985

Mar 9	Gwynedd
Mar 30	York National
Apr 20	Granite City
May 11	Manx Stages
Jul 13	Peter Russek Manuals
Aug 25	Mewla Stages
Sep 7	Lindisfarne
Sep 28–29	Cumbria
Oct 19	Audi Sport National

Golf GTi ⊕

112bhp. 0–60 in 8.3 seconds. 119mph.

FURTHER INFORMATION FROM VOLKSWAGEN SALES ENQUIRIES, YEOMANS DRIVE, BLAKELANDS, MILTON KEYNES MK14 5AN. TELEPHONE: (0908) 679121. EXPORT AND FLEET SALES, 95 BAKER STREET, LONDON W1M 1FB. TELEPHONE: 01-486 8411.

The car on the left is the ultimate sports car, the *£60,000 Audi Sport quattro, which will be one of only twenty in the country.

It's for the driver with everything.

The car on the right is the Audi 80 Sport.

It's for the driver with everything, except *£60,000.

The 80 Sport offers many features which owe a great deal to its big brother.

As well as £51,293 change.

Under the bonnet lurks a 112 bhp fuel injected engine, developed through Audi rally success.

This, with the help of a five speed close ratio gearbox, will whisk you from 0-60 in 9.2 seconds†, then on to a top speed of 115 mph.

The performance is matched by the kind of sporty equipment that you won't even find on some rally cars.

One unsportslike quality, however, is the rather frugal fuel consumption.

One day.

GOVERNMENT FUEL FIGURES FOR THE AUDI 80 SPORT 25.9 MPG (10.9 L/100 KM) URBAN, 45.6 MPG (6.1 L/100 KM) AT 56 MPH, 34.9 MPG (8.0 L/100 KM) AT 75 MPH. *PRICE ESTIMATE AT TIME OF GOING TO PRESS. †MANUFACTURERS FIGURES.

At a steady 56 mph you can expect over 45 mpg, which with a 15 gallon petrol tank, means you'll complete more than 500 miles between fill ups.

Like all Audis, everything about the 80 Sport is designed with safety in mind.

The self stabilising steering system helps keep you in a straight line should a tyre blow.

There are diagonally linked dual circuit brakes.

There are also front and rear seat belts and a laminated windscreen fitted as standard.

And should it come to the crunch, rest assured that the passenger compartment is contained within a steel safety shell, with crumple zones front and rear.

Finally, from a practical point of view, may we add that the £8,700 Audi 80 Sport has a distinct edge over the *£60,000 Sport quattro.

It has four doors and ample leg and headroom for five adults.

Money can't always buy you friends ■

Today.

PRICES AND BROCHURES FROM AUDI MARKETING, YEOMANS DRIVE, BLAKELANDS, MILTON KEYNES MK14 5AN. TEL. (0908) 679121. EXPORT AND FLEET SALES, 95 BAKER STREET, LONDON W1M 1FB. TEL: 01-486 8411.